SPEAKING OUT

SPEAKING OUT

Lessons in Life and Politics

Ed Balls

HUTCHINSON
LONDON

1 3 5 7 9 10 8 6 4 2

Hutchinson
20 Vauxhall Bridge Road
London SW1V 2SA

Hutchinson is part of the Penguin Random House group of companies
whose addresses can be found at global.penguinrandomhouse.com.

Penguin
Random House
UK

First published in Great Britain in 2016 by Hutchinson

www.penguin.co.uk

A CIP catalogue record for this book is available from the British Library.

ISBN 9781786330390

Typeset in 12.5/16.75 pt Quadraat
by Jouve (UK), Milton Keynes
Printed and bound by Clays Ltd, St Ives plc

Penguin Random House is committed to a
sustainable future for our business, our readers
and our planet. This book is made from
Forest Stewardship Council® certified paper.

FSC
www.fsc.org
MIX
Paper from
responsible sources
FSC® C018179

To my Mum and Dad, for giving me the best start in life

To Ellie, Joel and Maddy – the next generation – for
putting up with all the madness

And above all to Yvette, because we've truly been
all in this together

CONTENTS

Part Three
Learning The Hard Way

Part Four
Learning To Move On

Period	Governing Party and Key Cabinet Ministers	Ed Balls' Timeline
September 1990 – April 1992	Conservative **Prime Minister:** Margaret Thatcher/ John Major **Chancellor:** John Major/Norman Lamont	**September 1990:** EB graduates from Harvard and joins the *Financial Times* as a leader writer
April 1992 – May 1997	Conservative **Prime Minister:** John Major **Chancellor:** Norman Lamont/Ken Clarke	**January 1994:** EB leaves the FT to join Shadow Chancellor Gordon Brown's Labour Treasury team
May 1997 – June 2001	Labour **Prime Minister:** Tony Blair **Chancellor:** Gordon Brown	**May 1997:** Yvette Cooper (YC) elected as MP. EB joins the Treasury as the Chancellor's Economic Adviser **January 1998:** EB and YC are married in Eastbourne **May 1999:** EB appointed chief economic adviser to the Treasury **June 1999:** EB and YC's eldest daughter is born
June 2001 – May 2005	Labour **Prime Minister:** Tony Blair **Chancellor:** Gordon Brown	**August 2001:** EB and YC's son is born **July 2004:** EB selected as Labour candidate for Normanton and leaves the Treasury. EB and YC's youngest daughter is born
May 2005 – May 2007	Labour **Prime Minister:** Tony Blair **Chancellor:** Gordon Brown	**May 2005:** EB elected as MP for Normanton **April 2006:** EB appointed Economic Secretary to the Treasury
June 2007 – May 2010	Labour **Prime Minister:** Gordon Brown **Chancellor:** Alistair Darling	**June 2007:** EB becomes Secretary of State for Children, Schools and Families **December 2007:** EB publishes the first ever National Children's Plan
May 2010 – April 2015	Coalition (Conservative / Liberal Democrats) **Prime Minister:** David Cameron **Deputy Prime Minister:** Nick Clegg **Chancellor:** George Osborne	**May 2010:** EB elected as MP for Morley & Outwood and becomes Shadow Education secretary **June 2010:** EB stands for Labour leadership against Ed and David Miliband **August 2010:** EB delivers economic speech at Bloomberg **September 2010:** EB appointed Shadow Home Secretary **January 2011:** EB appointed Shadow Chancellor **April 2012:** EB runs first London marathon **July 2012:** EB passes Grade 1 piano exam
May 2015 – June 2016	Conservative **Prime Minister:** David Cameron/ Theresa May **Chancellor:** George Osborne/Philip Hammond	**May 2015:** EB loses his parliamentary seat **September 2015:** EB returns to Harvard Kennedy School as a Senior Fellow **December 2015:** EB joins board of Norwich City FC as chairman

Milestone Political Events

October 1990: Britain enters the European Exchange Rate Mechanism (ERM)
November 1990: Margaret Thatcher resigns as prime minister and John Major is elected
January 1991: Commencement of the First Gulf War, UK joins US-led coalition to invade Iraq

April 1992: Labour loses the general election, John Major re-elected as prime minister, Neil Kinnock resigns
July 1992: John Smith elected leader of the Labour Party
September 1992: Black Wednesday; Britain exits the ERM
November 1993: Maastricht Treaty enters into force
May 1994: John Smith dies
July 1994: Tony Blair elected leader of the Labour Party
February 1997: Gordon Brown announces 'Five Tests' to determine whether the UK should join the single currency

May 1997: Labour wins a landslide, Chancellor Gordon Brown makes the Bank of England independent
October 1997: Gordon Brown announces Britain will not join the euro in the first wave of members, based on an assessment of the 'Five Tests'
July 1998: Government passes the National Minimum Wage Act
September 2000: Blockades and protests against rising fuel prices

June 2001: Labour wins a second term
September 2001: 9/11 terrorist attacks
October 2001: UK sends troops into Afghanistan
March 2002: Budget announces National Insurance tax rise for the NHS
March 2003: Start of the Iraq War. UK joins the US-led invasion of Iraq
June 2003: Britain decides not to join the euro, based on a new assessment of the 'Five Tests'
May 2004: Britain opts not to have 'transitional controls' on migration from eastern Europe

May 2005: Tony Blair wins a historic third term
July 2005: 7 July London bombings
September 2006: Tony Blair commits to serving for a full third term. Labour MPs call for him to resign. Blair concedes he will resign within a year
May 2007: Labour leadership election. Gordon Brown is the only candidate to receive the required number of nominations

June 2007: Tony Blair stands down, Gordon Brown becomes prime minister
September 2007: Problems emerge at Northern Rock building society
October 2007: Gordon Brown cancels plans for an early general election
September 2008: Lehman Brothers collapses, the global financial crisis intensifies
November 2008: Mother of Peter Connelly (Baby P), her boyfriend and their lodger found guilty of causing his death
May 2009: MPs Expenses scandal erupts, based on information disclosed by the *Daily Telegraph*
June 2009: Labour suffers heavy defeats in the local and European elections, James Purnell resigns

May 2010: Labour loses the general election, coalition formed with David Cameron as Prime Minister
September 2010: Ed Miliband elected as Labour leader
July 2011: News International phone hacking scandal reported in the *Guardian*, leading to public outcry
January 2013: David Cameron says the Conservatives will hold a referendum on EU membership before end of 2017
September 2013: Ed Miliband announces Labour's plan for a two-year freeze on energy prices
September 2014: Scotland votes to remain in the UK in the Scottish Independence Referendum

May 2015: Labour loses election. Ed Miliband stands down
September 2015: Jeremy Corbyn elected leader of the Labour Party
June 2016: Britain votes to leave the European Union, Jo Cox MP is murdered in her West Yorkshire constituency
July 2016: David Cameron resigns as prime minister and Theresa May is chosen to replace him

PREFACE

Being present at your own funeral isn't all it's cracked up to be.

Mine took place early on 8 May 2015, in the living room of a large house in Morley, West Yorkshire. The mourners trooped in one by one to give me their condolences, telling me what a great job I'd done, what a good innings I'd had, and how I'd be remembered. I comforted them and said it would all be OK.

I turned to Neil, my election agent, and said: 'This is ridiculous. I'm still here!'

Overhearing me, his wife Jayne disappeared into the kitchen and returned with a tray of thirty small sherry glasses, so I could pour out measures of Harveys Bristol Cream and hand them out to my campaign team. We all began to laugh. When the toast came, it was 'To the late Ed Balls.'

I realised how often this happens in Westminster. When you've held a senior position, and will in all likelihood never rise that high in politics again, the end of your career is treated like a death.

Gordon Brown, Tony Blair, John Major and now David Cameron have all been able to read supposedly definitive accounts of their lives while they're still very much with us, as though nothing they do or say after leaving office will ever matter.

Over the next few days, as I read some of my own obituaries, I kept thinking: 'I'm only forty-eight; I'm not dead; I'm not dead.'

I'd come into this life aged twenty-seven, giving up a career in economic journalism because I'd finally decided I wanted to be 'doing it', not writing about it. And back then I rather brashly believed that I knew exactly what needed doing.

I like to think I was right in some respects – championing Bank of England independence, and working to keep Britain out of the euro among them – but in so many others I had a huge amount to learn.

At the end, I'd had twenty-one good years in politics, but I had to see it that way: twenty-one memorable years out of a life that will – touch wood – last four times that long, and contain many more great experiences and opportunities.

So this is my fond farewell to that part of my life; a reflection on what I've learned in those twenty-one years, recorded while the memories are still fresh. I hope it can reveal something about the realities of political life: how good and bad decisions come to be made; what the modern politician needs to survive (and occasionally succeed); and the strange challenge of trying to remain a proper person at the same time as being a politician.

There are a lot of things I wish I could tell my 27-year-old self, the one who left the *Financial Times* to go and work for Labour; but he had to find them out the hard way.

It was a very different political world back then: no 24/7 news channels; no social media; I'd never sent an email; and the only mobile phone I'd ever seen in the flesh was owned by Gordon Brown, so large that it took two hands for him to hold. It was a world in which there was much less commentary, much more privacy, and much more time to think about how to deal with an issue or a story.

There is no doubt that politics is more challenging now because of all the changes since then. We live in an era where trust in mainstream political leaders and parties has slumped to an all-time low. Outsiders to the extremes of right and left have been making the political running. And politics is more short-termist, more populist, more unstable, more risky than at any time in my life, as the current uncertainty over the impact of Brexit makes abundantly clear.

But it is now, at a time when politics is more diminished and unpopular than ever before, that we need it most. Whatever else may have changed in the last two decades, politics is still essentially the same beast. People put forward ideas, they try to win arguments, they try to gain trust. Sometimes you win, sometimes you lose, and when it's the latter, politics is just as unforgiving as it has ever been.

And in the end, for all of the bizarre moments and terrible misjudgements, it is still a noble calling; still a pursuit of important causes; still a profession which needs, more than ever, the best and the brightest to join it in the years and decades to come.

I hope this book will inspire some of them. I hope it will show why politics matters and how it can help make a difference. And I hope, too, that it will provide some interest, ideas and entertainment for everyone interested in what life is really like inside the political jungle.

PART ONE

Learning Who You Are

I discovered much about myself over my career in politics —
my strengths, but also my flaws and vulnerabilities. These
chapters set out some of the lessons I learned along the way,
most importantly about how politicians can succeed, survive
and stay human.

I

Defeat

Every politician strives to climb the political ladder – but what happens when you fall off?

At 21.59 and 59 seconds on 7 May 2015, anything seemed possible. Outside of opening exam results, or waiting on news from a doctor, there aren't too many moments in life where your whole future hangs on what you're about to see or hear.

I was standing with Yvette in the living room of our home in her Yorkshire constituency waiting for the general election exit poll to flash up. I thought the chance of Labour taking power the next morning was significantly less than 50 per cent; but the chance of the election producing a very tight hung Parliament with all to play for was, in my mind, close to 100 per cent. Anything under 290 seats for the Conservatives and it was anyone's guess.

Anything under 280 and we had a real chance of forming the next government.

When Big Ben sounded ten o'clock and David Cameron's face flashed up on the TV screen next to the caption 'Conservatives Largest Party', that was fine – not inconsistent with what I was expecting. But then the projected seats flashed up. 316 for the Conservatives. 239 for Labour. Nineteen fewer than we'd won in 2010. We both stared at the screen flabbergasted. I turned to Yvette and said simply: 'That's it . . . that's it.'

We stood there in silence. And in my mind, I was back in 1997, in the house we were renting on the edge of Castleford, a year before we were married, sitting with her mum and dad, all of us wearing big red rosettes and ready to go off to her count for the seat of Pontefract and Castleford, where she was standing for the first time aged just twenty-eight. We thought Yvette was going to win that night, we knew Labour was going to win, but when we saw the scale of the projected landslide at ten o'clock, our jaws just dropped. Eighteen years later, I was experiencing the opposite. The unexpected shock of catastrophic defeat.

They say it's the hope that kills you. And for a long time before the 2015 election campaign, I'd almost deliberately stayed pessimistic about whether it was really possible for Labour to win.

I thought that the burden we carried from the past and the challenge we faced in the present were going to be too much, and there were times in the build-up to the election when I believed we had no chance. At the beginning of the year, on a trip to Washington DC, I spent a gloomy hour with Tony Blair in his hotel suite. Forget the polls, he told me, in the end when people go to vote they just won't put Ed Miliband into Downing Street.

But as the campaign went on, and the polls stayed so tight, it was impossible not to think that it could be done, and feel that hope rising. The day before the election, I'd gone up from London to Yorkshire via three Tory-held marginal seats in Stevenage, Peterborough and Lincoln, meeting three brilliant Labour candidates with huge campaign teams. There was a real buzz and excitement on each of those stops, a real sense of optimism.

You can always tell when a crowd is with you. I'd supported Gordon Brown on visits like this back in 1997. Even a renowned doom-monger like Gordon would come away from campaign meets on that trail, and say: 'You know, I think we're going to do this.'

In Peterborough, a seat I had assumed we couldn't possibly win in 2015, I was amazed to see the level of confidence. Our polling experts said that UKIP were surging at the expense of the Tories. All we needed was one last push. In Lincoln, a seat which we lost in 1992 but won in 1997, we had an enthusiastic rally in the campaign headquarters, a real tribute to our candidate's leadership and hard work. Of course everyone was nervous, but I heard nothing but confident expectations that we were going to win.

Back in my own constituency on polling day, the mood was good. We had hundreds of people out from first light delivering 'Remember to vote' leaflets, knocking on the doors of our supporters or phoning them from our three campaign hubs across the constituency. Our vote felt solid and Jo Coles, my experienced campaign manager, was confident that we'd win with an increased majority.

But we were mistaken. When the exit poll emerged, it felt like falling into a big black hole. It wasn't just that our hopes were dashed, it was that dreadful feeling that everything we thought we knew was wrong.

Yvette and I immediately had to go to our counts and our pre-agreed media appearances. I thought back to that feeling in 1997, a night we'd been able to share and celebrate together, and as we went our separate ways on what was going to be a very different night in 2015, I felt a desperate wrench that we were going to go through it all apart.

One of my team picked me up to drive to my count at the Leeds Arena, where I was to do a round of television and radio interviews at 11 p.m. I'd thought it would be a good time to speak: if the result was still close, I could parry any questions about Labour's tactics in a hung Parliament by saying the interviewers were being premature. I hadn't ever envisaged that things would be so clear right from the beginning.

As we drove to the count, I texted my brilliant media adviser, Alex Belardinelli, to ask if there was a line prepared from the campaign – something for me to say. Alex always embodied strength, calm and common sense, so when he was agitated or annoyed, you knew it was with good reason. He said that he was pressing for a line. However, Ed Miliband's team had prepared advance interview scripts for every eventuality, except the one we were facing.

We arrived at Leeds at 10.45 p.m., and checked into a

Premier Inn over the road from the Arena. The proposed line eventually came through from Labour HQ: 'Pour water on the exit poll – say we think it's wrong.' They suggested pointing to YouGov's alternative poll, which had the Tories on 284 seats and the election 'too close to call'.

Certainly a straw to clutch at. But the exit polls had been pretty spot on from 1997 onwards, and I thought it would look foolish to dismiss this one. I decided that I'd say there were a couple of polls out there, that we'd have to wait and see which was correct, but if it was somewhere in the middle then we were in hung Parliament territory and David Cameron had not secured the majority that he'd set out to achieve.

Over at the packed Arena, Tracey Paul, one of the most professional and experienced Labour operators, had already managed to befriend the security guards and secure a secret way into the main hall, avoiding the media scrum at the entrance. We were ushered down a few back corridors and onto the broadcast stage, where I proceeded to do my interviews, trying to sound as upbeat as I could.

It didn't feel very convincing, although half an hour later Charlie Falconer texted me from Labour HQ to say my interviews had been a huge boost. At least I had given them a script that would get the party through the next couple of hours.

At the end of my BBC interview, David Dimbleby asked me whether the rumours on Twitter were true: that I could lose my seat. That was the first I'd heard of any threat in Morley & Outwood, and although it was obvious from the exit poll that it was going to be a terrible result for Labour, I hadn't really computed the local implications. I was worried for the party, but not yet for myself.

Nestled around the junctions of the M1 and M62 between Leeds and Wakefield, Morley & Outwood is a constituency created after the latest Boundary Review, which came into effect for the 2010 election. A prime commuter location on the edge of Leeds, the area had seen a great deal of new housebuilding over the previous two decades and more. It was demographically very different – more affluent and much more marginal – from the old mining constituency of Normanton where I was first elected in 2005.

Back in 2010, with Tory pressure mounting, the invaluable Alicia Kennedy, assistant general secretary and campaign coordinator at Labour HQ, had told me the national campaign was worried that my seat was at risk, and would allocate me extra resources. The Tories fought a very aggressive and personal campaign, but we won with a majority of just 1,101 – the smallest in the Shadow Cabinet, but for me a big victory.

This time round, there was never the slightest indication of any concern about Morley & Outwood. Instead, Labour HQ had me on a non-stop tour of marginal seats all around the UK, which I relished. With the race so tight, I could see the importance of focusing on the battlegrounds where the election would be decided.

Nevertheless, we had taken nothing for granted in Morley & Outwood. It was still a marginal seat, and my campaign team had worked incredibly hard: door-knocking both days at weekends and most weekdays; organising regular public meetings with me on local and national issues; and hand-delivering over 250,000 letters and surveys in the year before the election. Every few months we had Campaign Saturdays where, in return for lunch cooked by me – lasagne, boeuf bourguignon, spaghetti Bolognese – often seventy-five or more students and volunteers from across Yorkshire and beyond came to deliver our mailshots.

As in 2010, my assumption had always been: if the Tories win a majority nationally, then I will lose my seat locally; if they don't, I'll win. So when even the BBC exit poll showed the Tories short of a majority, I'd assumed I was fine. I scoffed to David Dimbleby that he should probably spend less time reading Twitter and more time reporting the facts, which was one of the more foolish things I've ever said in an interview.

Election night in Leeds is manic. With so many seats being counted in one place, there are always reporters everywhere. In 2010, when my seat seemed in the balance, I was followed for an hour and a half by Michael Crick with a camera in my face, trying to read and report on my mood.

So this time, I went back to the hotel room with my press officer, Steph Driver, to watch the live programme. When we switched on, the BBC exit poll guru, John Curtice, was explaining that the early results from Sunderland were consistent with the exit poll, but there was still a huge amount of scepticism around. That was compounded when Jeremy

Vine went through a detailed projection of what the exit poll would mean for individual constituencies. I watched his list of seats turning Tory, and thought, 'This can't possibly be right.' I knew we'd lost and clearly weren't going to be in government, but I just didn't believe it could be that bad.

Then came the result from Wrexham. My Labour friend and colleague, Ian Lucas, had increased his vote by twenty from the last election, but the Tories had gone up by 2,000. Ian held the seat but only just, with an almost 3 per cent swing to the Tories. For the first time I properly realised what was happening. UKIP were surging in some parts of the country, but not by nearly as much as people had thought and without damaging the Tory vote in any serious way in key marginals like mine. But it was the Lib Dem vote I was looking at. Not only was it collapsing far more than expected, it was splitting to the Tories, not to Labour, which nobody had seen coming.

Since 2010, Labour, the Tories, the media and the pollsters had assumed one thing: if a traditional Lib Dem voter was so disillusioned at the role their party had played in coalition with the Tories, then their vote would have to go to Labour, or perhaps to the Greens, or the SNP in Scotland. Nobody had thought they would go to the Tories – but however illogical, that's what was happening. And if anything, the exit poll now looked to be understating David Cameron's victory.

In my seat, a similar one to Wrexham in terms of demography, my campaign team were still confidently telling me that we'd held on to our vote from 2010. And in all of our thinking in the previous five years, we'd concluded that if we could hold the Labour vote in a seat like mine, then we would be fine. We'd benefit from voters fleeing the Lib Dems, and any Labour losses from UKIP's rise would always be outweighed by the damage they did to the Tories.

Plus the Tories had thrown everything at my seat in 2010 – including numerous visits from David Cameron and George Osborne, and mass leafleting campaigns – so I assumed that had to be their high point in the seat. Before the campaign started, I'd thought to myself that the Tory vote would go down about 3,000, and mine would hold. But the lesson from Wrexham, and from Swindon North and Nuneaton which quickly followed, was that holding your vote wasn't enough if the Tories were increasing theirs thanks to Lib Dem switchers.

I realised the Twitter rumours might turn out to be correct. I kept texting my agent and campaign manager at the count, asking them to forget whether our vote was holding up and tell me what was happening to the Tory vote instead, but they could only reply that it was too close to call.

I sat there in silence, thinking about all the times in the previous couple of weeks when I'd been canvassing in better-off areas in my constituency, and in similar areas around the country. Normally, you're lucky to be given five minutes on someone's doorstep, but unusually in those last few days before the election, I was meeting undecided voters in those areas – many of them ex-Lib Dems – who'd spend half an hour asking what would happen in a hung Parliament – would we do a deal with the SNP, and if so, would Nicola Sturgeon be able to tell a Labour government in Westminster what to do?

As the results came through, I could hear the echo of those conversations, people worried that if Labour held the balance of power, the SNP were going to come down, demand increased public spending, and make them pay more tax. Vote Labour, get Sturgeon, get screwed.

By 4.30 a.m., the full scale of Labour's defeat was unfolding, especially in Scotland. I'd watched Jim Murphy's and Douglas Alexander's defeat speeches, given with great grace, magnanimity and calmness, and I realised they had probably been thinking about what to say for weeks.

In 2010, I'd prepared six different speeches: three for a defeat; three for a win in the event of an overall Labour victory, a Labour loss, or a hung parliament. This time I hadn't thought about my speech at all. My plan was just to thank my campaign team and my fellow candidates, say that I was honoured to be re-elected as the MP for Morley & Outwood, and reaffirm that the picture of politics was very uncertain and we would see how things would unfold in the coming hours, days and weeks. It didn't seem to be a particularly difficult speech to give, and not one that was likely to attract much attention.

But suddenly all the attention was on me, and lying on the bed in my Premier Inn room, I felt very isolated. Yvette was in constant touch, but it wasn't the same as being with her, the children were in London and all my other MP friends were busy worrying about their own counts, speeches and media interviews.

As the night wore on, I started to get an increasing volume of messages from different colleagues and my own advisers down in London, asking what was going to happen in Morley & Outwood. I could only say that I wasn't sure.

Eventually, one or two people started gently suggesting I prepare a concession speech.

I lay on the bed thinking about what I'd say, words jumbling in my mind, and every now and then drifting off to sleep, as I waited for news and a summons to the Arena. Just before 7 a.m., Tracey called and said they were getting close to the end, but the result was still far from clear. We made our way back to the Arena, finding another route to avoid the cameras. As I came through the door, I saw the other candidates and their agents and the returning officer, Leeds Council chief executive and an old friend of mine, Tom Riordan, waiting by the stage.

I greeted the Conservative candidate, Andrea Jenkyns. A former teacher, musician and businesswoman, Andrea was nice and decent with no side to her at all. We had first met at the Remembrance Day parade soon after she was selected as a candidate. I'd told her then that – as with my opponent in 2010 – I would never say anything aggressive or personal about her. To my surprise, and unlike her predecessor, she immediately promised to do the same, and had been true to her word.

We went into a dressing room behind the stage, and Tom said he would read us the provisional results. Back in 2010, despite the attentions of Michael Crick, one of the election officials had sidled up to me five minutes before the official result, and managed to whisper 'You've done it'. That was a huge relief then, but this time, I had no idea.

Tom read the names in the order they'd appeared on the ballot, so I heard my number of votes first, and knew that, as expected, it was basically the same as I'd achieved last time round. Then he read out Andrea's name and her number of votes. The Tories had gone up by 1,500 since last time, giving

Andrea a majority of 400. She gave a rather polite and modest whoop.

Even though my mind was racing, that typically English instinct kicked in: when you receive bad news in public you have to demonstrate your decorum, and under no circumstances betray any emotion. You just thank people, smile, shake hands, and – especially when someone else is celebrating – behave like a good sport.

We went through the formality of a recount, given the closeness of the vote, which gave me time to go and tell my campaign team what had happened. I carefully positioned myself with my back to the cameras, and told them all not to react.

It's an incredibly difficult thing to tell people who've worked so hard and so tirelessly for weeks and years that it's all been in vain, but they were typically professional. While the recount was going on, we stood and chatted about whether there was anything more we could have done, and recalled all those conversations we'd had with swing voters in middle-class areas which now seemed so revealing.

After forty minutes, the signal came and we went back behind the stage to see Tom Riordan again. So much for the recount; the new tally had actually increased the Tory majority. I was told, later, that I had been ahead on the returning officer's tally after every box was counted, right until the very final one, a big village to the west of Morley, which shifted me from winning to losing.

Andrea was in a nervous state, realising what a huge media moment this would be. Turning to me, she asked: 'Do I have to make a speech?' I thought about the elation of that night in

1997, when Yvette had first been elected, and the night in 2005 when I'd followed her into the Commons. I thought about my hard-fought win in 2010, when I'd applauded my Tory opponent for helping to put the constituency on the map, and – even though he was clearly upset to lose, and as bitter as the contest had been – he'd nodded along warmly.

So I told Andrea: 'It'll be fine. This only ever happens to you once – it's the first time you ever make a speech as a Member of Parliament. All you've got to do is thank people, and remember the moment. Just enjoy it.'

We went onstage. I was conscious of not wanting to give the cameras their picture by looking ashen-faced or annoyed. I certainly didn't feel that way. My mind went back to recent conversations with Yvette about the potential election outcomes. I'd confessed to her a couple of times that the only scenario that haunted me was the possibility that the Tories could end up winning a majority and I'd be stuck doing another five years in opposition. And standing on that stage, I thought, whatever the future does hold for me, at least it's not going to be that.

Looking at Andrea take the applause after the result was announced, I realised that, while she was experiencing some-thing that would never happen again for her, the start of her career as an MP, I was facing the end of mine, and that I'd even-tually start something new as well. I found myself smiling, thinking about beginnings, endings and new starts, and enjoying Andrea's combination of nerves and exhilaration.

When they invited me to speak, I stepped forward, unable to see anything in front of me because of the blaze of camera lights. I think being unable to see the audience made me, if anything, more reflective and conversational in my tone. I began to say aloud the thoughts that had been running through my head. I wanted, first and foremost, to pay tribute to the way in which Andrea had run her campaign. I went on: 'Any personal disappointment I have is as nothing compared to the sense of sorrow I feel at the result that Labour has achieved across the UK tonight.'

I also felt it was important to talk about the risks the country would face from a Tory government, and how important the Labour Party would continue to be in standing up for working people. I'd been talking about those risks – to the union with Scotland, to our European membership, to the NHS – for eight weeks, but I'd never really managed to get either the media or Ed Miliband to pick up the theme. So I thought at least if people are watching, I'll finally get my point across.

A couple of times I felt my emotions welling up, speaking about my campaign team and about my pride at having represented the area, but I pushed them back and got through it, ending with a declaration that I was sure Labour would be back.

And then it was over. I was whisked offstage and taken out by the back route into my agent Neil Dawson's waiting car, and from there to the sherry wake at his house. I looked at my old Nokia phone a few times, but there were so many text messages coming through that it became totally blocked up.

My first concern was for my family. With her count also done and majority increased, Yvette came to pick me up from Neil's, and it was only then that I learned that our son had stayed up all night with Yvette's dad, starting the evening with such hope and ending it by seeing my own defeat. It was also the morning of our eldest daughter's first GCSE exam. She got to a point where she couldn't stand the tension of waiting any longer and left the house to go to school. A second later she came back: 'I need to watch it before I go or I won't be able to think about anything else.'

Hearing about the children watching me lose made me more emotional than anything else. I managed to get my phone working long enough to send all three of them texts and voicemails, something that I found very hard. I then rang my dad who was equally emotional about everything that had happened, and I found myself comforting him, telling him it would all be fine and not to worry, that I had achieved a lot that I was proud of in the time I'd had, and who knew what the future would hold.

Just as my defeat was the Tories' symbol of their election-night joy, I found that for many distressed colleagues and Labour supporters I became almost a totem of their emotion, and I spent a huge amount of time consoling those who managed to get in touch with me. None of it was particularly personal, I didn't think – I just happened to be the climactic scene in a tear-jerking movie.

Yvette and I decided quickly that we had to go somewhere where we could be away from the cameras and where the children could come to meet us without feeling that they were being watched, especially with our daughter needing to concentrate on her revision. So Yvette rang some good friends of ours, whom the children knew well and whose house, well away from both Yorkshire and London, was helpfully tailor-made for avoiding the cameras, and we headed there by car.

During the journey, Ed Miliband called – we hadn't spoken throughout polling day or after the exit poll and he had clearly been absorbed in his own wake that morning. I'll admit my first instinct was to ignore the call. I said to Yvette: 'It's all done now. What's the point?' But she urged me to answer. Ed told me briefly he was sorry about my result and then explained that he was about to resign as Labour leader. I said that I understood, and commiserated. Before we said goodbye, I said: 'I did my best but it wasn't enough and I'm sorry about that.' There was nothing more to say.

Once we got to our friends' house, I tried to read and respond to the many warm and sad emails and texts people had sent. I was struck that no one seemed to know quite what to say. If you resign, retire or are sacked from front-bench politics, it usually doesn't happen out of the blue, and there are time-worn phrases that we all know to use – 'You're a great loss to the Cabinet', 'I hope you'll continue your campaigning from the backbenches', 'I'm sure you'll be back very soon'. Whereas when a high-profile figure is unexpectedly shunted out by the voters, it's treated more like a political death – hence some people were actually getting in touch with Yvette, rather than me, to pass on their condolences.

Strangely, it was friends outside Westminster – from business, or American politics – who were most bullish about ringing me up, sharing their own stories and giving me advice. Former US Treasury Secretary Larry Summers, a long-standing friend, left me four voicemails, and kept texting me until I rang him back. He said: 'Ed, this has happened to me a number of times, suddenly ending a job I was doing before, not always at the time and manner of my choosing, but there are some really, really important lessons which I've learned. This is an ending, but it's also a beginning, and you'll recognise in time that this is an opportunity. It will take you a while, but you'll get there.'

From my experience on the stage at the Leeds Arena, I was probably already more in that place than he realised, not necessarily knowing what would happen next, but accepting that it was the start of new things.

Looking back now, the big lesson I learned that night is that power – supposedly that most precious of commodities – is always a second away from turning to dust in your hands. I had so often joked, talking about what I'd learned over two decades in politics, that you always simultaneously have to plan ten years ahead and treat every day as if it was your last. I never thought that joke would become my reality.

At 21:59:59 on 7 May 2015, I thought there was a chance I'd be delivering Britain's next Budget. A second later, my political career was over. But what I realised is that while my life certainly changed when that exit poll came out, I didn't. Nor when I lost my seat a few hours later. Winning and losing may be very different things, but you must react to them just the same – as Kipling famously counselled.

Every politician strives to climb up the political ladder. But if you let power define who you are, you probably won't know what to do with it when you get it, and you almost certainly won't be able to come to terms with losing it.

2

Loyalty

Relegation is bad in football and politics – but is there ever a time to walk away?

Much has changed in British politics since that night in May 2015, not least within the Labour Party, following the surprise election of Jeremy Corbyn as Labour leader a few weeks later.

If I'd still been in Parliament, I don't think I could have served in Jeremy's Shadow Cabinet; not because I believe in sulking in tents, but because it would have been impossible to serve in any kind of senior position if I had fundamental disagreements with the leadership on core policy issues, and I suspect there would have been many.

I know many old colleagues and traditional Labour supporters who were in anguish about Corbyn's election, and I myself reacted with a mixture of trepidation and bafflement about where it was going to lead. However, when I saw talk of Labour MPs giving up on the party or ordinary supporters cancelling their membership, that's what really made me despair.

I could never walk away from my family or from my football team. But nor could I easily walk away from the Labour Party. And there's a reason those loyalties are so intertwined for me. Because when I was growing up, family life revolved around two things: football and politics, with our collective colours firmly pinned to two masts, Norwich and Labour.

My family was born and bred in Norwich. My mum grew up above the butcher's shop on Unthank Road and attended Notre Dame girls' school; my dad lived in a terraced house off Newmarket Road, and won a scholarship to the City of Norwich School. All of their many brothers and sisters grew up in the city, and pretty much all of them were avid Norwich City fans. So much so that when the day I was due to be born – 18 February 1967 – clashed with a fourth-round FA Cup tie at Manchester United, the family decided that my dad was better off going to the game. I'm sure my long-suffering mother would have just rolled her eyes. Luckily, I arrived a week late, so Dad could both watch a famous 2–1 victory at Old Trafford and be there for the birth.

I never met either of my Norfolk grandfathers. My dad's father passed away when my dad was just ten years old, my mum's when she was sixteen. But walking to Norwich's Carrow Road home ground before a game, my dad would talk to me about how his father, a lorry driver for the local gas company, would walk down Gas Hill on a Saturday morning after his shift, earn some more money for the family working on the turnstiles at Norwich and then get the bus to the Speedway in the evening to do his third job of the day, working as a steward.

We never had much money as a family. We never took a holiday abroad and didn't get a colour TV for years, and growing up in a small village just outside Norwich, there was nothing much for me to do except spend hours alone in our back garden winning imaginary cups and scoring goals in a full Norwich City kit. I was in the back garden one Saturday when my uncle John came out and said: 'We've had a discussion and we think you're ready to go to a game.' He had bought tickets for Norwich against Leeds in the FA Cup third round.

First, though, I was to be given a trial run to see whether this six-year-old could sit still for the full ninety minutes. The following Saturday, we drove over to Cambridgeshire, and I was sent off with my dad, Uncle John and my cousin Robert to watch March Town United versus Wisbech Town. I had a scarf, a hat, a huge rattle, a comic and a large bag of pear drops. I think they thought I was going to be bored to death. While I can't remember anything about the game at all, I did watch it avidly – and passed the test.

The next weekend we went to see Don Revie's mighty Leeds take on Norwich at Carrow Road. Norwich drew 1–1, but I most remember walking to the ground in a growing surge of supporters, all of whom were at least twice as tall as me. Inside the ground, I recall the noise, the smells, the passion, the way the singing bounced around the stands. It was the beginning of a lifetime of watching Norwich, and my initiation into our family love affair with the club.

It was only after we moved out of Norfolk in 1975, when my dad took up a position at the University of Nottingham, that I discovered quite how unusual and exotic it was to be a Norwich City supporter. Everyone in my Bawburgh primary-school class was a Norwich City fan. At my new school in Nottinghamshire, I was the only one. We were one of only two families with our distinctly Norfolk surname in the phone book, unlike in Norwich where our name had covered two pages. We were also marked out by our accents, with our new East Midlands friends continually calling out 'Oo-aah' whenever I or my sister Joanna spoke.

I had an inauspicious start at my new school. At first break on my first day, I joined in a game of football in the playground and was tearing down the right wing like Norwich winger Graham Paddon, when I put my foot just over the edge of the concrete and went flying on what turned out to be very wet grass. I was escorted back inside by one of the older girls and sat, coated in mud, on newspaper for an hour until my mum arrived with a change of clothes.

Later that week, I decided that I would turn up for the school assembly 'Show and Tell' in my full Norwich City kit. I stood decked out in yellow and green in front of three hundred bemused children explaining where Norwich was and why I supported the Canaries. I didn't care a jot if they laughed, not least at my surname or my funny accent and rather halting speaking style.

After we moved to Nottingham, we regularly made the long and winding journey back to Norwich – through the Fens, via Thorney, Swaffham and Downham Market – for family gatherings: weddings, christenings, summer get-togethers. Invariably, these occasions clashed with Norwich City matches, and while we weren't allowed to escape to Carrow Road, we did always spend more time in the car park listening to Radio Norfolk than standing round the buffet.

Having been initiated into Norwich City by my family, I took on that role myself when my little brother Andrew was born. Seven years younger than me, he'd been only eighteen months old when we moved to Nottingham so had no memories of Norfolk, but he was a Norwich City fan before he could walk or talk. I made certain of that.

This was when Nottingham Forest were in their pomp under Brian Clough, and Norwich were in their familiar struggles against relegation, but it would never have occurred to Andrew to switch teams. Norwich was at the heart of who we were as a family. It was our collective passion.

Norwich never left me either, not when I went to Oxford, then Harvard; not when I started my career in London, working for the *Financial Times* and then for Labour as adviser to Gordon Brown and then the Treasury; not when I became a junior minister and then a Cabinet minister with a young family; and certainly not after my election defeat in 2015. That October, I was approached to become a non-executive director, and had gladly accepted, but when shortly afterwards the chairman announced he was standing down, the club's majority shareholder, Delia Smith, asked if I'd step into the vacancy.

A whirlwind week later, I was sitting in a press conference before the Aston Villa game as my appointment was announced. It was only after that press conference, and after

I'd posed for a photograph holding a Norwich scarf in the tunnel, that I realised quite what I was letting myself in for. Sitting in the stands, I was hit by the rather obvious truth that there was absolutely nothing I could do at all to influence the course of the game that afternoon.

If we'd lost to Aston Villa, it would have been a bad result for Norwich but a disastrous start for me – and I knew my Norfolk surname would have provided plenty of headline copy for the newspapers. Luckily we won – emphatically – and we went on to beat Southampton the following Saturday.

If I'd resigned then, I would have been the most successful chair in Norwich City's history, but what followed was a deeply emotional roller coaster, encapsulated in a 4–5 last-minute home defeat to Liverpool that has left me scarred for life, and sadly ending in relegation from the Premier League. But we'll be back. And nothing has diminished my love for the team. Certain things consume you. Certain loyalties are unshakeable. And usually, the most permanent of the lot are the ones instilled in you from the cradle.

Politics can also be tribal. But it's about much more than that. It can be about where you come from, but it's also the values you are brought up to respect and the vision of a better society which inspires you and drives you on. Mum and Dad were both staunch Labour supporters and campaigners, their politics shaped by their upbringing, and growing up in that politically febrile time in the 1970s and early 1980s, debates about education, strikes, the economy, civil rights and apartheid seeped into my brain long before I was old enough to take part in them.

But as soon as I was, there was an expectation that not only would I understand the issues, but that I should also be able to form an opinion and defend it in the constant discussions that went on round our kitchen table and in front of the television. I can imagine many teenage boys thinking of nothing worse than sitting debating the Brixton riots with their parents, but – like Norwich City – it was just what our family did.

My dad was chair of our local Labour branch in the constituency where Ken Clarke was the Tory MP, and I joined the party as soon as I turned sixteen. At Nottingham High School I ran the Politics Society. And while Edwina Currie drew the biggest audience – it was a fee-paying school, Michael Foot had just lost the 1983 election and Labour supporters were in the minority – my most vivid memory is of three striking Nottinghamshire miners coming into school one lunchtime to talk about pit closures and police roadblocks.

Fortunately, my passion for Norwich City prepared me well for a career in politics. I've known great triumphs while supporting Norwich: watching the Milk Cup final in 1985 on TV with Andrew, and waiting for our dad to come back and tell us what Wembley had been like; seeing Norwich become the first British side to beat Bayern Munich on German soil in 1993; the many successful promotion campaigns. However, there have also been numerous lows and disappointments. We have been on the end of many heartbreaking defeats and painful relegations, and being able to come to terms with those occasions is not a sign that you don't care, it's simply a fact. You'd drive yourself mad if you tried to pretend otherwise.

One person who has steadfastly refused to get caught up in my football passion is Yvette. Growing up in an equally passionate political family, she too liked a debate round the kitchen table. That's partly what drew us together when we shared an office when I first worked for Labour in Parliament in 1994. But when it comes to Norwich City, she has scarcely engaged at all over the last twenty-three years – other than to ask on a Saturday afternoon, as I come in looking glum, 'So, have they lost again?'

But after every disappointment, you have to move on and start afresh. That's how it's been for Norwich City after each relegation; that's how it was when, against all expectation, and despite the opinion polls, Labour lost the 1992 election and John Major was returned as prime minister; that's how it is for anyone who supports Labour after the 2015 election defeat; and that's how it's been for me after losing my own seat.

Our society has changed hugely over my adult lifetime, and no political party can simply rely on old class allegiances and expectations of continued loyal support, especially when divided into warring factions. But for me personally, brought up in the Labour Party and having worked for it most of my adult life, that allegiance runs deep in my bones, and my belief still burns strongly that only a Labour government – with its shared values, history and purpose – can offer everyone in our society a fair chance in life.

Of course, my own roles as a Cabinet minister and as an MP were by essence transitory, and the same will be true of my chairmanship of Norwich City. But the club and the party go on, their values endure, support for them continues to be passed from generation to generation, and a new group of fans, players, party members and politicians will get their chance to do them proud.

My abiding memory of my first season as City's chairman will be the chants of the home crowd as we were relegated, the singing echoing around from stand to stand; the support for the manager; the anticipation of Ipswich derbies to come – it was a sight and sound that took the breath away, and brought home to me the essence of loyalty.

As my young son – who was bribed for years to come to games with promises of Cokes and hot dogs, but has now fully inherited my obsession – said to me the previous time we went down to the Championship: 'Dad, it's only when you lose at home and get relegated that you realise you're a true fan.'

Labour has not just been my team. It's been my purpose. It stands for the values I believe in, the vision I aspire to. Labour is enduring a period in the doldrums and doesn't look like getting promoted any time soon, but that's exactly when it needs its fans the most.

3
Family

———————

Many politicians want to keep their family life private – must it always be a losing battle?

Wednesday, 23 December 1998. The political world was absorbed in the intrigue of Labour MP Geoffrey Robinson's undisclosed home loan to Peter Mandelson, creating an apparent conflict of interest, given that Geoffrey's financial dealings were under investigation by Peter's trade and industry officials. The scandal was threatening to bring down Geoffrey, Peter and, in the process, Gordon Brown's media adviser and my good friend, Charlie Whelan, who had been accused of leaking the details.

I was simultaneously absorbed in my and Yvette's usual last-minute dash to the airport to fly out for a Christmas break in Italy, where my dad had moved for work. Our luggage was packed full of assorted presents and foodstuffs, including a carefully chosen, very expensive joint of British beef, my mum's favourite. Yvette's father was behind the wheel as we pulled into Heathrow when my pager bleeped with a text: 'CALL ME URGENTLY GORDON'. I called him, while tripping through the usual travel checklist in my mind: passport, wallet, presents, and realised with a sudden jolt that we had left the prime joint back in the fridge at Yvette's parents' Hampshire home.

Gordon's voice blared out from my phone: 'Have you seen the news? Mandelson's resigned!' I barely heard him. I just looked across at Yvette with horror, and said: 'Where's the beef?!' As Yvette began a frantic and fruitless search of the back seat, Gordon yelled down the phone, incredulous: 'What do you mean, "Where's the beef?" That is the beef! Mandelson's resigned!' I looked helplessly at Yvette. 'What are we going to do?' An increasingly exasperated Gordon shouted: 'There's nothing to be done! He's gone!' Calculating the timings in my head, I asked Yvette: 'Is it too late to turn back?' Gordon's voice boomed out from the speaker on my phone: 'THERE'S NO TURNING BACK NOW!'

There wasn't always such a stark juxtaposition between the goings-on in our political and family lives, but it's something that every person in politics has to face, not just in terms of the competing demands on your time and attention, but also – from a media and public perspective – as politics in Britain becomes increasingly personality-driven. Compared to three or four generations ago, there is now a widespread expectation that a politician's family will be part of their 'story', as it has been in the United States for far longer than here. And as a result, any modern politician who tries to keep their family life private is not only considered an oddity, but is also fighting a losing battle when it comes to the media's respect for that decision.

Once we decided to get married, Yvette and I knew one thing: our 'private life' was always going to be public property as far as the media were concerned, and we would have to be careful about what that meant, for ourselves, our friends and any children we had. But we thought we were ready for the disruption and anguish that would cause; we had each other for support, advice and comfort when times got tough, and we were determined to do everything we could to protect our family as we climbed up the political ladder.

Even before the birth of our first child in 1999, we'd seen the pitfalls. But the issue properly reared its head when Yvette had our second child in 2001, and became the first ever minister to take maternity leave – appropriately enough, given she was in charge of maternity services and public health at the time.

Early in her pregnancy, Yvette went to Alan Milburn, the then Health Secretary, to ask about arrangements for maternity leave. He said he had no idea, and suggested she speak to the Permanent Secretary, the civil servant in charge of the department. He had no idea either. There were no precedents. Formally speaking, Yvette was directly appointed by the monarch, but no one thought it was a good idea to ask the Queen what the rules were. In Sir Humphrey-style, the Cabinet Secretary, the most senior civil servant in the government, said Yvette should decide what she thought the appropriate rules should be, implement them as she wished, and set the precedent herself.

It wasn't long after the birth that we faced our next big challenge. Debates were raging at the time over the MMR vaccine and its safety and, given Yvette's ministerial position, we knew we would be under intense scrutiny. It was Yvette's view that she couldn't do her job without being willing to say to other parents what she as a parent had decided for our children. When asked, she therefore confirmed that our daughter had been given, and our son would have, the MMR jab and that she believed that following the advice of the Chief Medical Officer was the right thing for parents to do. The trouble was that this was not a view shared by all in the government, most notably Tony and Cherie Blair, who had refused to answer that question.

We discussed our approach to the media and our children at length at that point, wanting to make sure we got the balance right. We felt other politicians had got into difficulty when they tried to have it both ways in terms of their privacy: happy for some photos to emerge, unhappy with others, and therefore unable to enforce any kind of line. We took the view that the only way to try and protect our children from unfair coverage when they were older was to protect them from any coverage when they were very young too.

Our rule would be that decisions we made as parents on behalf of our children would be fair game: the MMR jab, the choice of schooling, our approach on smacking. If we were expected to comment publicly on those kinds of live political debates, we couldn't expect our own decisions to stay private. But we thought that the children's lives and their photos should be protected. They weren't political figures, and if they couldn't make those decisions for themselves, we shouldn't do so for them. That was the approach we took from the beginning, one newborn baby photo aside, and it's what we have tried to stick to ever since, even more so once I was elected an MP and after we became the first ever married Cabinet minister couple.

That said, I think it is an incredibly tough decision for a prime minister or leader of a political party to shield their children entirely from public view. If you're the American president, there is an expectation that the voters will want to judge the whole individual, from the state of your health to how you spend your holidays, and as our political system has drifted in that direction, it's become harder and harder for our party leaders to resist putting their families on show. Personally, I've always thought our party leaders should adopt the 'Prince Charles on holiday' approach: agree to one photo opportunity and that's it. It's the only compromise that works for the media, the public and, most importantly, the children.

In a way, politics and the media have always been a part of our children's lives. When they were very young, Yvette was increasingly asked to appear on GMTV or BBC Breakfast. One unusual morning absence quickly became routine: the children would come down for breakfast, say 'Where's Mum?', and I'd turn the TV on so they could see her. It's weird how quickly something like that can become normal.

But our determination to shield them from media attention hasn't been easy. Their privacy has been protected, but not without a few fights. When I was Children's Secretary, we accepted that our decisions about where we'd send our children to school were always going to be fair game, but – given we were committed to using the state system all the way – we didn't expect them to be particularly controversial.

When Yvette was starting out as an MP, and I was working in the Treasury, we moved our London base from Hackney to Vauxhall, to be closer to Westminster and Whitehall. But we'd always regretted leaving Hackney, where we'd lived for several years, and where we still had a network of good friends. So shortly before Gordon became PM in 2007, we moved back to east London, and enrolled the children in a local primary school.

One right-wing newspaper immediately wrote an article about the move, describing us as typical New Labour middle-class parents moving house in order to get our children into better schools. It was nonsense, but the kind of story where you just sigh and take it on the chin. However, shortly after, the school got put into special measures after a bad set of results, and the head teacher resigned. The very same paper then carried a piece saying we were typical New Labour politicians willing to sacrifice our children's education by sending them to a substandard school.

Worse was to follow. They then ran a series of stories about the school, culminating in a ludicrous claim that the head teacher had been forced to resign by a cabal of middle-class parents, led by me and Yvette. I talked to journalists at the paper and sent a long handwritten letter to the editor, saying that while decisions over where politicians send their children to school are arguably fair game, writing unsubstantiated stories about the goings-on inside a particular school simply because our children went there was unfair to both the school and our children.

I also asked the Press Complaints Commission for advice. They sympathised, but said they couldn't help; if newspapers decided there was a public interest in writing about our children, it wasn't very easy to stop them. That struck me as ludicrous, but it may just be a reflection of how toothless our press watchdogs were at that time. I found out subsequently that they promptly telephoned the paper's managing editor to warn them about my call. The paper wouldn't back down, and we just had to live with it.

An even more troubling story followed when an employee in Yvette's department was arrested for an alleged serious offence, leading to our being asked by the police whether that individual could have represented a risk to our children. We said an emphatic 'No', and that should have been the end of the matter.

But it is a depressing fact that any police matter involving high-profile individuals is likely to get leaked to the newspapers. There are just far too many people involved in investigating and processing each case for that not to happen. Sometimes, as with my rather too frequent dealings with the police and the courts over traffic offences, I knew I had only myself to blame. But on something serious like this involving the children, I thought it was completely beyond the pale.

Predictably, a week after the arrest, we had a call from a reporter at a tabloid newspaper to say they'd received a tip-off about it. I immediately rang the then editor, whom I knew pretty well, and said to him that as far as we were concerned they could write anything they liked about us but there was no public interest in writing a story with any connection to our children. I reminded him we'd always protected them from media exposure, even trying hard not to mention their names in public, so that they could be as anonymous as possible at school. The editor agreed, said there was absolutely no public interest, it wasn't a story he was going to touch, and indeed he was happy to intervene with editors of other newspapers if someone else looked like writing the story.

Three days later, on a Saturday afternoon, I was due in Brighton to make a speech to the annual conference of primary-school head teachers, a difficult assignment given at the time they were calling for industrial action to boycott SAT testing. On the train, I got a call from my media adviser, Alex, to say a Sunday newspaper was now planning a story about the employee's arrest and the supposed risk to our children. I asked him to go back and explain that there was no public interest in writing anything about our kids, let alone a story that was wholly inaccurate.

My office went backwards and forwards with the journalist for the next hour or so, and when I spoke to Alex again in Brighton, he said he was fearful they were still planning to write some version of the story, probably as the front page. I told him to go back and ask that the editor phone me directly. My speech was due at 4 p.m., and with five minutes to go, a call came through to say the editor was waiting on the line. With all my staff in Brighton urging me to get into the conference hall and avoid a potentially hostile audience turning even more restless, I had to put my foot down, and say: 'No, this is the most important thing, we must do everything we can to stop this story appearing. The heads are just going to have to wait a bit.'

I started off how I always did with editors whom I'd met a number of times, talking in a very reasonable way: thanks for taking the call; we both know the issue; and I'm sure when you hear what's actually happened, you'll see there's no story here. I repeated what I'd said to the editor of the tabloid newspaper: you can write what you like about me and Yvette, but there is no public interest in you writing any story about our children, especially one that is just wrong. He listened, and said bluntly that he didn't agree: 'In our view, there is a public interest; it's a government employee; there's a link to your children; people have a right to know about this.' I became a little heated: 'There is absolutely no public interest in our children's names being on the front page of the newspapers, so when they go to school on Monday, people can point at them in the playground and say "you're the kids", when they're not remotely involved in this. They've not chosen to be in politics. You shouldn't do this. How would you like it if it were your kids?'

He wouldn't agree, but insisted they'd write the story in a careful way. I came off the phone and went straight onto the platform to deliver my speech. I managed to keep my emotions in check at the conference, but spent the journey back to London trying to contain the damage. With any Sunday newspaper story, the problem is always compounded if the TV and radio news bulletins pick it up, so I focused on persuading the BBC and Sky News not to do so. Their respective political editors, Nick Robinson and Adam Boulton were both sympathetic to my arguments about the children's privacy, and said there was no way the BBC or Sky were going to touch the story.

Waiting for the story to drop, as I travelled to Yorkshire, was agonising. Eventually, the call came through from Alex around 10 p.m. just as I was pulling into our drive. The story was inside the paper not on the front. It was very carefully written. The children were not mentioned. I felt a huge wave of relief. Alex said: 'That's the good news. Do you want the bad news? The paper's splash is "Charles Clarke: Ed Balls must be sacked".' Charles had an article in the paper which had no bearing on me at all, but seemed to have had one sentence shoehorned into it at the last minute to generate the headline.

I went into the house and told Yvette the good news about the story, and the bizarre news about Charles Clarke. Yvette smiled, and said: 'I've think you've just taken one for the kids.'

As the children have got older, we've been increasingly glad we took the stance we did. As they continually remind us, they should be defined by what they do, think and say, not by who their parents are.

And we were naturally sympathetic and supportive of Gordon and Sarah Brown when they took the same view for precisely the same reasons, even after Gordon became Prime Minister – a fierce desire on both their parts to protect their children's privacy. It was certainly painful for Gordon when his pollsters gave him focus group feedback from many parents saying that he couldn't relate to their lives because – as far as they knew – he didn't have children. But he and Sarah can be rightly proud that they stuck to their principles.

George Osborne has faced the same dilemma. We've never spoken about our respective approaches, but it's clear he and his wife have so far taken a similar stance. Given we regularly used to appear on the same interview programmes, and both had kids who liked coming to the studio with us, George and I got to meet each other's children. One Sunday morning, I had to do an interview with John Pienaar on Radio 5 Live after we'd both appeared on *The Andrew Marr Show* together. George kindly offered to take my son up to the post-show breakfast, while I went and did my interview.

Once I was finished on *Pienaar*, I was chatting to the other guests in the studio with the microphones off, and I casually said: 'I've got to go because I've left the Chancellor babysitting my son,' which they all found funny. But one of them then casually tweeted what they thought was a nice and harmless tale. I was mortified because I felt I'd crossed the line in respect of my own son, and inadvertently put George in a difficult position if his press people got calls asking them about his new role as my babysitter.

I quickly got my press officer on the case with the journalists asking them not to report it. I called Yvette to say I had made a mistake but was trying to fix it. And then I rang the Treasury to apologise to George. He said it was no problem, but the fact that both he and I wanted to stop this story running shows how counter-intuitive it is for senior politicians to keep their children out of the media. Looking after my son was a very kind, avuncular, and – to use the pollsters' jargon – humanising thing for George to do, and yet I had to apologise to him for it becoming public.

Of course, in the last twenty years, the revolution in camera phones means that it's not just newspaper photographers you have to worry about; it's people in the street taking pictures of you to post on social media. And whereas you can more or less control the former, there's no sense trying to control the latter. The only way to do so would be never to go out in public with your kids, and then you're denying them a normal childhood, which defeats the whole object.

Not that I always get it right. I still shudder when I think about Nicole Scherzinger shouting out 'Vote for Balls!' after Dermot O'Leary read out one of my tweets on *The X Factor*. I was very excited. But any momentary pleasure was immediately wiped out by the kids' total mortification as friends started messaging them on Facebook about what had happened.

Inevitably, the children find it annoying when they can hear people talking about us or taking pictures in the cinema queue or going to the football, but it just becomes part of life after a while. But it does affect some of your choices: it feels more relaxing going on a camping holiday in America than a beach holiday in Spain, because you know there are going to be fewer people around who recognise you.

It's one thing making decisions for your children; it's a different matter for your siblings and parents. They're in the same position: they haven't chosen to be public figures just because you are; but it's harder to tell a group of intelligent, free-thinking adults how they should go about protecting their own privacy.

It's a terrible thing to admit, but sometimes politeness can be your downfall. In 1996, I was with Gordon and Charlie Whelan in Gandhi's restaurant in Lambeth on the eve of the Confederation of British Industry (CBI) annual conference. Gordon had given an interview overnight, and – as part of talking up his credentials – he'd spoken about his mother's business acumen, saying she had 'business in her blood'.

Of course, a Press Association reporter then doorstepped Gordon's mother up in Scotland and asked for her views. Polite woman that she was, she agreed to speak to them, and modest woman that she was, she played it all down, saying she had no business experience at all and she really didn't know why Gordon said these things. That was enough for a *Times* front-page story, and poor Gordon was in agony when we got the news. I've never known a man with a bigger appetite, but he didn't touch his lamb bhuna that night.

As much as siblings and parents really want to help and be supportive, they don't have the same cautious instincts about the media that are bred into you as a politician, so their natural behaviour is just to answer the door or the phone, and deal with questions politely, because what they're most worried about is coming across as rude or angry, and that reflecting badly on you.

All politicians start out the same, but after you've been turned over once by the media, you learn that sometimes you just have to hang up the phone or close the door in someone's face. As with your children, it makes you feel very defensive and protective when you hear that reporters have turned up at your parents' house, or rung up your brother or sister.

For me as Education Secretary, that was particularly so when there was any coverage about the fact that I'd been educated at the fee-paying Nottingham High School. Here was a decision my parents had made on my behalf when I was young being used three decades later as a stick to beat me with politically, and I would regularly get asked by the media whether I regretted my parents' decision. They made huge sacrifices to send me to that school. My mum put aside all the money she earned working in the pharmacy at the local hospital, and that education was the only luxury we ever had as children.

We live in different times now, and today's Labour politicians will make different choices. But I'm still so grateful to my parents for the sacrifices they made, and I would never dream of saying I regretted my education. My parents went for the option they thought was right for me and my brother and sister, because wanting the best for your children is what every parent wants. Each parent has to make their own choice about what that is, and no one else has the right to second-guess those choices.

And that's what I've always said to my former colleagues, especially those at the start of their careers. Decide right at the outset what's best for you and your family based on their needs, not yours. And once you've taken that decision, stick to it as best you can.

4

Vulnerability

We all have flaws and imperfections – but can a politician really admit theirs in public?

My first live television interview as a politician was on *Newsnight* in 2004, the same evening that I'd been selected as the Labour candidate for Normanton. More than 120 people had come to vote at the final meeting which, after seven years of careful preparation, I'd won by a landslide. But they were all long gone when I finally got to do my interview – I stood alone outside Normanton Community Centre for an hour in the cold before finally speaking 'down the line' to Gavin Esler.

It was a big moment for me, a 'coming out' after years of backroom politics. I wasn't sure how well I'd done on the TV, however. I guessed from the muted response of Yvette and the local council leader that it wasn't a flawless performance, but I just put this down to nerves and a lack of training.

When I called Damian McBride, the Treasury's head of communications, to ask what he thought, he said: 'Was it really freezing there or something? There were times you sounded like it was too cold to get your words out.' 'Yeah,' I said, 'it must have been that – it was really cold.'

It was the start of a decade-long struggle, one that I didn't realise I was fighting at the time, and which I didn't understand for a long while to come.

A few weeks later I was preparing to appear on Radio 4's *Any Questions*, the day after Tony Blair had announced that he was going into hospital for heart surgery and also that he intended to serve a full third term. That bombshell put paid to any hope Gordon Brown had of fighting the 2005 election as leader of the party, a move he believed Tony had promised him earlier that year. Tony's announcement was dubbed the 'African coup', after some loose talk by Gordon's aides when they discovered the news that night after landing in Washington.

I'd spent the whole day working out how I would answer the inevitable Blair–Brown questions. They came up, and I answered them as best I could, feeling that I hadn't put a foot wrong. As the programme continued, and the subject moved on from the leadership battle to the Iraq War, my answers became less convincing, my voice more hesitant and faltering, with a couple of unplanned pauses. I knew it hadn't gone that well, but I left the studio to drive back to Yorkshire not really knowing what the public perception of my performance would be, and just wishing I had thought more about my answers on Iraq.

The next morning, I got a phone call from my dad. 'Ed,' he said, 'I heard you on the radio last night.' He paused. 'I think you've got the same thing as me.' 'What thing?' I asked. 'The speaking problem,' he said. I was suddenly – and sickeningly – aware of what he meant, but I needed him to tell me. He explained: 'It's the reason why I've never been able to read out a speech. I have to deliver all my lectures without notes. It's the reason why when I was on television in the old days, I was sometimes a bit hesitant. I don't know what it is but I think you've got it.'

Even after the conversation with Dad, I tried to convince myself that there was nothing to worry about: that it was all just about gaining confidence and experience. Soon afterwards, I appeared live on *Channel 4 News*. After a perfectly ordinary start, Jon Snow asked me a question and I suddenly froze, silent for what seemed to me like a lifetime. It was probably only a second, but it was enough for me to see this mixture of concern and bafflement in his eyes.

Over the next few months it happened again and again. Every now and then in a television interview, I would just freeze, my words wouldn't come out, and I would look at the interviewer with a slightly bulgy-eyed look of surprise. It didn't take long for people to pick up on it. A coruscating column dedicated to my media performances appeared in the *New Statesman*, and I learned I'd acquired the nickname 'Blinky Balls' in Conservative Central Office, supposedly courtesy of David Cameron. But I still brushed it off, and continued to try and find conventional ways to blast through it. Through Sarah Brown, I was introduced to a theatre vocal coach, who said I just needed to breathe more deeply. I tried, but if anything, it made me more nervous.

Things didn't get worse, but they didn't get better. I got through my maiden speech as an MP OK, but often when I stood up to ask a question, I'd feel that same sudden tension and pressure, causing my speech to halt. My eyes would stare, my hands would reach out to grip the bench in front of me and sweat would prickle down my back as I tried to get the words out. But it didn't *always* happen – sometimes I was really fluent – so I just used to feel irritated at myself and a bit confused when it did.

In 2006, I was appointed to my first ministerial job as Economic Secretary to the Treasury with responsibility for the City and financial services. As the Tories got a chance to see me up close across the dispatch box, a new phenomenon started: if I hesitated when answering a question, they'd shout 'Errrr', which made me hesitate more, and the laughter and mocking 'Errrr's would grow louder. When he'd get up to speak, Gordon Brown would always be ferociously angry and protective of me, like a big brother rolling his sleeves up. He would roast the Tories in those sessions, but I always felt embarrassed that he was having to do it on my behalf.

I did quite a lot of media that year, and – while it continued to be hit-and-miss – I was learning various lessons as I went along, probably better called coping mechanisms: making sure I was totally on top of my subject; starting every response with the word 'Look . . .'; never arriving out of breath; and getting into certain rhythms and routines at the different studios. A year on, I was appointed to my first ever Cabinet job, Secretary of State for Children, Schools and Families. The pressure and responsibilities grew exponentially. I still had a reputation for not being the most fluent on television, and still had not been properly tested, with only a few big set-piece interviews and speeches under my belt. At the back of my mind the question remained: sometimes my speaking went wrong, and I still didn't know why.

About three or four weeks into my new job, I was expected to give my first speech about our new Children's Department to a large audience of 600–700 experts from education and children's policy at the Design Centre in Islington. It was a frantic period and with so much else going on I hadn't really had time to work properly on what I wanted to say, but my advisers had done enormous amounts of work on the speech, and I'd just about managed to rehearse it. Plus I was pretty confident – I knew what I wanted to say. Or rather I thought I did.

As I stood up and began to speak, I noticed my sentences were getting bumpy. I had a couple of halting pauses, but I eventually got through it. I was exhilarated, but I was the only one. Afterwards, my expert policy adviser, Francine Bates, said to me: 'What was wrong? You didn't look as though you believed in it, you were so hesitant, there was no passion. What happened?' Those listening couldn't work out why I'd been so flat and uninspiring, and just felt disappointed.

A few weeks later, answering questions in Parliament with the rest of my ministerial team, I was the first up to speak, and only needed to read out the short prepared answer to the question on the order paper. But for seconds, I couldn't say anything. As I eventually sat down, I heard the late, great

Gwyneth Dunwoody lean over and say to the person sitting next to her in a very loud voice: 'He's supposed to be the Secretary of State and he can't even get his words out.'

I knew something had to be done. I sat down with my closest advisers back in my office and said: 'There's something wrong and I don't know what to do.' A week later, Francine came into my room. 'I've done some research, and I want you to read the link I'm going to send you, and see what you think.' I clicked through, saw it was the website of the British Stammering Association, and thought: 'Why am I reading this? I don't have a stammer. I don't speak in a stuttering way.'

But the page Francine had sent me was about 'interiorised stammering', commonly known as a block. It described people who didn't overtly make a sound when they stammered, they just blocked, and couldn't get any words out. An American academic described it as being like an iceberg, where a small amount of the problem was apparent above the ocean – the silence, the stare, the clenching of the throat and the fist – but under the surface there was a huge mass of churning emotions, tensions, worry and avoidance.

I read this and thought: 'Here I am, aged forty-one, a Cabinet minister, and I've only just found out I've got a stammer.' I called Francine back in and said: 'You're absolutely right, what shall I do?' She said: 'I've found the best person for you to speak to. Her name is Jan Logan, and she's a therapist from the City Lit College in central London. I've spoken to her and she's looked at some video clips of your speeches and interviews and thinks she can help. So let's get her in.' I'm ashamed to say I was both sceptical and a bit worried at the prospect. It all felt a bit Cherie Blair and Carole Caplin.

I said: 'Come on, I'm a Cabinet minister, I can't start seeing a therapist.' But Francine said: 'If you don't, things aren't going to get better,' so rather reluctantly I agreed.

That first meeting with Jan was the beginning of a huge transformation.

She told me straightforwardly that she thought I had an interiorised stammer, and the normal way of dealing with it would be to enrol me on an eight-week course with a group of similarly affected people to work out how best to deal with the problem. She said it was normal in those group sessions for things to get worse before they improved, but she was confident that at the end of it I would be more able to do my job. I tried to explain my predicament: I had to run a department. I made speeches and appeared on television most days. As much as I wanted to follow her advice, I didn't have time to go to group therapy, and couldn't afford for things to get worse.

I thought that might be the end of it, but she very kindly developed a solution for me: weekly solo sessions at her house in Islington. Instead of group practice sessions, I got to 'practice' in public on a regular basis in the House of Commons and live on TV. Jan filmed me speaking and watched a couple of performances, and we realised that when I was feeling tense and worried, I was also speaking much faster. So the process began to find a way to slow my tempo, calm down and get in control. She also talked to me about a process of therapy called Neuro-linguistic Programming, which was about understanding the bad mental states when the stammer or block occurred and the good mental states when it didn't, which fitted my experience exactly.

Through those regular meetings, I began to develop a set of strategies which made life increasingly easier. I realised that I found speaking to an audience I'd never met really hard, so I'd always try to arrive at an event early and speak to a few of the audience members in advance, so when I started my speech, it would feel more like continuing a conversation.

I also learned that if I arrived late and rushed straight onto the stage I was much more likely to stammer. Whereas if I simply spent ten minutes, preferably more, sitting in the audience watching the previous speaker or panel discussion, then I would start to feel more in tune with the mood of the audience and not feel destabilised when it was my turn on the stage.

Trying to read from a text didn't really work for me either. Whereas if I wrote the speech in advance, spent two or three hours learning it and then stood up without any notes and just spoke, I could deliver it pretty much word-for-word but my speech would be much more fluent and conversational.

One particular revelatory occasion happened a year in when I was talking to Jan about doing clips for the television, the kind of twenty-word soundbite which every politician is supposed to be able to deliver with ease. I could always do that fine in the context of a longer interview, but when it was the soundbite alone, I'd have to really focus hard and grip my hands together to get the words out.

Jan said: 'Gripping your hands like that is making things worse not better; it's causing tension to rise through your arms, up through your body, and making you block. The next time you do a clip for television, put your hands in your pockets or waggle them by your side, but just stay relaxed.'

Things certainly weren't solved overnight. One time, doing a live interview with Jon Sopel, out on College Green, I had a block for so long that he looked at me with fear in his eyes, wondering what the hell to do if I didn't start speaking again. And I know in that early period, I deliberately avoided some situations when I was feeling under pressure, and knew it would be a bad time to do an interview stammer-wise, even if it was necessary politically.

So for all the strategies I was learning, I still lived with this fear that blocks could just come out of nowhere, and that one would happen at a time that would be disastrous both for me and for the government. I told Jan about this, and she gave me perhaps her most important bit of advice. 'The best thing you can do is be open and go public about it. It will relieve the pressure and make a block much less likely.'

The trouble was, at the time, I just didn't think that was a possibility. It felt like admitting a flaw or a weakness, and that's just not what politicians do, especially not someone like me who projected a robust, commanding image. I just didn't have the confidence that speaking about the problem could be part of the solution.

I did speak privately to a few people, besides friends and family. I told Michael Palin, whose name adorns the Centre for Stammering Children in London, and the Speaker John Bercow, who had attended the centre with me. I also confided in the BBC's Nick Robinson; I thought it was important that at least one senior person in the media knew, just in case I had a real meltdown in public and nobody knew why.

When I made my next speech to the Labour Party conference, I did my usual trick of delivering it without notes, but distributing it in advance to the journalists, who could see I was reciting it pretty much word for word. At a certain point, as almost always happened during my speeches, I had a block. *The Times* columnist Ann Treneman speculated the next day that my recall of the speech was so accurate, I must have had someone reading it to me through an earpiece, and when I'd paused, it was because I was 'awaiting instructions from Mission Control'. Little did the writer know what was really going on, and it was on those kinds of occasions I felt increasingly frustrated that – in my own mind – I couldn't or wouldn't talk about the real problem.

The key breakthrough on that front happened a few months later in a primary school in Islington. As part of my increasingly regular discussions with the Michael Palin Centre and the charity Action for Stammering Children, I'd commissioned a DVD of children talking about their stammers, as a tool for teachers about how to handle stammering in their classrooms. It was called 'Wait, wait, I'm not finished yet'.

I arrived with Michael Palin to launch the DVD to an audience of 150 or so people. I'd been given a copy the night before, foolishly hadn't watched it, and when I saw for the first time these incredibly brave primary-school children speaking about their stammers and saying to teachers, don't interrupt us, don't finish our sentences, don't undermine our confidence, just give us the space to speak, I was incredibly moved and tearful.

I had to stand up straight afterwards to say a few words of introduction, and I was so shaky and thrown, it was one of the hardest speeches I've ever had to make, and I was blocking throughout. Afterwards, a man came up to me and said: 'Can I just ask you, do you have a stammer yourself?' And I said: 'It's not really about me today, it's about the children.' And the man said, with a lot of emotion in his voice: 'My son is one of the kids in that video, and what he's done there speaking about his stammer is really brave. And I think you're being a coward by not doing the same. Why don't you give these kids some hope and confidence that you can have a stammer and become a Cabinet minister?'

I stood there mortified. I went back to the department and wrote a personal letter to every one of the twenty or so children who'd appeared in the DVD, thanking them for what they had done and telling them that I had a stammer too, and that they had inspired me. And that was the moment I realised I had to be open about it.

A few weeks later, after much internal debate and with my media team still very cautious, I did a long feature interview with the *Telegraph*'s Mary Riddell, where I told her I had a stammer and explained how I dealt with it. A few weeks after that I went live on GMTV with Michael Palin and a child with a stammer and spoke openly about my own problem, and that afternoon I did a live interview with Kay Burley on Sky, which was just me on my own talking about the issue.

The response was amazing. Many people got in touch to

say well done, but most importantly, hundreds of people with stammers, or with children who stammered, wrote me letters and emails to thank me for speaking out, and to tell me that it had helped. It was the beginning of a hugely valuable process for me. I continued to speak publicly at stammering events, and did a number of other interviews, and every time I was able to speak out, it felt so liberating. I also learned the importance of always striving to be conversational and relaxed in interviews, even if they were on the most serious political programmes and with the toughest interrogators.

It made me a much better political interviewee because I couldn't over-rehearse, I just had to react to what I was asked and respond on the hoof. It turned my flaw into a strength. And the process of being public about it not only helped me to deal with it, it also made me a stronger individual. When I'd have the occasional block, I was able just to shrug it off. The less pressure I put on myself, the less I would block. And when people would write on Twitter 'Why does he say "Look" at the start of every sentence?' it was easier for me just to think 'Don't you know I've got a stammer?' rather than taking it to heart.

Because the stammer never goes away, and sometimes it can hit me very hard. One of those occasions was the Autumn Statement of 2012, the second biggest financial statement of the year, delivered by the Chancellor live on TV, with the Shadow Chancellor having to give an immediate reply.

Right at the end of George Osborne's speech, I was thrown by a sleight of hand he had pulled on the numbers. I stood up, still trying to work out what he'd done, mixed my words, and had to begin again. I suddenly had a really bad block, and there was a gale of noise and mockery from the Tories, with

David Cameron leading the laughter. I gradually pulled things round, but the media verdict was that it had been a total disaster, and my own side were clearly demoralised.

The next morning I was on the *Today* programme, and Sarah Montague started the interview by repeating the Tory line that my halting response showed I lacked confidence in Labour's economic arguments. At the end, she went back to it, challenging me to accept that I had let George Osborne off the hook, and then asking, 'And you did your job well enough yesterday?' And live on the radio, I had a choice to make. I could have blustered it away, but I thought, 'I'm just going to tell the truth.'

So I said to Sarah: 'Everybody knows that I have a stammer and sometimes my stammer gets the better of me in the first minute or two when I speak, especially when I have the Prime Minister, the Chancellor and 300 Conservative MPs yelling at me at the top of their voices. But frankly that is just who I am and I don't mind that . . . and I don't apologise for one second. I'll keep making the arguments.'

I came out of the *Today* interview, my phone exploding with messages saying 'That was brilliant'. But then as tears welled up I sat disconsolate in a room on my own for ten minutes, thinking: 'Why have I done this? Why make myself so exposed?' But I had to pull myself together, and go and explain the situation again live on BBC *Breakfast*.

It was another watershed for me. It was the first time in which something had really gone so publicly wrong, and I'd chosen to explain that my stammer was part of the reason. Plus I had to accept that, for all the progress I'd made, I would never be free of the problem, and my opponents would exploit it whenever they could. The following year in the Autumn

Statement, the Tories had worked out that if they laughed, screamed and yelled incredibly loudly, they could try to put me off my stride and force me to block. I tried to be strong and robust in response, but it just came over as me shouting. The year after, I decided just to ignore their shouting and baiting, and be much more straight and forensic and questioning and it proved much more effective.

The most important thing I learned, though, was that I had a stammer and it was just part of who I was. It wasn't something that I'd caught, it was not something that could be cured, it wasn't something which was going to go away. There's nothing that annoyed me more than people writing in newspapers 'Ed Balls, who used to have a stammer', because I still have it today but I accept it as part of who I am.

The year after the election in 2010, Colin Firth won his Oscar for *The King's Speech*, playing George VI, who was probably the most famous person to deal with an interiorised stammer, and in an even more public setting. I wrote to Colin to congratulate him and said that I would like to talk to him about work we could do together to support stammering children.

We met in the House of Commons, and I told him my favourite exchange of the film was right at the end, when the King delivers his great speech to the nation on the eve of war, and his therapist Lionel Logue says drily: 'Very good, Bertie . . . You still stammered on the w . . .' And the King replies: 'I had to throw in a few so they knew it was me.'

I told Colin those words meant so much to someone with

a stammer, because it's not just that the speech itself was a triumph, it's the fact that he's so at ease with himself and his condition that he's able to joke about it. Brilliantly, Colin said that was included in the film because he'd found it in Logue's diaries, and realised what an important and illuminating moment it was.

Since that time, Colin and I have been a number of times to visit children and parents at the Michael Palin Centre. When you meet the parents early on in their two-week course, they're often still extremely stressed by the reality of the stammer, what their children have been going through, and sometimes feel terribly guilty looking back at occasions when they've interrupted or got annoyed at their kids.

But by the second week, you can see the difference it makes as they watch their children improve. And for us to be able to say: it worked for a king; it worked for me as a politician; it will work out all right for your kids too – that has been one of the most affirming experiences of my life.

All these experiences showed me that, even though I had turned the weakness to my advantage, it remained a weakness to deal with. The reality is none of us are perfect. Every politician, every adult, every child has some flaws, some challenges and some imperfections. But the more honest you are with yourself and other people about the struggles you face, the easier you'll find them to cope with; the more help, support, understanding and tolerance you can access, the closer you'll come to turning those weaknesses into strengths.

And best of all, in the process, you might be able to help some other people too.

5

Friendship

─────────────

You meet hundreds of contemporaries in politics – but can you become and remain true friends?

For me, sitting down with Denis Healey wasn't just like being a kid in a toy shop, it was like being locked overnight in Hamleys.

A few months after I was appointed Labour's Shadow Chancellor in 2011, I travelled down to Sussex with my old friend the *Observer* journalist Bill Keegan to seek advice from Labour's oldest surviving Chancellor, and one of the towering figures of post-war politics.

Over our mid-morning gin and tonics – Denis was from an era where a drink before lunch was a very important part of the political process – I knew I wanted to ask about his 1974 and 1976 Budgets, the IMF negotiation, the leadership battles, and of course his relationships with all the other big beasts of the time. But there was only one place to start: 'Tell me how things were with Tony Benn', thinking most of all about their bitter contest for the Labour deputy leadership in 1981 and their intense rivalry. His answer surprised me.

He didn't say a word about their respective political careers and ideological clashes, or the acrimony and animosity of that famous election battle. Denis just recalled how, after the love of his life, Edna, had died in 2010, just shy of their sixty-fifth wedding anniversary, his old foe Tony Benn was one of the first people to call him.

Tony had lost his own wife Caroline ten years before, and Denis said he took huge comfort from their conversations around that time, and that they'd continued to speak at length in the years since, about politics, history, family, and how much they both missed their wives. Denis said that friendship with Tony Benn, very late in both their lives, had been very important to him, and all their past differences had disappeared from his mind, because when it came down to it, they were fundamentally on the same side and had a kinship which could outlast any conflicts.

Time heals, Denis told me, rivalries fade, and friendships emerge, if you let them. But it can take quite a long time.

As I talked to Denis, I was reminded vividly of Gordon Brown's belated reconciliation with Robin Cook. Back in 1994, when I first arrived to work for Gordon, he had an incredibly difficult relationship with the then Shadow industry spokesperson. There was an antipathy which went back to their early days in Scottish politics which I never fully understood.

But there were also differences on policy. Robin wanted to announce a huge German-style industrial investment bank. Gordon thought that was far too 'big state' for the modernised Labour Party we were trying to project. So Robin's adviser and I came up with a compromise: we would announce plans for what Gordon would describe as a 'Small Business Development Bank' designed to help entrepreneurs, while Robin would claim that it was in fact a small 'Business Development Bank', the prototype for something much larger. It was one of many unhappy compromises and repeated clashes between the two. Gordon was always convinced that Robin Cook was briefing against him, and undermining him with colleagues.

But that all changed after Robin left the Cabinet over Iraq in 2003. The pair started to meet up more often, regularly sitting up talking into the early hours. Around 2004, Robin invited me round to his office, a large room overlooking the Thames where eminent backbenchers were situated by the whips, and we had a wide-ranging conversation about the purpose of politics and government, my own plans, and what Gordon should do in the future. As well as getting to know each other, it was clear to me that Robin believed he was going to be working more closely with Gordon in the years to come, and felt it important to establish a relationship with his key advisers. It was the first time I'd realised what a close confidant Robin had become.

So when he suddenly died in the summer of 2005, it was not just a huge loss to British politics and to the Labour movement, it was a real body blow for Gordon. And I'm sure it wasn't just the loss of someone who was integral to his future plans, it was the real sense of grief and frustration at wasting the years of friendship they could have had before.

I had a similarly difficult relationship with Jim Murphy before he became the leader of Scottish Labour. Jim and I were obviously on different sides of the Blair–Brown divide, and he was always deeply distrusted by Gordon, again for reasons lost in the mist of Scottish politics. He made an amusing but slightly pointed remark about me when he decided to run the 2013 London Marathon, which was going to be my second. Asked if he would beat my time from the previous year, he answered: 'I could beat Ed Balls' finishing time with Ed Balls on my back.' We were never on opposite sides in the annual party conference football match, but I imagine it would have got rather feisty if we were.

But when he took over in the wake of the Scottish referendum, I decided I would try and do everything I could to support him; deep down, we had always been on the same side and what was happening to Labour in Scotland was so difficult and so crucial. I went up a few times and we did a number of joint events together. We had some good times and great fun together on our visits. A few months after the election, Jim thanked me for being there for him at a time when I think he felt very alone.

Again, it left me thinking how daft politics can be sometimes, when you imagine yourself into a rivalry or enmity, regardless of all the more important things you have in common.

★

It is well known that one of the great political battles of recent history was fought between Blair and Brown. But ironically, if any two people demonstrated the ability to maintain their essential kinship whatever their own rivalry and the day-to-day difficulties, arguments and conflicts going on beneath them, it was Tony and Gordon.

I first met Tony Blair in the autumn of 1991. He was the Shadow employment minister at the time, and we struck up an easy relationship. I went down to his tiny office in Parliament to talk to him about the American welfare-to-work programmes, and the minimum wage, and the research I'd done on these issues at Harvard.

As a journalist and then as I regularly went down to Westminster to meet Gordon, I often saw the two of them together, and the closeness and depth of their relationship was obvious. They had come into Parliament together in 1983 and shared both an office and a political project – to make Labour electable again.

When John Smith died suddenly in 1994, Gordon knew from the beginning that powerful forces were pushing for Tony to be the candidate and for him to stand aside. It was painful for him and for Tony, both because they were friends and because Gordon's own desire to lead the Labour Party was deep and long-standing. It was going to be a difficult conversation.

They finally decided to meet in the Granita restaurant in Islington to resolve the issue. Gordon didn't know where Granita was, he wasn't sure it was his kind of place, and he was worried Tony might be late, so I was brought along as his guide and chaperone. He told me and his core staff that he wouldn't eat too much, and that we could all go for a steak back in Westminster to debrief afterwards.

When we arrived, Tony was already at the table. The three of us sat down. It was the first, but certainly not the last, time I was to play gooseberry in a one-to-one meeting between Gordon Brown and Tony Blair. Polenta was famously on the menu that night, and I recall it because Gordon had to ask me what it was. I stayed until their starters arrived, at which point I made my excuses and left.

If I'd stayed for the full dinner, people say it could have solved a lot of problems down the line with disputes over what was said, not least I'd be able to tell the media and biographers what was right and wrong and whether a deal was offered on the leadership. But they needed to sort things out themselves, in a way that would allow them both to carry on.

In reality, I don't think Tony was offering a promise about the future leadership, and I don't think Gordon was asking for one. Gordon's sole focus going into that meeting was to agree a partnership between them, with him having control of the broad range of economic policy – and that was certainly the version which was agreed and briefed the next day to the newspapers.

But I think what was really going on at the dinner was something more important: they were not going to let the issue of the leadership destroy their friendship, they were going to find a way to make it work and not just rip it all up. That's why I've never bought into the notion that if Tony had encouraged Gordon to stand and then beaten him fair and square, a lot of their future troubles could have been avoided. It's a complete misreading to think Gordon didn't accept the outcome – everyone knew who was in charge. The point was that they had a deal on how they would work together. So if there was a sense of resentment in Gordon that the 'deal' at Granita was not being honoured, it was on those increasingly frequent occasions when it felt as though they were not working together properly, and Tony wasn't confiding in him. Inevitably, those occasions usually coincided with speculation about Tony's future and Gordon's succession, so it's no wonder the two things become conflated.

That the relationship between Tony and Gordon deteriorated badly from 1997 onwards is, of course, one of the worst-kept secrets in British politics. Time after time, junior ministers were sent out to tell the world what a strong and close partnership it was – the rock on which the government was built. But everyone knew that the tensions and rows and genuine policy differences were only growing. Each got frustrated and angry and resentful towards the other and the people around them magnified the disagreements.

And yet, having seen it all up close for years, I don't believe the conventional wisdom that their relationship simply collapsed. For all those difficult times, I believe there was a deeper truth that even many of the people who worked closely with them didn't fully appreciate: that while their friendship was often stretched beyond breaking point, their underlying kinship never fully disappeared.

Take 2004, when some were urging Gordon to strike against Tony as the Iraq War and the domestic fallout reached a crisis point. Gordon's reluctance to do so was not only because he feared the division that would follow, but because he thought it would be an unforgivable breach of their comradeship.

But during that whole period, with the Tories ineffective, the prism of politics in Britain was all about the Blair–Brown relationship, and it was very easy for the supporters on either side to feed and deepen that perception of division via the media. It was a failure on Tony and Gordon's part that they never acted to stop that briefing, and sometimes fed the flames: Gordon ranting about Tony screwing him over on some policy issue or telling Robert Peston he no longer believed Tony's promises; Tony openly calling Gordon 'impossible' to deal with. But the biggest failure on their part was that, in those first few years after Tony became leader, they did not reveal more openly the reality of their comradeship, both internally and externally.

It wasn't just the public and press who didn't understand the strength of that personal bond, it was also some of their closest colleagues. As the years passed, the number of supporters on either side who knew the others grew fewer and fewer. The vitriol really flew between the younger or less experienced members of each camp.

For someone like me or Sue Nye, who'd known Tony and Gordon for years, it was very different. The same was true of Jonathan Powell, Alastair Campbell, Anji Hunter, Peter Mandelson and the late, great Philip Gould in their dealings with Gordon. Perhaps the only person in that older inner circle who was openly hostile and rude to Gordon, and the rest of us, was Cherie.

Of course, I had my occasional disagreements over policy with Tony, but there was always a mutual respect between us, and he shared the fatherly pride that Gordon had in all of us who had been their young advisers in opposition. So at the end of even quite difficult meetings on pensions or

Europe, Tony would ask me how I was getting on with standing for selection and how we were managing to balance work and family life, and would advise me and Yvette on how to cope with the travelling between Yorkshire and London.

On the day when I received my first ever ministerial job in the reshuffle of 2006, I sat in my office up in Yorkshire waiting for the call I'd been told to expect. The phone rang: 'We have the Prime Minister for you.' A second later, the familiar voice said: 'Ed, it's Tony. I've been thinking very hard about how to use your skills, and I think you should go to work on investment and small business in Northern Ireland.' I paused, thinking: 'Bloody hell, I know nothing about Northern Irish politics. How are we going to manage that with the kids? What's Yvette going to say?' But it was the Prime Minister appointing me to a job and I told him it would be a great honour to accept the position. There was a pause and Tony laughed and said: 'Gotcha! Only joking, you're going to the Treasury. Good luck and enjoy it, I'm sure you'll be brilliant.' And that was that.

For Tony and Gordon, things finally reached their nadir in September 2006. Tony had returned from his holiday and did a weekend interview with *The Times* where, unexpectedly, he repeated his pledge to serve a full third term, sparking a huge rebellion from MPs, including many normally considered Blairites. The parliamentary party went into turmoil for days, with different groups of MPs compiling letters urging him to reconsider in the wider interests of the party.

On the Wednesday morning that week, as I sat in Gordon's office with Ed Miliband and Douglas Alexander discussing Gordon's conference speech, a call came through to my phone from our close ally and my friend Tom Watson. Tom told me that he and a group of other ministers had just tendered their resignations. We were all shocked. 'Can we stop them?' Gordon asked. I told him it was too late.

There's a myth that everything which took place that week was coordinated from Gordon's office, but Tom's resignation was a case in point. Tom was certainly one of those putting pressure on Tony to retract his 'full third term' statement, and we were happy enough with that, but we had no indication that he was planning to resign to force the issue, and it was at that point – with things clearly snowballing out of control – that Gordon contacted Tony to try and restore some unity, and sanity, to the party.

The following morning, 7 September 2006, Tony decided he had no choice but to announce he would be standing down as leader within a year, and I was in Gordon's flat when they spoke on the phone. They spent a long time talking through the statement, and the way it would be made. And despite all the acrimony of the preceding days, the tone of Gordon's voice in their conversation that morning was tender, friendly and sympathetic, and I could tell from his long pauses and embarrassed laughs – he always chuckled whenever anyone praised him – that Tony was almost certainly reciprocating at the other end.

And that was the truth: many times, I saw the two of them together having conversations with a closeness that belied the caricature of their relationship in the press and in the public domain. And if anything, several of us old-timers sometimes thought that the friendship between them got in the way of good decision-making. I certainly heard Blairite friends of mine complain that when it came to the crunch,

Tony was always inclined to agree with Gordon rather than back his own team.

And that was evidence not just of their kinship, but also of their common purpose. Given what I know of Michael Gove, it seems to me he genuinely convinced himself that, despite past friendships, his principles and convictions prevented him working with David Cameron and Boris Johnson and justified the way he acted during and after the Brexit referendum. Whereas with Blair and Brown, for all the differences they had over the detail of policy over the euro, tuition fees and foundation hospitals, there was never a fundamental issue of principle between them.

Both Ed Miliband and I had similar experiences of being close up to Tony Blair. We had both arrived to work in Westminster only a few months before John Smith died and Tony became leader – Ed with Harriet Harman, me with Gordon, her boss. Over the years, as we worked closely together, we saw the jealousy and resentment which the Blair–Brown relationship created in the people around them. I often wonder whether Ed drew a lesson from that, and perhaps the wrong one.

We'd become good friends, close friends, after we started working together in 1994. We had a close partnership, both inside and outside work, and Yvette and I regularly used to go out for the evening with Ed and his then girlfriend.

However, I think the lesson Ed took from the Blair–Brown relationship ultimately convinced him that it was one thing to be friends when working together in a strong and cohesive team at the Treasury, but doing so as MPs, ministers and potential future leadership rivals was something altogether more difficult. Things were already complicated enough for Ed because of the sibling rivalry with his brother, David, who had been Tony Blair's head of policy and was now an MP.

After Ed took a sabbatical to teach at Harvard in 2002 and then became selected as an MP in his own right, I felt he very deliberately withdrew. The whips put Ed and me in next-door offices again – just like in the Treasury, just like the young Tony and Gordon – but I barely saw him, and when we did speak, it was all very cordial but slightly formal. Yvette and I often invited him to come over to our house twenty miles up the road from where he was in Doncaster, but he never did.

Nothing had happened between us; I just think he wanted distance, to separate friendship and politics. I was competitive and driven, but so was Ed, and he was weary of being seen as my junior partner. He knew tricky times were going to come along, and already having one older brother with whom he had a strained relationship, he didn't need a second. And maybe he was right. The only times I felt short-changed were when the growing distance between us seemed to affect his professional judgement. He was in charge of writing the 2010 manifesto, and I'm sure he took the counsel of many people, but that didn't include me, despite the number of times we'd worked successfully on such documents in the past.

When it came to the leadership election, he made the highly controversial decision to challenge his brother, a sibling battle that became the defining soap opera of the campaign. Ed and I hadn't been colleagues or friends since 2004, and six years later I didn't bat an eyelid at the idea of us competing with each other. If anything, it just made more sense of the distance he'd created over that period.

That same distance made it easy for him not to make me Shadow Chancellor in 2010 when he won and became the leader. I told him the day after his election that he'd won fair and square, that I was going to back him 100 per cent, but I also made clear what job I wanted. I'd spent the previous few months formulating the economic strategy we could adopt.

When I saw him a week later, he asked me to be Shadow Home Secretary. I told him I thought that was the wrong decision. He smiled and told me these were his decisions to make, not mine. I was frustrated, but I also understood: he was trying both to break with the Gordon Brown era and to keep David and his people on side, and making me Shadow Chancellor would have made both tasks harder. He knew I could be forceful and determined and probably wanted to put me in my place. But when he eventually decided to appoint me to the job a few months later, after Alan Johnson's resignation, we began a new working relationship which was professional, disciplined and respectful, if not particularly friendly or open. I yearned for us to be the kind of team we had been back at the Treasury, united in battle against a common adversary.

What I learned is that – rather like Gordon – he was the kind of politician who relied far more on his inner circle than on fellow Shadow ministers, and we would go for days, sometimes weeks, without a conversation; equally, when members of that inner circle would brief against me from time to time, he clearly found it painful and offensive, and would apologise in a very heartfelt way. But as with Tony and Gordon years before, his apparent dismay didn't stop it happening again and again, including just a few weeks before the general election when, in the middle of a difficult negotiation over tuition fees, his team briefed that he was considering sacking me, a story which splashed a Sunday newspaper.

Having kept me at a distance in the run-up to the election in 2015, I think we probably only spoke twice in the whole four-week election campaign. That was astonishingly dysfunctional when I compare it to how Tony and Gordon worked; back then, whatever the differences we'd had in previous months, there was no doubt that when the election was called we would all come together, with Tony's most trusted advisers, Peter Mandelson, Alastair Campbell and Philip Gould, working closely with Gordon's – Sue, Douglas, Ed and myself – all of us working closely together.

David Cameron and George Osborne took a different course from how Ed Miliband worked with me, and also from how Blair and Brown operated. And they managed to remain friends and maintain a close working relationship between Number Ten and Number Eleven, as long as they were both in office, although they may well now look back and say some of their policy mistakes – from premature austerity to the foolish referendum decision – might have been prevented if there had been a bit more grit in their relationship.

As for my own relationship with Gordon, it was only after he became prime minister that it became hard. After thirteen years when we had spoken every day and in which I had been there through many difficult and many great times, things changed. On one level, I had my own department to run and couldn't spend as long being on call for him. But he was also trying to run Number Ten – with dozens of new staff – in a functioning way, and he probably knew he couldn't operate as he previously had with me now on the outside.

As things got tougher for him politically, I felt he used me as a lightning conductor – whether it was being accused of supposedly running his 'brutal' media operation or becoming the target of attacks by Cabinet members as a proxy to attack him. And even if Gordon wasn't happy for that to happen, he didn't stop it, even when in early 2010, with Geoff Hoon and Patricia Hewitt calling for him to resign, I was one of the only people still out defending him in public. When many of his team ended up shifting over to work for Ed Miliband and let it be known that Gordon had decided to back Ed because he thought he was the better prospect to defeat David than I was, I felt pretty hung out to dry.

But time heals. And even though neither of us is in Westminster and our paths don't often cross, we still make time to see each other and chew the fat.

In politics, trust is such a big issue. It is rare to have friends with whom you can have a close conversation, revealing your doubts and worries and asking for advice, without having to fret that what you're going to say will be recycled into the media or to other politicians.

There's a risk – as I saw with Ed Miliband and to some extent with Gordon – that as you reach the highest levels in politics, you end up trusting only your close circle of advisers and officials, and while that's very important indeed, it can never replicate the benefits you get from a friendship with a fellow or former MP, someone who understands the same pressures. Those are the political friendships you value the most. But they are hard to come by and you can never be sure. Times change, alliances shift. Nights spent in a Soho karaoke bar singing the old favourites – important bonding times as they are – don't guarantee loyalty. A trusted conversation one month can become a ticking bomb a few more down the line.

There will always be stresses and strains in any working relationship. But in politics, where you have to set out competing visions, deal with the media and win votes, sometimes against each other, it is inevitable there are battles – personal and ideological. That's the nature of the game.

But as Denis Healey showed me, it doesn't always have to be that way. And when I say always, I mean that, whatever the knocks and bumps along the way, the experiences we share, our common values and the kinships forged in past political battles also make it possible to come back together again.

The friendships you sustain throughout a political career will likely be the strongest you ever make. But as with Gordon and Robin Cook, or Denis Healey and Tony Benn, in politics you can put things back together again. I hope I'll also be able to say the same of Ed Miliband one day.

I'll keep some gin and tonics in the fridge.

6

Flowers

———————————

Politics gives you experiences that you never imagined – but is that the reason to do it?

The moment when Dolly Parton placed her hand on my inner thigh and whispered in my ear 'I hope you don't mind me hitting on you' will always remain one of the highlights of my life in politics. If you think I was taken aback, you should have seen the look of surprise and amazement on the face of my Permanent Secretary.

Dolly Parton is a hero to me and to millions around the world. She has a brilliant foundation in America and one of its programmes is sending books – one a month – to young mums to get them reading to their kids. We had a similar programme called Bookstart, but Dolly had teamed up with Rotherham Council – don't ask me how – to trial her own programme in Britain.

So she was really trying to 'hit on me' for my department's money. I knew as much but I didn't care. I was the young lad from a small village in Norwich who'd grown up on 'Jolene' and '9 to 5', and now here I was sitting next to the legend who'd sung them.

The reality of politics and government can be tough and arduous with long days and late nights. But it's also a fantastic privilege and opportunity to meet people, see sights, and do things you'd never have dreamed would be part of your life. And for me, having never stepped on a plane until the age of twenty-one, the biggest thrill of all was being able to visit new places.

My very first trip on Concorde took place straight after the election back in 1997, when – almost as an ostentatious expression of our confidence strutting onto the world stage – Tony Blair decided we should hire the plane to fly out to the G8 summit in Denver, Colorado.

The night we arrived, there was a welcoming musical show and celebration event to which we were all expected to go in specially prepared buses. We arrived at the hotel and went up to Gordon's room, where on his bed was a pair of jeans, checked shirt, cowboy boots and cowboy hat, ready and waiting. He took one look and said: 'I'm not wearing any of that.'

When we went down to get the bus, Gordon remained in his usual blue suit and blue tie, while Robin Cook had gone the whole hog. Tony had made do with the jeans. The rest of us were still in our crumpled plane clothes.

The event was packed when we arrived and we had no pre-assigned seats, but Charlie Whelan and I had developed a standard rule on foreign trips: look like you know what you're doing and where you're going, and no one will ever stop you. So we marched straight in and took a pair of seats in the second row from the stage, only for President Bill Clinton, German Chancellor Helmut Kohl and the Japanese PM Ryutaro Hashimoto to come in and sit directly in front of us. As the woman sitting next to us began leaning in to the conversation and whispering in Kohl's ear, it dawned on Charlie and me that we were sitting in the interpretors' seats. But our rule worked – no one asked us to move.

I'm not sure Jonathan Powell, Alastair Campbell and the rest of the Number Ten delegation were very impressed though, sitting twenty rows back on the other side of the room. But they probably didn't notice – they couldn't take their eyes off Robin's cowboy hat.

I learned a few more rules about international travel over those years. Always keep your coat and bag with you in case the minister you're with suddenly decides he or she has had enough and wants to leave to catch the plane; and never let your briefing papers – or your minister, for that matter – out of your sight.

In 1999, we went out to Helsinki for a meeting of the European Council, at a particularly tense time in our negotiations over proposals for a European savings tax, completely isolated and under pressure to concede. We arrived, went through security at the conference centre, attended the first meeting, went for dinner, and headed back to the hotel – a typical long day on the EU summit trail.

The next morning, we were summoned to Tony Blair's room at 7 a.m. for a discussion on the tactics for the day. I arrived to find Tony in a white dressing gown, and Gordon in his full suit, as tended to be their way. As I sat there, I realised with a mounting sense of panic that I didn't have my huge Treasury briefing file containing our highly confidential negotiating strategy. Nor could I remember the last time I had seen it.

I excused myself and walked over to the conference centre not quite sure what to do, went through the security scanner, and there – still sitting on the conveyor belt where I'd laid it down twelve hours ago – was the file. Thankfully I never had to own up to Gordon or Tony. I would like to say I never made that mistake again. But to the great horror of my staff, and doing no favours for my blood pressure, I became a serial offender over the years. Leaving an important and confidential government report in a BBC make-up room and a mobile phone, unlocked and brimming with text messages in the back of a black cab, are just some of the memories that make me shudder.

Losing my summit briefing pack was bad enough. But worse was to come. Unable to fly from New York to Washington DC because of a raging storm, Gordon decided we should take the three-hour train ride instead. Eight hours of delays and floods later, our train crawled into Philadelphia and – despite the protests of the train guard that we would get to DC in the end – most passengers disembarked. As did Gordon's excellent private secretary, Tom Scholar, and I in order to stretch our legs and find out what was going on. Suddenly, without warning, there was a loud whistle and, as we ran waving our arms down the platform, the train pulled out of the station with Gordon and an eminent senior official, Jon Cunliffe, on board.

'Tom, what have you done?' I wheezed. 'You've lost your Chancellor.' To make matters even worse, we realised we had left our bags, passports, money and mobile phones with Gordon on the train. Thankfully, we managed to blag our way onto the next train for what became the final six hours of the journey, with Tom fretting all the way about how on earth Jon Cunliffe would cope with Gordon on his own. We found out later that an American soprano had got into Gordon's carriage, already half cut, and proceeded to rally her fellow flood-affected travellers with a selection of well-known arias before passing out with her head on Jon's lap. Oblivious, Gordon just got on with writing his speech.

Another valuable lesson I learned came in a meeting with Helmut Kohl in 1998, during Britain's presidency of the EU, when Tony Blair had to chair a session to decide who was going to be the first head of the European Central Bank. It seemed to be the usual choice between the French or the German candidate.

The big problem was that the German representatives were themselves arguing over who they should support. It looked like their governing coalition might fall apart on the spot. In those situations, the Civil Service instinct is to break up the meeting, take it into various small groups, and hope a solution can be brokered. However, the political lesson is that you must keep the politicians in the room as long as it takes to reach a compromise, on the grounds that if you let them leave, it will be much harder to get them back in again.

And this is where hunger and tiredness eventually take over. As the meeting dragged on all through the afternoon and into the evening and eventually to 10 p.m., the mood among the frustrated, fatigued and famished leaders rapidly turned to mutiny, with the Belgian prime minister, Jean-Luc Dehaene – who looked like he had a good appetite – trying to lead a walkout.

As we stuck at it, the leaders' anger turned to desperation, and around an hour later, a compromise was reached to appoint the head of the Dutch Central Bank, Wim Duisenberg, for half a term, on the understanding that he would then voluntarily stand aside for the French candidate, Jean-Claude Trichet. A classic European fudge.

We had found agreement easier to come by at a Commonwealth Finance Ministers' Meeting in Mauritius in September 1997, when we launched what we called the 'Mauritius Mandate for Debt Relief'. Our idea was to secure the backing of the Commonwealth for the IMF to use its gold reserves to fund unprecedented debt relief for the poorest countries in return for an agreement to tackle corruption, and then take the agreed proposal to the IMF Meetings a few days later.

It was a strange place for a summit – a rather idyllic tourist hotel half full of newly-wed couples and half full of Finance Ministry officials in suits. Every morning, the other aides and I would meet in Gordon's room and stroll down the shore-front path to breakfast with the honeymooners. (At home, we were in the middle of a row over our insistence on capping Cabinet ministers' pay as part of our commitment to fiscal discipline. Some of our disgruntled colleagues would have choked on their cornflakes if they could have seen us walking along the beach to get ours.)

Following the meeting, we were due to travel from Mauritius to Bangkok for the Asia-Europe Meeting and then on to the IMF Meetings in Hong Kong. Due to the timing, we had to fly to Johannesburg to make our first connection. We went to the airport and found an extremely small plane waiting for us with just four seats. The in-flight refreshments consisted of four cheese rolls and a cool box full of South African beer.

As we set out, the pilot told us we were facing unexpectedly big headwinds, and not long afterwards informed us that we'd have to make an unexpected stop in Madagascar to refuel. That was fine by me – I'd never been there before so was rather excited to visit somewhere new – but Gordon made it pretty clear we were not going to be stopping over for a look around.

We soon landed on the almost deserted tarmac, and our plane slowly taxied towards the kerosene truck. Before we knew what was happening, a car came racing from the terminal towards us, screeched to a halt, and out stepped one very tall man, and one very short round man, who beckoned to the pilot.

The pilot nervously got out and spoke to them, then rapidly returned and clambered into his seat. He turned to face us. 'I'm afraid we have a problem: we can only refuel if we pay these gentlemen a hefty "refuelling fee" in US dollars.' The pilot explained that he certainly didn't have that kind of cash, and wasn't sure we'd be able to leave if we couldn't pay.

Gordon looked at us and said: 'This is a real problem. We've just agreed a Commonwealth statement of our collective commitment to tackle corruption. We can't pay a bribe a few hours later.' We deliberated for a little while, before Gordon stood up. 'OK, here's what we'll do, I'll get out and speak to them and explain the position of the Commonwealth finance ministers. And if that doesn't work you lot look in the bags and see how many dollars you can find.'

So Gordon got out of the plane to go and read the finance ministers' communiqué to our two friends, while Gus and I began a frantic search in the back of the plane to try and find enough US dollars to do the deal in case Gordon's powers of persuasion failed. As we were searching, we heard the sound of another plane overhead and looked out of the window to see a large Aeroflot jet approaching the landing strip. Clearly the two gentlemen concluded there was a lot more money to be made from the Aeroflot plane than from us, and they wouldn't need to listen to a Scotsman lecture them on the corrosive impact of secret commissions to get it.

They told Gordon to wait where he was, jumped in their

car and sped off towards the Aeroflot. At which point our pilot turned to us and said: 'I can fill the plane up myself – no need to pay the bribe, we'll just do a runner.' So he raced to do that, and then – without clearance from air traffic control or anyone else – we shut the doors and jetted out of Madagascar with the integrity of the Commonwealth Finance Ministers' commitment still just about intact.

A year into government, we were starting to flex our muscles in the big international negotiations. It soon proved vital. In the summer of 1998, financial crises in Asia and Russia led to big knock-on effects in the European jobs market, and rumours of a major hedge fund struggling, which was beginning to destabilise the stock market.

By the time we got to early September, it was clear that the global economy was entering a very tricky phase, and Gordon decided that – as chair of the G7 Finance Ministers' Meeting – he was going to address the problems head-on, and make sure it was Britain putting forward the solutions, and leading the negotiations to agree them.

First, rather than trying to cobble together proposals with our international partners through some endless circulation of drafts, we sat down with the Treasury's international director, Sir Nigel Wicks, and his brilliant team, to diagnose the weaknesses in the financial system and set out recommendations for reform. Second, we undertook a roadshow of all the key governments and institutions to whom we needed to sell our 'British plan'. Occasionally, we'd find ourselves flying halfway around the world just for one or two crucial meetings.

Two such meetings took place that autumn, in Japan and South Korea. The first leg in Japan was even more pressured after we ran into what seemed to be our perennial plane problems, aborting a landing at Tokyo's Narita Airport even as we could see the British ambassador's Rolls-Royce waiting for us on the tarmac, and only finally getting to the Finance Ministry six hours late.

Gordon's agitated mood was made worse by the fact that when we arrived, it seemed we weren't even getting to meet the finance minister but a senior official instead. As we were going up in the lift, he turned to me and the UK official who had greeted us, and said: 'This is totally ridiculous. Why are we not meeting the finance minister? It's a bloody shambles. Get me the ambassador on the phone, I need to tell him this isn't good enough.' The UK official coughed, and said: 'Chancellor, excuse me but, er, I *am* the ambassador'.

However, eventually we did see the finance minister for dinner that evening, and it perhaps became clearer why his officials were doing the negotiations for him. In a beautiful Chinese restaurant, the old chap – already in his late seventies and tired out from a day sitting in the Japanese parliament – had a couple of scotches and then fell asleep.

We were worried he was ill, but two of his aides came in, took an arm each, carried him out, and returned to tell us the dinner was over and to wish us a good night.

After our Asia trip, we flew out to Washington for the annual meetings of the IMF and World Bank, armed with our new plan for global financial reform: a new financial stability forum to act as an early-warning institution to spot financial crises coming sooner, and codes of practice in monetary, fiscal and financial policy to safeguard financial systems and allow adequate international surveillance.

It has to be understood what a rare thing this was: a British finance minister coming to the Americans' backyard to set out a plan with radical implications for financial management in every major country.

Our resolve was strengthened at a meeting with Alan Greenspan, the chair of the US Federal Reserve, just a day before the Washington meetings. Alan, whom we'd met many times before, was hugely spooked by what was happening with the hedge funds and the international credit markets, and said it was the most dangerous period in the world economy he'd seen in his professional lifetime.

Gordon was left even more determined to get his plans agreed, so much so that he took the unprecedented step of obtaining the mobile phone numbers of all his finance minister colleagues in order to persuade them personally, bypassing the usual conventions.

I remember him trying to track down Dominique Strauss-Kahn, then the French finance minister, while Dominique was at the opera in Paris. It said everything about Gordon that he was annoyed to have to wait until the interval to be able to speak. He was tenacious, like a dog with a bone, and he got a truly impressive set of reforms agreed by the G7 and then the IMF; the implementation of which I had the responsibility to oversee when, a few years later, I became the chair of the IMF deputies.

In the end, the problems of 1998 were obviously just a small precursor of a much greater financial crisis, which exposed all kinds of hidden risks in the banks' lending activities that even the Financial Stability Forum was powerless to see or to stop.

But the economic leadership role which Gordon assumed then among the biggest nations – they immediately appointed him head of the IMF Ministerial Committee – continued right until the 2008 financial crisis hit, when he used the same skills, techniques and force of nature to drive through the global agreement that stopped recession turning into depression.

The only other finance minister I met who had such an immediate impact was Nicolas Sarkozy. He attended his first meeting of the G7 Finance Ministers in Washington DC in April 2004, barely a month into the job, and immediately started lambasting the central bankers for not pursuing growth and employment creation with sufficient vigour, and said it was time that the finance ministers took back control of setting interest rates.

This caused great consternation, not least to Jean-Claude Trichet, the president of the European Central Bank, to whom most of these comments were directed. Even more surprising, Sarkozy then didn't come back after lunch, instead requesting a meeting with the president of the United States, George W. Bush. Given Mr Sarkozy was determined to be the French president, he thought it only right that he should meet his soon-to-be counterpart.

Protocol demanded that didn't happen, but he nevertheless secured meetings with Vice President Dick Cheney and National Security Advisor Condoleezza Rice, which he considered more important than attending the rest of the G7 meeting.

Soon afterwards, I sat next to him at an IMF Finance Ministers' lunch. Gordon was chair so I was occupying the UK seat. There was a big debate round the table about whether the US was wielding too much power on trade and quota issues, and needed to accept that emerging market economies should have a stronger say.

Next to me, I could see Sarkozy growing increasingly angry and animated. Eventually, he leaned over and rasped: 'This is ridiculous, these Americans, do they know what they are doing? This is no way to run things.' I listened intently, waiting for him to expand on his views on trade reform, but he just gestured angrily towards his lunch plate. 'Do they expect us to eat this?'

If these international meetings can seem like one adventure after another, with getaway planes, idyllic hotels, flagging finance ministers, and the like, it's because that's often what they were.

Of course they were extremely important: from the huge steps we took to tackle global poverty to preventing the slide into global depression.

But if you didn't stop and appreciate the wonderful countries you were lucky enough to visit, the characters you met, the exotic food you ate, and the odd funny or hair-raising experiences you had along the way, then you were missing out on half of what made the job we did such a privilege and an experience.

And you never knew when it might end – which it almost did on my final trip on Concorde. It was April 2002 and we were travelling out to Washington for the spring meetings of the IMF and World Bank. It was always a bit of an alarming experience flying on Concorde: a plane that took off like a rocket and quickly rose to 56,000 feet, according to the vast altimeter counter at the front of the cabin.

We were an hour into the flight, working intensively on the speech Gordon planned to make during the IMF Meeting, when suddenly there was an enormous noise, a huge jolt throwing us around in our seats, as though the plane had hit a wall, and we felt ourselves begin to plummet. From the back of the aircraft came the terrible sound of screaming.

The altimeter counter was tumbling down: 55,000, 54,000, 53,000. I don't know much about planes, but I knew they weren't meant to lose a thousand feet every thirty seconds. The steward came over the intercom, and the desperation to know what was happening quietened the commotion. He said there had clearly been a major incident, and that the captain was trying to work out what it was. When he found out, he'd let us know. He didn't sound very calm, and none of us were after hearing that. But the eerie silence remained, as we continued to watch the numbers tick down: 33,000, 32,000, 31,000.

Gordon turned to me and said: 'Well, here we are,' and I said: 'Yep, maybe this is it.' We had a really nice conversation about our families, about the good things we thought we'd done in our lives, and what we'd be sorry to leave behind. By this point, the plane was down to 24,000 feet. Gordon paused, turned to me, and said: 'What do you think? Should we finish my speech?' I looked at him with incredulity.

But at 20,000 feet, the plane levelled out and stabilised. One of the engines had blown out, but the plane could carry on flying at half the power, half the speed and at a much lower level. When we got to Washington, it was the most relieved I have ever felt on touching solid ground and I never got on Concorde again. But I'd also discovered that Gordon Brown was a fine companion when facing imminent death.

My time in government didn't end that day in a plunging plane. But the final scene, when it came, was equally memorable.

A question I'm often asked is what contact I had with the royal family, and whether they had any input into the job I was doing. Given Prince Charles' passion for education and propensity for writing letters to Cabinet ministers, I unsurprisingly heard a lot from him, attended a number of seminars he hosted on education, and met many representatives from The Prince's Trust and The Prince's Teaching Institute at his request. As far as his letters go, I always found him hugely constructive, helpful and incisive. I regard myself as very lucky to have had his counsel and advice; and I believe anyone who objects to him playing that role is frankly wrong.

I didn't have the same kind of relationship with HM the Queen, although I was honoured to meet her a number of times at Privy Council meetings and receptions. I never had an opportunity to discuss education policy with her until – to my surprise – I received an invitation to attend Buckingham Palace shortly after Labour had been turfed out of power in 2010.

The Palace explained that Her Majesty liked to have a meeting with all outgoing Cabinet ministers, and unlike previous times where I had rolled up through the Buckingham Palace gates in the departmental Jaguar, this time a black cab dropped me off at the outside security cordon and I walked through the courtyard to wait with the lady-in-waiting before going in to see the Queen.

I obviously won't reveal the contents of our conversation, other than to say that while these were entirely voluntary meetings – there was no constitutional reason for her to meet outgoing Cabinet ministers – Her Majesty had a depth of understanding of the issues I'd faced, and the decisions I'd taken, which took my breath away and left me rather speechless in response. Prime ministers often say what a great adviser and counsellor she has been throughout her reign, and that day I saw at first hand that insight and wisdom, and how much she cared about the issues of schools and child welfare.

At the end of our meeting, I walked back across the courtyard and into St James's Park. I bought an ice cream and wandered along the path, no longer responsible for the education system, no longer a Cabinet minister and with no department to go back to. But as I licked my ice cream and passed all the tourists walking up to look through the gates of Buckingham Palace, I smiled to myself at the knowledge that I had just come from a meeting with the person they all wanted to see.

As I literally slowed down in the park that day to smell the flowers, feeling both a swell of pride and also a sense of loss, I thought how lucky I'd been in my career – from talking to Britain's Queen to being 'hit on' by Nashville's, and I was so glad I'd always taken time to let it all sink in.

And as someone who's had the experience of sitting on a plummeting plane thinking my time was up, I'd always want to be able to look back at all the things I was proud to have accomplished, and all the people and places I was lucky enough to have encountered, and take real satisfaction in both. I only know it would be terrible to be in that situation, and realise I had missed out on one or the other.

PART TWO

Learning What Works

I came into politics because I wanted to be on the pitch, not just commentating from the sidelines. I believed a progressive government could be both trusted on the economy and change the world, and tried to show I was right. These chapters are about what I learned trying to deliver that change.

7

Reform

_____

Saving the NHS was New Labour's greatest achievement – so why did it all go wrong?

On the night of 11 May 1994, I was at a Labour fundraising dinner at the Park Lane Hotel in central London where our leader, John Smith, was the speaker, inspiring the audience with a rallying cry in defence of the NHS. It was a great evening and in the early hours he was still having a drink with the rest of us. When he was finally persuaded it was time to leave, he gave me one of his great bear hugs and said: 'Ed, listen: we must get all the thinkers together, plan the future.' That's what I'd come into politics for and I felt really chuffed. I didn't realise at the time how much that moment meant.

The next morning, as I travelled along the Embankment in my small Renault 5, the news came over the radio that

John had suffered a heart attack and had been rushed to hospital. By the time I arrived in the House of Commons, it was confirmed that he had died. Gordon was so grief-stricken, he just hid away in his nearby flat and poured himself into writing an obituary, while the political ramifications swirled around Westminster. It was a terrible shock for all of us.

No one thought it for a very long time to come, but there is no doubt that John's death had a significant impact on the direction of the Labour Party in those crucial years. After 1992 and Black Wednesday, John Major's government was lurching from crisis to crisis over the Maastricht Treaty. Labour was ahead in the polls, and John Smith was confident that – if he could hold the party together and avoid any pitfalls – we were on course for victory next time round.

For that reason, in his conference speech of 1993, he had promised the restoration of workers' rights from day one in government, signalling a sizeable repeal of the 1980s trade union legislation, and said he would use all the levers of economic policy to deliver full employment – everything, essentially, that the unions and the party wanted to hear. However, Gordon Brown and Tony Blair were deeply nervous, worried that the fabled 'one last heave' wasn't going to be enough to put Labour into government, and that the need to show the party had changed from the 'bad old days' of the late 1970s and early 1980s was undiminished.

In their respective areas, they were constantly pushing the envelope in terms of demonstrating their commitment to modernisation – whether it was Tony's 'tough' language on crime or Gordon's ditching of John's 1992 pre-election 'Shadow Budget' and his insistence that we would never tax for the sake of it. But that clearly irritated John and his office, who thought they were creating fights that didn't need to be fought. After four election defeats, Tony and Gordon thought those fights were essential if Labour was to get rid of its past reputation for wasteful spending, taxing for its own sake and bending to placate vested interests rather than putting the country first.

On a flight to Geneva for a meeting of the Socialist International, just a few weeks before he died, John became enraged reading a front-page story suggesting Labour was planning to scrap Clause IV of its 1918 Constitution: a commitment to 'the common ownership of the means of production, distribution and exchange'. The story was based on an interview with John Prescott, the then Shadow employment minister, who had called for a new relationship with the private sector to deliver infrastructure – yet another example of the 'obsession' with modernisation that John Smith thought would upset the party for no benefit.

But it was immediately clear that John's successor was going to be a moderniser: embracing globalisation and the dynamic market economy, rejecting renationalisation, and controlling public spending. For all of the difficulty between Tony and Gordon about which of them it would be, they were agreed that they were going to pursue this modernising agenda with a vigour that they felt had stalled in the previous couple of years.

But I never felt that either Tony or Gordon lost sight of our core values. On the economy, and with Tony's blessing, we were determined that Labour would make the economy stronger and fairer, make work pay, end child poverty and save the NHS, hence Gordon campaigning against the fat-cat bosses of the privatised utilities making a killing off the taxpayer, demanding a national minimum wage and exposing Tory privatisation of public services. It was important for the Labour Party, and the country, to see that this modernisation was not detaching the party from its history and beliefs, but was instead – in John Prescott's words – traditional values in a modern setting.

Even though the expression 'The Third Way' to describe New Labour came later, that's what we were trying to do back in 1994: find a path between the old ideological statism of Labour in the 1970s and the excesses of free market economics seen under Margaret Thatcher. And, greatly influenced by Philip Gould's focus groups, we believed the general public and the mainstream of the Labour Party could be persuaded to join us there.

With the NHS approaching its sixtieth anniversary, and Labour, the party which founded it, now enjoying a solid polling lead on who was best to save it, the initial approach to health care was very cautious and steady-as-she-goes. But after the election victory, as we sat down to make a reality of our commitment to stick to Tory spending plans for the first two years, we were clear that the NHS was an exception.

Indeed, I had told the Treasury before the election that we would allocate an extra £1 billion to the NHS in the July Budget. Over that first Parliament we found ourselves continually allocating money from the Treasury reserves to the NHS to cope with winter pressures; although – ironically – it would be Tony demanding the cash, no questions asked, while Gordon would agitate about whether it was being spent effectively and whether reforms of NHS management were required.

Regardless of those debates, I think we all came to understand in that Parliament that this incrementalist strategy in health was never going to work. We'd inherited a health service in which people were waiting up to eighteen months or more for hip operations or knee replacements. And those waiting times weren't going to come down unless we did something radical and raised the money to pay for it. But simply relying on economic growth to deliver sufficient funds to save the NHS wasn't going to be enough. After the 1992 election defeat, many people had wrongly concluded that Labour raising taxes to invest in public services was politically impossible. But with the NHS under pressure, and the whole idea of a publicly funded, free-at-the-point-of-use health-care system being openly questioned, it was time for New Labour to step up and deliver.

The plan was to fight the 2001 election on the slogan 'A lot done. A lot more to do', and there were lots of achievements we could highlight to illustrate the first point. But very few of them were in health: there hadn't been really big injections of resources; there hadn't been big changes; and there hadn't been big improvements. Something new was needed to break out of the tax and spending straitjacket that we had inherited from the previous Conservative government. We needed to make the case for a tax rise, not to fill a budget gap but to deliver on our commitment to a world-class NHS.

That crystallised for me when travelling with Ed Miliband

over to meetings in Washington DC. We ended up discussing the need to have a big 'moment' on the health service, something which would allow us to move into a different realm, similar to our seismic decision on Bank of England independence. But we agreed that couldn't just be about finding the big extra injection of money that the NHS needed from within existing budgets or the proceeds of growth in the economy; it had to be deliberately funded through a tax increase. We had to make a virtue out of that – renewing the principle of a publicly funded NHS free at the point of use – and turn it into a big political argument and debate that we could decisively win, to settle the future of the health service once and for all.

When we met up with Gordon stateside, we told him what we'd been discussing, and he agreed. We spent most of that trip working out how we'd get to that end point: make clear that the NHS needed more money; commission internal work to consider the tax options; launch an independent review into the future of the NHS; then steadily escalate the debate on the NHS so it would be the central issue at the next election, giving us a mandate to act afterwards.

Gordon spoke to Tony, who was understandably nervous on the tax front but they agreed on the principles. That was fine, but – as sometimes happened with Tony – he then jumped the gun. He went on *Breakfast with Frost* and, to our immense surprise, said that he wanted health spending in Britain to match the EU average, something that raised all sorts of immediate questions about how much that would cost, and how we'd pay for it.

For all the later media characterisation of our 'battles' with Number Ten on NHS reform, we were also frustrated that, by making this just about money, Tony had missed the opportunity to talk about how the NHS needed to change, and what outputs we wanted in return for all the extra cash. But at least it meant we had a clear direction of travel for the government, and we decided to make this look as coordinated as possible by agreeing with Number Ten that the day after the 2000 Budget, we would commence our long-term reform initiative and Tony Blair would lead that in a statement to the House of Commons.

In the following, pre-election, Budget, we announced the launch of an independent financial review, led by Derek Wanless; and in the election campaign, we were clear that the NHS was our top priority, and that if we could keep the economy strong, that would release more resources for investment in health. We were also careful not to bind ourselves in with commitments not to increase taxes. The only wobble on that front was when Patricia Hewitt, Secretary of State for Industry, appeared to rule out changing the upper ceiling for National Insurance contributions. That was clearly one of the top options we had for raising the extra revenue for the NHS, so we had to quickly stamp on what Patricia had said, which just increased the suspicions about our plans. Fortunately we were swiftly bailed out by John Prescott punching a member of the public in Wales, which rather distracted the media for a few days.

Once the election victory was in the bag, we cranked up the Wanless review, with a superb team in the Treasury supporting Derek's work, led brilliantly by Anita Charlesworth. While they worked on their interim report, we worked on the inclusion of some significant phrasing in Gordon's 2001 party conference speech, an event otherwise dominated by the aftermath of the 9/11 attacks. In typical Gordon fashion, he didn't want to go too far, so his speech simply contained a highly elliptical phrase about our task in the next Budget being to combine reform of public services with providing 'the necessary resources for the future'.

After his speech, as always, I spoke to a big gaggle of lobby journalists and commentators, and I stressed the importance of the phrase 'the necessary resources'. 'What does that mean?' they naturally asked. I said we would take whatever action was needed in the next Budget to provide the NHS with the resources it needs. 'Tax rises?' they asked. I repeated myself: 'Whatever action is necessary.'

As far as I was concerned, the earlier a tax rise for the NHS was priced in by the papers, and the sooner we could start a public debate and political argument about it, the better. And no surprise, when the morning papers dropped, they had all gone very heavy on the story. Job done.

In the morning, I went round to Gordon's room, and found him in an absolutely furious mood. 'You've just lost us the next election!' he fumed. 'Why?' I asked, a bit taken aback. He said: 'The papers are all saying we're going to raise taxes for the NHS.' 'But we *are* going to raise taxes for the NHS!' I replied. 'And we agreed two years ago we were going to make a virtue of it. What the hell's the problem?'

Perhaps it was just the reality of the front pages, but Gordon was very sceptical that morning, and when there was a similarly heavy and hostile media reaction to the publication of the interim Wanless report alongside the 2001 Pre-Budget Report, that scepticism probably increased. Derek Wanless held a press conference in the morning, setting out what kind of NHS we needed for the future and how much money we'd need to get there – a sustained 7.5 per cent real-terms increase in funding. It helpfully moved us off the hook of having to match the EU average, but the papers could still easily work out what level of tax rise it would mean.

These are crucial times in politics, when you have to ignore the front pages, stick to your strategy, and trust that you can win the argument you've started. Most importantly, you have to stay on the front foot, because as soon as you even look like you're reconsidering, you're sunk. Staying on the front foot meant arranging breakfasts, lunches, dinners and coffees with every key journalist and media outlet in that period, taking the argument to them. The day after the Pre-Budget Report, we went to the *Sun* to see the editor David Yelland. The day after, we did the same at the *Daily Mail*.

Our narrative was simple. Any alternative to the NHS – for example, an insurance-based system like America's – would end up costing more in terms of the burden on employers and the public. We had to keep the NHS, we had to reform it, but we had to fund it properly, and that meant a tax rise. We would argue openly that their readers and the country would support this because every poll showed how valued the NHS was, right up there with the Queen as a symbol of what made people proud to be British.

These were some of the most difficult and robust meetings we ever had with the right-wing media. They were telling us they hated it, but we told them their readers were going to love it. If they wanted to be on the wrong side of this argument that was up to them, but it was one we were going to win.

★

To retain public support, we needed to be very careful about how to raise the revenue we'd need. It was no good doing anything which looked too good to be true, or unsustainable in the long-term, like saying we'd get the money from tackling tax avoidance. The preference of Number Ten and Treasury officials was to raise VAT, but the idea appalled Ed Miliband, Gordon and me, and – based on our polling – the public felt the same. An increase in income tax was slightly less unpopular, but an increase in National Insurance Contributions (NICs) to fund the NHS actually commanded a substantial majority in favour.

It was the symbolism of National Insurance that made the difference: the feeling that you pay in when you're working to ensure that when you lose your job, when you need the NHS, when you retire, you're going to be protected and looked after. And that's why we ended up going for the NICs increase. Tony was incredibly anxious about it. The idea that we would raise taxes on employers and earnings right up the income scale seemed to him like the reverse of what New Labour was about. He was also scarred by the impact that the threat of an NICs increase had had when Neil Kinnock announced it before the 1992 election.

It was my job to keep the strategy on track. And having worked closely with Gordon and Tony for a long time, I was used to saying things they didn't always want to hear, even if it was sometimes a bit uncomfortable. In one pre-Budget meeting with Tony during that period, he claimed that our preferred NI rise would hit average earners too hard and I decided to challenge him by asking what he thought the average household income was. Tony said that it was around £60,000 a year; I said it was actually closer to £20,000. He countered that the statistics were clearly not telling the real story.

When we had the crucial final meeting to make the decision, just days before the 2002 Budget, Tony said that his chief civil servant aide, Jeremy Heywood, had an alternative suggestion. That wasn't the only time we'd heard that line, but we'd learned that the key was to watch Tony as Jeremy spoke to see if he was nodding along or not. On this occasion, as Jeremy talked about how much revenue could be raised from removing the VAT zero rate on new greenfield housing and taxing it at 17.5 per cent instead, Tony wasn't nodding. He just turned rather pale.

So we stuck to our guns, we made the NICs change in the 2002 Budget, and – just as Ed and I had always planned – we made a virtue of saying we were doing it to ensure the NHS was properly funded. The polling for that Budget was the best we ever had when Gordon was in the Treasury.

When people say New Labour ducked big, brave decisions and that we lost sight of our principles in that second term, I will always counter with the NICs increase for the NHS. In fact, I would go further and say that the Budget of 2002 was the high point for New Labour, when we were doing something hugely radical and difficult, true to the traditions of the best Labour governments of the past, but also alive to public concerns about how we raised the revenue, and alive to media concerns about the need for reform, all of which made a huge difference.

By the time of the 2005 election, although there were problems in individual hospitals and a worsening superbug crisis, the resources we had committed were bringing in the doctors and nurses we needed, reducing waiting times, and delivering a palpable improvement in the performance and reliability of the NHS, and the public were seeing the difference. And the tax rise barely got a mention throughout the whole campaign.

It was especially vital because not only did it provide the funding the health service needed for the next decade, but it killed – forever I hope – the debate about whether the NHS was the right way to provide and fund health care in Britain. The strong resistance that the Tories have encountered since 2010 to their various attempts to interfere with the NHS is evidence of that, and it's pleasing that the same right-wing papers who argued with us in 2002 have often led the charge in opposing their plans.

And that's why New Labour was so important: showing that we could mix tradition with modernisation, and use our political acumen and media savvy to deliver big, lasting reforms and break out of the fiscal straitjacket we had inherited.

But bizarrely and simultaneously, 2002 was also when things started to go wrong for New Labour, and the NHS – as much as Iraq – was a symbol of that.

In some ways, we were victims of our own success. The Tories were in a mess at the time, with Iain Duncan Smith in charge and the party seemingly going nowhere. Labour was the only show in town when it came to political news, and the biggest story was the rivalry and argument – whether real or imagined – between Tony and Gordon.

Were Blair supporters being promoted, or Brownites? Did Tony still command support in the Cabinet, or was Gordon getting the upper hand? Above all, where did we stand on the succession: was Gordon still in pole position or was one of his potential rivals gathering steam?

The tragedy after the 2002 Budget was that the big project we and Tony's team had worked on together throughout the eight years of New Labour – the NHS – became one of the big sources of friction between Number Ten and Number Eleven, and the symbol of an invented battle about whether or not Gordon was sufficiently committed to reform.

It didn't help that one of Gordon's would-be rivals, Alan Milburn, was the Health Secretary at the time, and deliberately set out to create a divide over the proposal for foundation hospitals, previously a joint Number Ten/ Treasury initiative, by suggesting hospitals had to be cut loose and allowed to borrow money on their own terms as if they were private entities.

From our point of view, that was both unacceptable and ridiculous. There was no way we would allow a local hospital to go bankrupt, so letting them borrow money willy-nilly was a recipe for local managers to spend whatever they wanted, knowing the government would bail them out if things got difficult. Apart from anything else, we hadn't put ourselves through the wringer to raise NICs, ensure the health service was properly funded, and win the argument on NHS funding, only to discard all that, and create a free-for-all where hospitals could borrow and spend what they liked. Alan also began to push arguments about using price mechanisms to drive patient choice in the NHS, taking us away from the vision of the health service on which the Wanless report and the 2002 Budget had been founded.

The madness was, that in that period, whenever it came to the crunch, Tony and Gordon never differed about what needed to be done. Six months after the 2002 Budget, at the party conference, Alan made a speech setting out his plans for 'reform'. I ended up in the press area afterwards, briefing one group of journalists that hospitals were not going to borrow off-budget and I was confident that was not what Alan Milburn had been proposing, while his media adviser stood twenty yards away telling another group of journalists the exact opposite.

But two weeks later, when we sat down with Tony, Gordon, Alan, Jeremy Heywood and the Number Ten health adviser Simon Stevens, Tony looked absolutely baffled by Milburn's plan. He said: 'Of course we can't have public hospitals borrowing off the books. We want them to have more freedom and flexibility, but they're not private institutions.'

Which is exactly what we'd agreed before, but that wasn't the point. The media weren't interested in any attempt to play down the row; they were revelling in the apparent Blair–Brown factional battle, and once that was established, Tony couldn't say publicly what he was saying in private, because it would have looked as though he'd lost.

And in the Treasury we were in the same bind. I did an interview at the time with the *Guardian*'s Jackie Ashley – an unusual thing for a backroom political adviser. It ended up on the front page and said there were limits to the role of markets in the delivery of public services. That should have been an innocuous statement for anyone in Labour to say but, in those febrile times, it was seen as a rebuff to the Blairites, and therefore became hugely controversial. Even at the time, that felt to me like a disaster.

New Labour had been created to persuade the Labour party that we needed a dynamic, flexible market economy to drive the growth and revenue we needed to fund our treasured public services, and to persuade the public and the media that we could be trusted to look after both. And I was certainly not opposed to the private sector playing its proper role in public service delivery.

My experience, as a Treasury adviser, minister and Cabinet minister, was that if you wanted to stop private sector contractors ripping off the taxpayer with work done over-budget, not on time and not to the right kind of quality, you needed to get them bound into long-term contracts. It's why any sensible modernising government of any political colour will always have some form of private financing arrangement for public service contracts; and while we made some mistakes with PFI in the early years, using it for inappropriate projects and the like, we learned the lessons and had it working pretty well by the end. George Osborne made a big song and dance of abolishing PFI when he came into the Treasury in 2010, but a few years later – with rather less fanfare – it was reintroduced, as he belatedly learned it was the only way to do things.

But New Labour was never, ever about trying to turn our state schools and hospitals into a marketplace where competition and profit would be the drivers of excellence; and yet people like Alan Milburn redefined it in that way, and made Gordon's support of that agenda the test of whether he was actually New Labour or not. The same thing happened in the debate about tuition fees.

In the end, even though Tony and Gordon were much more united on policy and strategy than people knew, all the public saw was Labour divided, betraying its traditions, forgetting its values, and compromising on its principles. And all with two fundamental myths: that Tony Blair was more interested in helping business than protecting the NHS; and that Gordon was fighting him because of his political ambitions rather than to protect our public services.

The fact is there was no betrayal or compromise. We just lost sight of what New Labour was for. We won the definitive argument in the 2002 Budget, and won it comprehensively. But instead of taking that success and applying it to other public services in need of modernisation and proper funding – policing and social care for example – we just invented a new argument on health, and turned on ourselves.

That, as much as Iraq, was the New Labour tragedy: that we allowed differences of opinion on tactics or arguments about strategy to be presented as disagreements over principle when in fact we were all united in our commitment to saving and renewing the National Health Service as a world-class health-care system, the best insurance policy in the world.

This takes me back to those last words John Smith ever said to me: 'We must get all the thinkers together.' He was right. You need to get them together, but you also need to keep them together and never let them lose sight of what's at stake.

8

Markets

Labour tried to be on the side of both business and working people – but is it ever possible to do both?

'So what's wrong with capitalism anyway?'

It was my first meeting of the Left Caucus at Keble College, Oxford, in 1985, and it's fair to say my question didn't go down too well. I shouldn't have been too surprised though; at my first meeting of the Oxford Labour Club a few weeks previously, the main item on the agenda was whether or not to include the hammer-and-sickle on the club's new banner.

I first started learning about economics as I studied for my A Levels in the shadow of the failure of early 1980s monetarism, with unemployment above three million, growing inequality, and huge social and industrial unrest, from the miners' strike to the riots in Brixton and Toxteth. I certainly wasn't a champion for the free market, right-of-centre, capitalist model that Thatcher and Reagan advocated.

But from those earliest days, I also saw and came to understand the huge power and potential for dynamism, innovation and creativity that a market economy can bring. And over thirty years of travelling around the world, I've seen the way in which market economies can transform societies and start to reduce systemic poverty. I've always believed in the power of economics, markets and individual endeavour to make the world a better place, and my enthusiasm for that market mechanism is undimmed.

Which isn't, of course, to say that markets always work in the public interest. It was the founder of modern economics, Adam Smith, who famously argued that whenever groups of businesses get together, the chances are they will be plotting to prevent markets operating, to undermine competition and fix prices. That has been the reality for centuries.

While John Maynard Keynes' contribution to economics is often caricatured as being about boosting demand through fiscal spending at all times and not just in a depression, he was equally important and influential in the 1930s in highlighting the inherent tendency of 'casino' capitalist market economies to short-termism while advocating reforms to secure more long-term investment in companies and infrastructure.

That is why the role governments play in making markets work for the long-term, in the public interest, is so important – and just as important as their responsibility to tackle inequality and create equal chances for every individual.

Even though every child has the opportunity to go to school, the fact is that the income of their parents, their access to books when young, and the type of neighbourhood and community they live in, will typically have a massive impact on their chances of educational success. Only government can intervene to address inequalities in those kinds of areas, build and support strong communities and give them the extra leg up they need to have a fair chance. That is why I'm Labour.

But being Labour doesn't mean that I can't also believe in a market economy which creates wealth and good jobs. Some people in business are always going to be sceptical of a left-of-centre party, which claims to be pro-business but also wants to use regulation and intervention to make the market work in a long-term and fairer way. And that was the challenge Labour faced in the 1990s, as Tony Blair and Gordon Brown sought to end nearly twenty years of Conservative rule.

Their insight was that you couldn't build a stronger economy or a fairer society through opposing business; it had to be a partnership between the dynamism of business and the helping hand of government. And my arrival from the *Financial Times*, the pink-papered global business newspaper, to work for Labour in 1994 was one symbol of that change they were pursuing.

Just a few weeks into my new role as Gordon Brown's economic adviser, I arranged a trip for Gordon to Washington to meet with the new Clinton Administration. It was the first time I'd met Jonathan Powell, who was at the time working at the British Embassy in Washington, and very plugged into the Clinton campaign.

We were due to meet George Stephanopoulos in the White House, and hold talks with Clinton's key Treasury team: Lloyd Bentsen, the veteran Democrat senator who was then the Treasury Secretary; Bob Rubin, chair of the US National Economic Council; and Larry Summers who was in charge of international economic policy, and with whom I had worked closely at Harvard a few years earlier.

We flew in economy class, and were quickly spotted by a BBC producer from *On the Record*, the Sunday-lunchtime programme, who was travelling to Washington to do a film previewing the upcoming Detroit Jobs Summit. At the time, unemployment had stayed persistently high across Europe, and in the United States the big fear was of corporate downsizing – large companies moving offshore and exporting American jobs to cheaper locations around the world.

The Detroit summit was the G7's response to those fears, and the debate rumbling on in the media was whether the answer was to impose tougher standards for employers to train their workforces and invest in their growth, or whether to go the opposite route and deregulate labour markets, making them more flexible in an effort to persuade companies not to move jobs offshore.

Ken Clarke, the UK Chancellor, was a big advocate of flexibility, and *On the Record* was eager to push Gordon on the issue. Once they spotted us they saw their opportunity. It was clear that the news line they wanted was for Gordon to say that he thought that a commitment to flexibility was an important test of Labour's modernisation. However, in early 1994 – before the advent of New Labour and the battle over Clause IV – this would have caused chaos inside the party.

So we began a two-day game of cat and mouse, with Gordon determined he wasn't going to say 'flexibility' on camera, and *On the Record* determined to doorstep him. This was a great frustration for Gordon. In the UK he lived always expecting a TV camera or photographer to be lurking behind every corner. A trip to the US should have meant a few days' liberation to go into bars or bookshops. But suddenly the BBC camera crew kept popping up, trying to grab a quick interview. Luckily we were able to dodge them, but it was not easy.

By the time we came into government in 1997, the issue had moved on. Labour's new view was established – that, with the right rules and regulations and the right policy for fairness and social justice, the market economy was the best system. A commitment to flexibility no longer seemed like siding with business against workers as we legislated for a national minimum wage and tax credits, and we'd gone a long way to reassuring both sides that we could be trusted to stand up for their interests, and build collaborative relation-ships for mutual benefit.

But this 'modernising process' was not easy, and business was far from happy. We had tough arguments over the windfall tax on the privatised utility companies, and the intro-duction of criminal penalties for business leaders engaged in cartelising behaviour. And we had to introduce the national minimum wage in the face of strong opposition from major employers and the Tories. Ditto measures like the climate change levy or our double taxation reforms.

But despite those difficulties, I think we could be counted on to make sensible decisions. We commissioned the management consultants McKinsey to show us how we could boost productivity, whether that was through promoting more competition and investment or tackling barriers to growth in the planning system. And we decided not to jump to populist conclusions. For example, back in 2003, after the Enron accounting scandal, we were careful not to follow the US path of imposing very rigid new regulations – called the Sarbanes-Oxley rules – which, by the way, did nothing to prevent the financial crisis a few years later. We took the view that following suit would be counterproductive; that the market economy in Britain was still too fragile; and that the right thing to do was to work with business, not to impose a new settlement, but to try and tighten accounting standards and improve the culture.

Our solution to that issue summed up our approach to business in the Treasury, as also symbolised by the work we did on the New Deal employment programme and our 'Productivity Partnership', with a series of working groups made up of business leaders and the trade unions working together to look at where they could agree changes in labour-market regulation, infrastructure, finance, and so on.

Margaret Thatcher would have been appalled at our attempts to build a consensus between business and the trade unions about long-term reform. But I'd like to think that John Maynard Keynes would have heartily approved.

The fact that by the early 2000s we were making such good progress to forge a new consensus between government, business and the trade unions to boost investment, productivity and wage growth makes it all the more depressing to me that we're so far away from that kind of consensus today. In the shadow of the global financial crisis, with wages stagnant for many people and growing insecurity in the labour force, it is perhaps no surprise that while politicians in Britain have probably never been more unpopular, the same is true for the business community.

When voters on the doorstep say 'I work hard and play by the rules and pay my tax, and I don't see why these people shouldn't do the same', they may often be referring to immigrants or to people who are not working and on benefits, but they are also likely to be talking about corporations not paying their fair share of tax, or company bosses being paid multimillion-pound salaries and bonuses even while their businesses are struggling and laying off workers.

But I'm not sure how many company bosses understood that. Just a few weeks after I became the Shadow Chancellor in 2011, I was invited by the City Corporation to a business breakfast with a number of people I'd known and worked with back when I was the financial services minister.

I talked that morning about the challenge of rebuilding trust in the banking industry after the gross errors and misconduct of the financial crisis. Big reform was still needed, I said, but I was also clear with them that I thought the UK financial services industry was one of Britain's vital economic assets. The City of London is a world-leading centre for accountancy, law and auditing as well as asset management and banking, and the wider industry provides hundreds of thousands of jobs and livelihoods across the UK.

But my line – don't throw the baby out with the bathwater – wasn't good enough for a senior executive from one of Britain's biggest banks. He suddenly grabbed the attention of the room by pointing at me, wagging his finger and reacting angrily to what I was saying. 'Why don't you politicians understand?' he said. 'People up and down the country are complaining about the price of food not mortgages – they're much more angry about the supermarkets than they are about bankers. But instead of tackling that issue, you're playing to the gallery and talking down the City.'

I was stunned that someone so senior could both miss the point of what I was saying and completely misread how angry the public were about the financial crisis. And when, a few weeks later, at my first meeting with the CBI, I was presented with research showing that the chief priority for Britain's business leaders was to cut the top rate of income tax for those earning over £150,000, I must admit my heart sank.

The public rightly felt that the government hadn't been tough enough on the banks before and were angry about the taxpayer bailout; but they also felt the bankers themselves had been irresponsible and needed much tougher regulation. People still don't think that has happened, and both the government and the banks would be kidding themselves if they feel this issue is resolved. It certainly is not.

But that doesn't mean that people want to elect a government of bank bashers. One of the important lessons I've learned in politics over two decades is that it's not only common for people to hold two seemingly contradictory opinions at the same time, but it also makes a good deal of sense.

So when I think of the conversations I've had with voters

in recent years, I recall people ranting about the bankers and what they had done to our economy and how angry they were about it. But when asked, the same people would agree that banks are important for our economy and just want them to work better in the future, not be permanently weakened. They know they matter for their savings and mortgages, and for small-business lending, and more widely for jobs and wealth creation in the economy.

I saw that when Stephen Hester, then the chief executive of RBS, came to a meeting with a delegation of Yorkshire business leaders in Wakefield. Some in the audience were certainly cross, but the majority were there to find out what RBS was going to do to make things better. There was one gentleman in attendance who was really angry about his experiences with RBS, and he promptly took a shoe out of his briefcase and threatened to throw it across the room at Stephen. But he was the exception that day: most people in the room really wanted to know what RBS was doing to repair the damage, and if it was going to do a better job of serving them and the wider community.

I'm not sure more recent Labour leaders have properly grasped the public's complex, and seemingly contradictory, attitude to business. Ed Miliband spent the leadership election in 2010 attacking the bankers and New Labour for being in hock to them, with great success among Labour Party members. He thought the mood of the wider country was just to throw shoes at the banks and the energy companies, and he didn't fully understand the fact that people could be angry but also think that it was the job of government to work with business to try and solve the problems.

Moreover, he was always inclined to see business as a group, as a section of society, and didn't recognise that in the end businesses are, top to bottom, made up of individuals. I used to say to him that when you went to the CBI conference and spoke to a thousand people, you couldn't see industries or corporations, you had to see a thousand very different people.

Obviously there are business leaders out there who only care about making money or who just want to be left alone to do things their way, and some of them are willing to break the law or play fast and loose with regulation to achieve that goal. There are bad apples in business just like there are in politics, or in any industry. And like governments, the business community as a whole sometimes gets things wrong. In retrospect, the CBI's dogged campaign in the mid-2000s to prevent better workplace protections for casual and agency staff by stopping the UK from enacting the EU Agency Workers Directive now looks deeply misplaced.

But the large majority of people at a CBI conference are trying to do things the right way, and justifiably resent being treated like crooks. Most of the business leaders who take the time to come to the CBI do so not just because they want their business to succeed but also because they see their business as making a contribution to the country; and their self-worth is, in part, based upon the worth of their company, the contribution it makes to wider society, the jobs it creates, and the pensions it funds.

So I felt you had to speak to people at the CBI conference

as individuals who themselves felt they had a moral purpose as legitimate in their eyes as your own moral purpose as a politician. Ed didn't see it that way. Which was why his proposed price cap on the energy companies was so unpopular with business when he announced it in 2013.

It reminded me of the windfall tax on the utilities we announced in 1997, and the one-off way in which we raised resources from a sector which had made excessive profits while we tried to put in place a new regulatory environment. And given the public anger towards the energy companies in the last Parliament over the high price of gas and electricity bills, it did seem to me that some kind of similar catharsis was needed.

My concern about the price cap was less the unpopularity of the policy with business but more that it was seen as some left-wing crackdown on the energy sector, despite the fact that over the next thirty years we need that sector to produce the largest volume of private investment in any part of our economy, and make a hugely important contribution to tackling climate change, neither of which would be possible without the willingness of private investors around the world to put money in.

Saying that the energy companies were getting too good a deal and that regulation needed to be tightened was fair enough, but to give the impression that profits were inherently exploitative and that these were intrinsically bad vested interests sent a negative message to those investors, to business more widely, and I believe to the general public. It was the opposite of working with business to agree mutually acceptable solutions.

The same happened with our proposal for a 'mansion tax' on properties worth over £2 million. In its own terms, it was a sensible piece of tax policy which would have affected a tiny minority of properties, and we needed to show we could raise money without hitting people on middle and lower incomes; but it was certainly seen by some as a signal that we thought rising house prices were something bad and that we were anti-aspiration.

Ed and I certainly agreed that a return to 'business as usual' wouldn't work. We just often differed on the changes that needed to happen.

I recall one Sunday morning in Wakefield knocking on doors and speaking to a mum who said that her son had gone to college, got qualifications, but found it very hard to get a job until being taken on by a local employer. However, the nature of his contract meant that each day he had to ring up his employer at 7 a.m. to find out whether they wanted him that day or not. If they didn't, he wouldn't be paid. His mum looked at me and said: 'He's my son and it breaks my heart, he shouldn't be treated like this, it's not fair.' And she was right.

Her son was one of the losers, hit by the way the labour market has changed in Britain, America and across the developed world. Minimum wages have fallen behind the cost of living, while many more private sector employees are now employed, not by corporations, but by subcontractors without the same wealth-sharing mentality towards their staff.

Yes, there are some people for whom zero-hours contracts do make sense. A retired teacher in their late fifties wanting to do some supply work while balancing looking after their grandchildren can sign a zero-hours contract with a local authority and only work on the days they want to. For IT professionals, zero-hours contracts are the norm so that they can be on a company's books but have the flexibility to choose where to deploy their in-demand skills.

But for young people starting work in factories, shops or restaurants, the advantages of that kind of flexibility are much less clear. And the disadvantages all too apparent. For a restaurant with poor bookings one night of the week, it's much cheaper to stay shut and tell the staff not to come in to avoid paying their wages. Yet in those circumstances it's the workers who are bearing the risk, not the firm. With so many more people these days employed on short-term, flexible, but often disadvantageous contracts, without proper pensions, paid holiday or sickness support, that is not only unfair but undermines wider public support for the way companies and markets operate.

That fairness issue equally applies to the taxation of global companies. In the era of globalisation, the old rules of the game for charging and collecting tax have failed to adapt. And in this new weightless world of digital goods and brands, finding ways to ensure that big global corporations do pay their fair share of tax in the countries where they operate is something which, in my experience, sensible business leaders know we need to work together to solve.

*

Building a new and inclusive prosperity, which people feel is based upon fair rules and equal chances, is not just rhetoric for a political manifesto but a business necessity for companies in the UK, US and around the world.

Ten years ago it was common for people in the business community to defend very high executive salaries as evidence of the market economy in action. Today, voices worrying about what executive pay is doing to our economy and society range from the TUC to the Institute of Directors and across both sides of the House of Commons.

Back in the late 1990s, New Labour proved it was possible to have flexibility and fairness with a minimum wage and improved rights at work, preserving the UK as a job-creating labour market without onerous regulation.

And while the situation is different and more difficult today, and demands new and more radical approaches, the solution will again require a coincidence of interests between job-creating businesses and workers demanding fairness and respect. That was a synthesis which was not available when Gordon was ducking the cameras in Washington in 1994. And it was a synthesis which by 2010, when he was elected leader, Ed Miliband decided to reject.

For the many business leaders who wanted reform, who knew that the system wasn't fair, and that you needed to have regulations in place to protect working people, it dismayed them to hear Ed describe all zero-hours contracts as immoral. It was the black-and-white nature of it which many found so infuriating. I lost count of the number of times friendly business people said: 'If only Ed would say profit is important, wealth creation is important, we need to be innovative and flexible. If only he would say we could do this with business, not against business.'

But balance doesn't exist in a black-and-white world, and the danger is that – for increasing numbers of ordinary people – belief in striking that balance may be waning, especially as they see more examples of unfairness, corruption or scandal in the open market economy going unchecked.

For the thirty-plus years of my adult life, I've believed that with the right rules and regulations and the right policy for fairness and social justice, the market economy is the best system. I like to think that my view is shared by the public at large. But if politicians and business leaders take that for granted, if they simply resort to populism on the one hand or bury their heads in the sand on the other, then that consensus won't last. And we will all pay the price.

9

Change

The Treasury is one of the UK's oldest institutions – so how does a young pup teach an old dog new tricks?

On your first day in any job, you can almost always tell what it's going to be like. You get an instinctive feeling about the atmosphere and culture of your new workplace, and it tells you a lot about whether you're going to fit in, get ahead and be happy. And you're very rarely wrong.

My first day in the Treasury was in the summer of 1989. I had just graduated, and gained a place on the Civil Service fast-stream scheme. But rather than start immediately, I'd asked to defer for two years so I could take up a Kennedy scholarship to do a post-graduate degree in America.

The Treasury took me up on my request for a summer internship in the middle of my graduate course and I turned up on a sunny Monday morning, and was taken down to meet my boss in the Monetary Economics Unit. He didn't say hello to me, but gestured for me to sit down in the chair opposite him. In silence, he produced from his drawer an envelope and handed it over to me. I opened it, and read a letter saying: 'Dear Mr Balls, Welcome to the Treasury.'

The letter explained that I was to work on a research project assessing the real impact of the Chancellor's attempt to support sterling in the foreign exchange markets in 1986. It said that I would be expected to support the wider work of the team, and it was to be hoped I would enjoy my time at the Treasury. It was signed by my new boss, who was still sitting across from me. 'Any questions?' he said. 'No, that's fine.' He nodded. 'Great, that's your desk. Off you go.' And that was my induction.

An hour later, there was a knock on the door and in came a woman in a big apron pushing a trolley loaded with cups and saucers. 'Would you like some hot water?' she asked. I said 'Yes,' because I assumed that was the done thing. Five minutes later she returned with two cups filled with hot water and put one on my desk, and one on my superior's. He looked at me rather perplexed. 'But you've nothing to put in it?' 'No,' I admitted. 'I suppose I can lend you a tea bag,' he said – I noted the world 'lend'. The next day I brought in a box of PG Tips and made my loan good. His generosity only went so far, however. That lunchtime he said: 'I generally go to the park for sandwiches – would you like to come?' We walked out to St James's Park, sat on a bench, I watched him eat his sandwiches, and we walked back.

It was a strange time. The department had to shut down every Wednesday because of weekly Tube strikes. But rather than miss work, a number of civil servants had old Second World War camp beds brought up from the cellar in order to be able to stay overnight. I chose not to take up the offer. Of course, throughout that summer, I never met the Chancellor, Nigel Lawson, or went anywhere near his private office. All policy advice was routed through the Permanent Secretary, each division was its own fiefdom and communication was distinctly Stone Age. To send a memo or respond to a letter, you had to write in longhand what you wanted to say, post it off to a member of the 'typing pool' – located in some distant office – wait for the typed-up copy to return, send it back with your corrections, and wait for a final proof. Only then could you submit your missive to your boss for approval – at which point the process would invariably begin again. Getting a simple letter sent out could take at least two weeks.

But for all the arcane practices, this was the Treasury, the beating heart of economic policy, the most powerful department in government, the place where economic and political history was made. And what struck me most about the Treasury back in 1989 was the sheer excellence of the people who worked there, the volume of data they had access to, and the quality of their research and analysis. My boss was a first-rate economist and a wonderful teacher. It was without question a Rolls-Royce operation, even if it was a rather vintage model.

I could have joined the Treasury permanently in 1990, but when the FT offered me a job as a leader writer, I decided to take that instead, simply on the grounds that the FT was somewhere I could make an immediate impact, and – based on what I'd seen – I wasn't sure the same would be true at the Treasury, at least for quite some time.

If you had told me then that ten years later the Treasury's Permanent Secretary would be asking me to take on the position of chief economic adviser and join the Treasury Management Board, I would frankly never have believed you.

Over the course of seven years there after the 1997 election, I was at the heart of planning eight Budgets, seven Pre-Budget Reports and four Spending Reviews. We made the Bank of England independent, introduced tax credits, raised taxes to save the NHS and kept Britain out of the euro.

At such a young age, I found myself at the centre of power, and everything that's happened to me since – becoming an MP, a junior Treasury minister, a Cabinet minister, my four years as Shadow Chancellor and almost becoming Chancellor before losing in 2015 – was shaped by those experiences. It was the time of my life, and I set out to use that time to change the Treasury – and Britain – for the better.

When the time came for Gordon's first day in the Treasury in 1997, I had some trepidation about how he would adapt to the culture that I'd seen there, and – more importantly – how they would adapt to working with him.

In the months before the general election, I'd met with the Treasury Permanent Secretary Terry Burns almost twice-weekly to prepare the policy agenda and first Budget of what looked increasingly likely to be the next Labour government.

Gordon was far too superstitious to hold those meetings

himself, having lost elections in 1987 and 1992. So almost all the preparatory work fell to me, including spending a lot of time studying Treasury history, and trying to learn from the mistakes of the past.

I wasn't the only one. It was clear that the Treasury civil servants had also spent a lot of time studying the past, particularly the transition in 1979; and the conclusion they'd drawn from that election was that they'd known the personalities of the incoming Tory administration quite well, but hadn't paid sufficient attention to the potential shifts in policy, which led to great tensions between Treasury ministers and their civil servants after Margaret Thatcher came to power.

But if anything, in 1997 they made the opposite mistake. They spent a huge amount of time preparing for the implementation of our new policies, but did very little to prepare for Gordon's personality, and that made things very tough when we arrived.

For example, we all had mobile phones and pagers and were used to being in constant touch, but the Treasury's head of communications and her team had no pagers, and one mobile phone which was passed to whichever press officer was on duty. It was the opposite of the 'rapid rebuttal' approach we'd been used to in opposition. Charlie Whelan, Gordon's press officer, couldn't hide his disdain.

Similarly, Gordon's working practices and methods were very different from the rather more laid-back approach of Ken Clarke, and we faced a constant battle in the early weeks and months, with the officials saying 'This is how *it* works', and us saying 'Yes, but this is how *Gordon* works'.

During that early period, I worked hard alongside Ed

Miliband and Sue Nye, Gordon's political secretary and personal manager, the model for anyone in the world who occupies that kind of job, to make the Treasury machine mesh with its new boss, and ensure that the advice going up to Gordon made sense, fitted with his objectives and could be delivered.

And I would like to think that, in that period, along with the policy decisions we made, we also helped to drive what was an evolving process of culture change in the Treasury, most importantly in terms of changing the policymaking process from an entrenched hierarchy into a true meritocracy.

It was a real culture shock for many senior civil servants when we scrapped the traditional away-day at Dorneywood, where the Chancellor was supposed to make his key Budget decisions in their company, but it reflected what we were doing across the department. We always insisted on having in the room the individuals who had actually done the work on an issue under discussion, not the people who had signed it off. And when Gordon wanted to discuss any particular point, we'd tell him whom we regarded as the best person to speak to.

Compared to 1989, when I never got near the Chancellor's office, the post-1997 Treasury saw junior civil servants in their mid-twenties becoming pivotal figures in the formation of our Budgets and Spending Reviews, and the talent-spotting which that enabled saw dozens of the best civil servants quickly elevated into more senior or central roles.

The Chancellor standing outside Number 11 Downing Street holding up the traditional red box is the image that will come to mind for most people when they hear the words 'Budget day'. Along with the usual groans if petrol and alcohol taxes go up that evening. For the Treasury, and the government, it is the most important day of the year. On election day in 1997, I met Terry Burns outside the Treasury to give him detailed papers on the windfall tax, the New Deal and other aspects of policy for the first Labour Budget that we'd been discussing over the previous months. We soon discovered we had a lot to learn.

The Treasury is rightly obsessed with secrecy in the run-up to the Budget. A leak about an upcoming tax change can cost the Exchequer millions of pounds. So every night we had to lock up all our papers in big safes in the corner of our offices. But I wasn't so careful. A few weeks before that July 1997 Budget, I realised I'd left the whole of the draft Budget document on the floor of a hotel room in central London, and had to dash back by cab, shredded with nerves, to make sure that it had not been filched. I tried harder from that point on, although there was another occasion walking back from Downing Street to the Treasury after a Budget meeting, when I sensed that the bag I was carrying was becoming lighter. I looked back and saw a great trail of Budget papers littering the street behind me. Once again I had to move with great speed.

Then, of course, there was the speech. It was only the day before the Budget in July 1997 that we realised we had a big problem. Gordon had been working for the past four weeks on the speech, with the help of his old friend and speech-writer, the veteran of US Democrat campaigns, Bob Shrum. In many ways, it was a very American speech that Bob and Gordon had prepared – more of a 'State of the Union' address in terms of its sweep and ambition, and very much intended to set out the mission of the new Treasury and new government, at least in terms of the economy, society and public services. I will never forget its opening line: 'We inherit a kingdom united in name only.'

But the day before the Budget, the official speechwriter in Gordon's private office presented us with an entirely different speech. It was something she'd been working on for weeks and which focused primarily on the measures that were actually being announced in the Budget, and one that had, most importantly, been cleared by officials across the Treasury, Inland Revenue and Customs and Excise. They were just continuing to follow Ken Clarke's working method, which was to wait until the day before the Budget, get the draft speech from the Civil Service, make a few handwritten amendments and then read it out. Gordon's approach was rather more hands-on than that!

When, in something of a panic, I looked at the two speeches together, I realised the speechwriter's draft was rather short on message but very long on policy announcements. Gordon's was very strong on message but included almost none of the actual Budget measures. I went into his office, and explained that there were a series of announcements we had to include, for example a 17p rise in cigarette taxes. Gordon replied: 'Why ever would I want to say that?' And I said: 'Because it becomes law at 6 p.m., and there might be an expectation you'll tell people before it happens.' I told him I understood he wanted to do things differently, but that there were some conventions – like actually announcing what was in the Budget – that you couldn't bypass.

We reached a compromise whereby Ed Miliband, the

speechwriter and I spent a frantic few hours putting the two speeches into one. We then took it page by page into Gordon, with a team of officials standing by in the anteroom. He'd make amendments, the officials would decide whether the amended version was sufficiently transparent and consistent with what we were actually doing, and slowly, eventually, at three o'clock in the morning, we had a speech ready to go. It wasn't a mistake we made again.

For all of his passion and brilliance on the big picture, Gordon was never very good at making the Civil Service machine work for him. That was our job. We worked on long-term policy planning, but we also made the internal wiring work. And in my time as an adviser at the Treasury, we established a pretty good method when it came to Budgets and Spending Reviews.

For months in the run-up to each event, we would meet weekly, sometimes daily, with the key officials who held oversight of the entire package; and by oversight, I mean a forensic understanding of every aspect of what we were announcing. You had individuals from the team responsible for the fiscal forecast; the officials from the tax and spending teams; our experts from the Council of Economic Advisers; and, crucially, the civil servants we'd hand-picked to run the Budget preparation unit – individuals who needed to be calm, efficient, methodical, expert proofreaders, and able to work eighteen-hour days for six weeks, surviving on nothing but snacks from the Treasury vending machines.

Ed Miliband and I would sit with those individuals and go through two sets of spreadsheets: one – the Scorecard – setting out every potential Budget measure; and the other – the Fiscal Tables, originally called the Fry Tables after my private secretary who devised them – setting out every aspect of the forecast and telling us whether we were on track to meet our fiscal rules. And we'd lead a remorseless interrogation of the figures, the assumptions, the impact on child poverty, the politics, the practicalities, and the alternatives. Every week, every day, analysing the same measures and numbers over and over again. The only thing I can compare it to would be those movies of American lawyers preparing for a big murder case: it's all the endless, mind-numbing sifting of the evidence, the transcripts and the photos, which means when you come to court, you're ready.

We didn't always get it right – the 75p pension increase being the starkest example, where we failed to spot the impact of what we were doing. And even worse, there were occasions when we were fully aware of the distributional consequences and still went ahead with the policy decision.

A classic of its kind happened in the spring of 2007, when Gordon told us he intended to abolish the lower 10p tax rate to pay for a 2p cut in the basic rate of income tax. It was absolutely clear from all the distributional modelling the Treasury did beforehand that it would, without question, leave a percentage of the population out of pocket. They were typically low-paid workers – many of them young or in late-middle age – with no children, or whose children had left home, who therefore could not have their income topped up with tax credits. We knew that group of losers was there, and that's why both Ed Miliband and I said to Gordon we shouldn't do it. But in the end Gordon thought the positive news of the basic rate cut was worth the risk. Ed and I should have fought harder and I regret that to this day.

The two days after the Budget were always the toughest because – even while coping with all that exhaustion – we'd still be hectically busy dealing with the aftermath of what we'd announced. The low point was invariably when Gordon would say: 'Can we discuss next year's Budget?' And I would roll my eyes and say: 'For goodness' sake, we've got 363 days to go, do we have to start now?' But he was right; it was like painting the Forth Bridge, you never stop and you've never finished.

The other key consideration around the Budget was Number Ten, and keeping them in the loop on what we were planning. While Gordon was always wary about giving Tony a final version of his speech, and Tony himself never really got engaged until the last few days, there was a big operation going on for months before, where I would meet with Jeremy Heywood and David Miliband, head of the Number Ten Policy Unit, and go through all our measures in detail.

What that ensured is that when Tony finally did engage and had his conversations with Gordon, there were no surprises in the package as far as Number Ten were concerned. So in all those years, we never had an occasion when there was a last-minute, disruptive stand-off over anything we were planning to announce.

That was especially important for the Spending Reviews which allocate public spending budgets to the NHS, schools, policing and other public services. The Treasury has all the clout and know-how on tax policy. But when it comes to public spending and delivery issues, and influencing other Cabinet members to take ownership of changes in their departments, the influence of Number Ten, the Policy Unit and the Cabinet Office is hugely important.

In particular, having a Delivery Unit outside the Treasury close to the Prime Minister, coupled with the weekly meetings Tony and Gordon would have with different Cabinet ministers to discuss how they were delivering better public services, worked incredibly well. It was a process which could never have been managed solely from within the Treasury.

Of all the reforms dismantled by David Cameron and George Osborne, I think one of the most retrograde steps was their scrapping of the Delivery Unit and the output targets for public spending that we introduced.

It was, at best, short-sighted of the Tories to scrap them, and, at worst, a cynical attempt to avoid comparisons with our record under the guise of cutting bureaucracy, but the quality and effectiveness of public services has suffered as a result.

Many of the changes we introduced at the Treasury – policies, structures, procedures and reforms – have stood the test of time. Alongside not joining the euro, the dramatic fall in child poverty that occurred over the years I was at the Treasury – in no small part as a result of policies we delivered in successive Budgets – will always be one of the greatest achievements of my professional life. But I am as proud of how, with successive Permanent Secretaries, we helped change the Treasury's culture.

The institution Labour left in 2010 was a world away from the one where I spent the summer in 1989. It still has a reputation in Whitehall for being arrogant, which may just come with the territory. But it has gone from an austere, arcane hierarchy where a 22-year-old could be asked to write a paper and leave with no idea what would happen next to his recommendations, to a friendly, modern meritocracy where – if their ideas and analysis are good enough – young graduates would find themselves invited to submit their proposals and make a presentation directly to the Chancellor.

My job was made infinitely easier by the extraordinary group of people I worked with: the successive members of Gordon's private office, the Civil Service heads of communication, my own private secretaries, and my diary secretary, Julie McCandless, whom I persuaded to move over from the old Treasury typing pool, where she once had the dubious pleasure of typing my scribbled memos in 1989, to come and manage my life.

Julie is one of the most professional, dedicated officials you could ever ask for – she has since been my diary secretary on and off for almost twenty years – and with a great sense of humour as well. On my last day as an advisor at the Treasury in 2004, she said to me: 'Ed, there's just something I have to confess before you leave. For seven years, every day you've come into this office, you've had two fresh bottles of Malvern water on your meeting table. I just need you to know that every day I've filled those two same bottles from the tap. So wherever you end up, just remember you don't need to spend money on spring water.'

I laughed and said: 'I can't think of any story which proves your dedication to the Treasury cause more than that,' and wherever I've ended up since, Julie has been kind enough to follow me.

In the final months before the 2015 election, I had a series of preparatory meetings with the Permanent Secretary, Nick Macpherson, and his senior team in case we won the general election. We talked about our Budget plans, further banking reform, a new energy policy, and fixing the UK's still dysfunctional housing market. It was very different from those same meetings with Terry Burns almost twenty years before, both in terms of our much better collective understanding of policies and personalities, but also in the sense that none of us seemed too confident this time round that there would be a change of government.

But even so, I would come out of those meetings and just allow myself a fleeting daydream about getting down to all that unfinished business, with Julie in my office and the same old bottles of 'Malvern' water on my table. I have a strong sense of what might have been, and what I've left behind.

10

Control

You come into politics because you want power – but is giving it away the best politics of all?

With just three days to go until the 1997 general election, Gordon Brown rang me and said: 'Let's meet this evening at the Grosvenor.' That meant Labour MP Geoffrey Robinson's suite at the Grosvenor House Hotel, where we'd met many times over the previous twelve months to discuss and plan what we would do if we took office.

Right until the last, Tony and Gordon stayed superstitious that some late event might throw us off course, but we were on course to win and there was much planning to do. And top of that list was the potential move to make the Bank of England independent, and remove the control of inflation and interest rates from politicians.

Gordon arrived in Geoffrey's suite, having been out on the

road campaigning, poured himself a cup of coffee and said: 'I think we should do it straight away.' 'It' could only mean one thing. He continued, 'You're right about this, and I don't want to delay. We'll tell them on Friday and we'll move quickly.' I remember at the time taking it in my stride, thinking: 'Let's see if he sticks with this.' But I could also sense he was serious.

Regardless of the timing, just the fact that Gordon seemed to have made his mind up was significant. For the past three or four years, we'd been discussing whether it was strengthening or weakening for the Chancellor to give up control of setting the interest rates. Gordon never took steps he thought were weakening, so I'd always expected him to be more equivocal on the risks, but this was him at his decisive best.

That evening I started work on a letter from the new Chancellor to the Governor of the Bank of England setting out how we would make the Bank of England independent and also move their responsibility for the regulation of banks to a new statutory financial regulator, abolishing a plethora of other self-regulatory bodies in the process.

It took me a day to get the content and tone right, during which I called a senior Treasury contact whom I could trust, to tell him what we were planning and read him the draft. I finished the letter, gave it to Gordon, and we were off. On polling day, Gordon talked Tony Blair through the plan over the phone, although, as often happened between them, Gordon most likely hung up thinking everything was squared off, while Tony most likely hung up not entirely sure what Gordon was on about.

In any case, for all the significance of that conversation, it was overshadowed for both of them by Tony's simultaneous insistence that Charlie Whelan should not be appointed to a role in the Treasury, something Gordon would never accept, not least because I regarded Charlie as so essential to our operation I would have resigned in protest.

The next morning, feeling weary but elated after staying up to see Yvette's election victory in Yorkshire, I met Gordon at his flat in Great Smith Street. He was still waiting for the formal summons to go to Downing Street to be appointed as Chancellor, which we were certain would come at any time.

Counting my chickens, I went over to the Treasury. There I was met as always by one of the aides to Sir Terry Burns, the department's Permanent Secretary. He took me up to Terry's office where I was given a copy of the full incoming brief for Gordon and left in the Chancellor's waiting room to read it, keeping an eye on the television and Tony's triumphant march up Downing Street.

In the middle of the afternoon, I had a call from Sue Nye to say that Gordon was finally going to Downing Street, and that she would let me know when he was heading over to the Treasury. Slowly, excited Treasury staff had begun to gather in the hall, piling row by row all the way up the main staircase. When Gordon pulled up outside, Terry and I went out to escort him in. Opening the doors, a huge roar of cheers and applause greeted us. It made the hairs on the back of my neck stand up, and still does when I think about it today.

We went up to the Chancellor's office and met the principal private secretary, Nick Macpherson, and sat down for what I think was supposed to be a session where Gordon would listen to Terry explain who everyone was and what big issues the Chancellor would be facing, as many other Permanent Secretaries would have been doing that day.

That wasn't quite how it worked. Terry barely got a word in edgeways. Gordon had decided to show who was in charge, and said: 'Terry, there's something I need to say from the outset, I'm very much looking forward to working with you and all your staff, but I want to make an immediate decision for announcement in the next few days. I want to make the Bank of England independent.'

Terry was taken aback, but even more so when Gordon then turned to me and said: 'Ed, do you have the letter?' And I produced from my file the draft letter for Gordon to send to Bank of England Governor Eddie George and handed copies around. Terry read the letter and said: 'Well, we'd better get to work then.'

Nick and Terry then went into the outer office to confer and ten minutes later came back to the room with Alan Budd, the chief economic adviser, and a young civil servant, the excellent Tom Scholar, now the Permanent Secretary himself. We gave Tom the letter, talked through its contents, and he went off to get a team together.

We had told the Treasury. Now it was time for a proper discussion with Number Ten. We went over to the Blairs' house in Islington, where Cherie had famously been snapped in her nightie receiving a bouquet of flowers. The place was a bustle of activity, with dozens of civil servants running around, but we sat down with Tony and the Number Ten civil servant responsible for economic policy, Moira Wallace.

Tony turned to Moira and blithely said: 'Gordon's going to make the Bank of England independent,' and Gordon said: 'Yes, the Treasury's getting on with the details now, and I'll see Eddie George over the weekend.' Moira was clearly gobsmacked by this decision, and the nature of the decision-making process.

She said: 'Prime Minister, I think we would usually need to commission a series of papers from the Treasury about whether this is the right decision, how it should be organised, how the Bank of England and the markets will react, and then have a proper discussion about all of this.' Tony looked back at her and said: 'Moira, Gordon thinks it's a good idea and it's fine by me. We'll let them get on with it.'

We met with the Treasury the following morning – a Saturday – and as well as some very minor, legalistic changes to the letter, there were some big issues of concern.

First was timing: there was a bank holiday on the Monday, and Wednesday was the regular meeting between the Chancellor and the Governor of the Bank of England. I was very keen to move quickly, have surprise on our side, and avoid too much market and media speculation about the outcome of the Wednesday meeting.

So I proposed, with Terry's reluctant acceptance, that we should move the formal meeting to Tuesday morning, and get Eddie in over the weekend to tell him what we were planning. That was where things got more complicated. The letter was clear that this was one whole package of reforms: independence; interest rates; the Monetary Policy Committee; a new inflation target; and responsibility for financial regulation and debt management moving to new independent bodies.

Terry didn't disagree with any of that, but was worried that it would be too much for Eddie to take on board in one go, and there was a danger he'd react badly, not to the policies being proposed, but to the pace of them. It was a very difficult conversation, because our instinct was 'full steam ahead' while Terry's was 'tact and diplomacy'. But eventually a compromise was reached, where we would prepare two letters to the Governor: one about independence and debt management, which would be made public immediately; and the other about financial regulation, which he'd receive at the same meeting but would be published at a later date. We were moving fast, but also trying to give everyone a bit of time and consideration.

We had the meeting with Eddie that weekend, and while he was concerned about losing responsibility for bank regulation – and simultaneously delighted about independence – there was no disputing that this was the plan, and he would go along with it. After the recent regulatory debacles at Barings and BCCI, I think he knew change was inevitable.

We met early on Tuesday morning in the Chancellor's office for the first and last meeting of the 'Eddie and Gordon Show'. It was agreed between them that there would be a quarter-point rise in interest rates – a move which Eddie had been urging for some months given the rising rate of inflation, and which Ken Clarke, in pre-election mood, had been resisting in his own monthly meetings. While Ken would doubtless have done the same thing if he'd still been in place, there was something hugely symbolic and important about the necessary interest rate rise – put off for months by the Tories – being made immediately before Labour then put those decisions out of political control.

We had a gap between the meeting and our pre-arranged

mid-morning press conference, during which Gordon spoke to a number of former Chancellors to tell them what he was doing, notably Nigel Lawson, Ken Clarke and John Major.

Then, at the press conference, Gordon announced the decision on interest rates and on central bank independence. And, as so often happens in politics and communication, the journalists sitting through the whole announcement and Q&A still had to huddle around me afterwards so I could explain to them exactly what we were doing.

As I spoke, it became clear that a number of the very esteemed economic journalists present didn't fully appreciate that the Bank of England was actually being made independent, right there, right then, in front of their eyes. And some of them were obviously thinking: this is all a bit rushed and reckless – have you thought it all through?

But for me, this was no spur-of-the-moment decision.

I had come back from Harvard in 1990 just a few weeks before Britain joined the Exchange Rate Mechanism, which was intended to lock the value of the pound against the D-Mark and other European currencies. And though I was very new on the *Financial Times*, and disagreed with the paper's supportive stance on the issue, I found some comfort in the fact that my fellow leader writers were also clear that it was an incredibly risky decision.

Two years later, we were proved right, and all those who supported it – the CBI, the TUC and the main political parties – were left struggling to defend their position. The

I've just cooked lunch for the team at the Morley Labour rooms on one of our campaign Saturdays before the 2015 general election (*Defeat*).

Jayne Dawson, my agent's wife, took this picture of our empty sherry glasses straight after the 9 a.m. 'Wake' we held following my 2015 election defeat (*Preface*).

At the 2015 general election count in Leeds. Andrea Jenkyns was trying to stay restrained but her smile just burst out (*Defeat*).

Me aged 6 in my first ever Norwich City kit (*Loyalty*).

My first ever official school picture – my mum was cross that I fell over running down our drive the weekend before and had a big graze on my face (*Loyalty*).

With my younger brother Andrew and my sister Joanna looking all very Duran Duran (*Loyalty*).

Our wedding day in Eastbourne, 10 January 1998. From left to right: Yvette's sister Nicky, her dad Tony, my mum, my brother Andrew, EB, YC, Yvette's brother David, her mum June, my dad, and my sister Joanna (*Family*).

Mr Speaker, John Bercow, has been a great supporter of my work with Action for Stammering Children (*Vulnerability*).

Walking down the sea front at Blackpool for the cameras at the TUC conference, September, 1994 (*Friendship*).

Right: With the Queen of Nashville, Dolly Parton, in my office at the Department of Children, Schools and Families (*Flowers*).

Below: The *Guardian*'s Steve Bell marks my 2004 departure from the Treasury in typical style (*Friendship*).

Peter Mandelson in full flow in the office, me being attentive and Gordon – as always – pretending not to listen (*Reform*).

'Third Way' summit, Chequers 1998 (from left to right): Andrew Cuomo, Larry Summers, Gordon Brown, Melanne Verveer, EB, Geoff Mulgan, Patricia Hewitt, Cherie Blair, David Miliband, Tony Blair, Sidney Blumenthal, Hillary Clinton, Tony Giddens, (obscured), Al From, Margaret Jay, Joe Nye, Franklin Raines, Don Baer, Peter Mandelson (*Markets*).

A young me, and an even younger Ed Miliband, clutch our big briefing folders as we lurk in Downing Street on Budget Day, 1997 (*Change*).

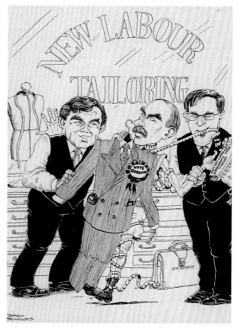

In 1997, Gordon and I set out to bring the twentieth century's greatest economist, John Maynard Keynes, back into fashion (*Control*).

Left: The days when my sceptical remarks at a seminar on the single currency could splash Britain's best-selling paper (*Decisions*).

Above: Three surprising amigos – George Osborne, Vince Cable and me – at RyanAir during the EU referendum campaign in May 2016 (*Identity*).

With my ministerial team: Sarah McCarthy-Fry, Jim Knight, Bev Hughes and Delyth Morgan (*Mission*).

With the End Child Poverty Coalition outside Number Eleven – Alistair Darling is Chancellor, I am Children's Secretary (*Ambition*).

Right: Eyeing up the Budget box in 2007 as Economic Secretary (*Ambition*).

Below: Standing in for Gordon Brown at the Helsinki Ecofin summit (*Ambition*).

Right: Politics loves a cartoon – and my build and reputation lent itself to lots of these kinds of images (*Image*).

Left: Raising a laugh from Vernon Coaker and Kevin Brennan in the House by asking Michael Gove to answer the GCSE science exam questions he said had been 'dumbed-down' (*Clowns*).

Right: 'Goosed!' – on a visit with pensioners in Glasgow in 2011. The picture splashed the *Daily Record* (*Assumptions*).

With my fellow candidates in the 2010 Labour leadership election (*Risks*).

ERM had never recovered from German reunification which, while a political triumph, was a massive economic shock; but because every country was so committed to the project, it continued even while short-term interest rates rose to double digits, and as our economy slumped into recession.

In August 1992, Norman Lamont announced he was going to issue a new government bond denominated in D-mark, the equivalent of putting a gun against the head of the British taxpayer if we decided to devalue sterling. It looked desperate, it was totally unconvincing, and we all knew the writing was on the wall.

But if things were bad for the government, they were also bad for the opposition. Neil Kinnock and John Smith had embraced a strongly pro-European position for the Labour Party at the end of the 1980s as an antidote to the Bennite anti-Europeanism of 1983. They were as hitched to the wagon of ERM membership as the Tories, and could never advocate devaluation. That was the most difficult period for Gordon as Shadow Chancellor. He was unable to argue against the government's policy, worried that to do so would damage his and Labour's credibility, but as a result, he was left unable to propose an alternative.

Throughout the summer of 1992, before Black Wednesday and with the blessing of the FT, I worked on a pamphlet for the Fabian Society entitled: 'Euro Monetarism: Why Britain Was Ensnared and How We Should Escape', which was deeply critical of the deflationary squeeze of the ERM. I argued that joining a single currency would be no long-term solution for Britain because it would lock us in even more tightly to a regime which could prove deflationary and politically unstable.

Instead, I advocated that the solution was to devolve power to an independent central bank, and that if Labour took up this proposal, it would transform the party's economic credibility. Alongside that, I said Labour should focus the Treasury's activities on a medium-term growth strategy to strengthen the underlying position of the economy on finance, skills and corporate governance; to move people from welfare into work; and to tackle inequality – all the areas where I thought the Tories were doing nothing, but where real gains for a Labour government could be made.

I'm not sure whether it was that pamphlet, or the various conversations I was having with key Labour figures at the time, but shortly after Black Wednesday I received an invitation to go and meet Gordon Brown. At our very first meeting, I told Gordon about my views on Bank of England independence, which – having spent ten years in opposition lamenting Labour's lack of control over the economic and fiscal levers – left him rather unconvinced.

He intrigued me enough in that first meeting, and in a number of others afterwards, that when he asked me to leave the FT and come and work for him, I was definitely interested. The crunch came when the FT talked to me about my next assignment. I said I wanted to be their Africa correspondent, working out of Nairobi. They said I could go to Washington, Bonn or Tokyo, but definitely not Africa. That was enough for me; I quit, and told Gordon I was coming to work for him.

When I arrived in 1994, we talked again about the Bank of

England plan; that autumn I wrote a long paper on the issue, and – at Gordon's suggestion – gave a presentation to Tony Blair and his advisers explaining that this reform was vital to Labour winning not just a first, but a second term in office.

I must have seemed a bit obsessive about my plan, and – at a time when people were so focused on what we needed to do to get into government – it was genuinely difficult to persuade them to concentrate on how we would avoid stuffing things up when we got there, in the way that previous Labour governments had done on inflation and interest rates.

But I plugged away, and in the summer of 1995 Gordon dipped his toe in the water, making a fairly dry speech at the Labour Finance & Industry Group in which he set out a plan for restructuring the Bank of England with a new Monetary Policy Committee, and said we would *consider* the case for independence once we had seen the track record of the new reformed institution.

It was a long way from that speech to announcing independence as a fait accompli two years later, but the journey had to start somewhere. Even so, by 1997 many people were still opposed to the move, from my friend Bill Keegan at the *Observer*, who was worried it would affect our ability to stimulate growth, to William Hague's Tory Party, who voted against the legislation when it came before Parliament. In all the commotion over the announcement on independence, what people missed was the importance of our decisions to make the inflation target symmetric, removing any deflationary bias by making it clear that inflation going too low below target was as big a problem as inflation going too high; and that we would appoint four external members of the nine-member Monetary Policy Committee, the equivalent of giving the US president just shy of a majority on appointments to the Supreme Court. We made explicit that it would be the job of these individuals to bring debates and disagreements about economic policy into the public eye.

We thought hard about who the best people would be. I think the press speculation was that we were going to appoint Labour lackeys, but we defied that by opting for Charles Goodhart, DeAnne Julius, David Currie and – a big surprise and potential risk – Professor Willem Buiter, known for his economic intellect and track record, but also for the stridency of his Keynesian views.

I rang Larry Summers, my old Harvard professor, to tell him we were thinking of appointing Buiter, and his response was: 'Well, he's brilliant, my goodness, but what on earth will Eddie George and Mervyn King say?' To which my reply was: 'Well, that's the point, we've got to make sure someone will challenge the consensus view, and make sure there's an open debate.'

In the months after the election, with inflation rising, Willem Buiter played a crucial role through his public utterances in ensuring the Bank raised rates regularly throughout that year to meet the 2.5 per cent inflation target, but equally – when the Asian and Russian crises of 1998 hit – he and the Bank harnessed that same proactive Keynesian instinct to get ahead of the curve to protect growth and stop a deflationary cycle with inflation under-shooting the target.

If a Labour Chancellor had presided over that much volatility in interest rates month after month, it would have been seen as an economic crisis out of control, as happened to Nigel Lawson in the late 1980s; but an independent Bank of

England was seen to be acting soberly and prudently as the circumstances dictated. In that sense, it was hugely empowering for Labour's economic credibility at the time.

The move had other significant benefits as well, which have been rarely understood. Pre-independence, in the weeks around each interest rate decision, senior civil servants in the Treasury would spend vast amounts of time worrying about what should be done, worrying about what the Chancellor would do, worrying about how the Bank and the markets would react, and very often trying to find a way to persuade the Chancellor to act in a way which was essential for the economy, but difficult politically. That disappeared overnight.

Relationships between the Treasury and the Bank of England also improved. Indeed, I had no idea before I arrived at the Treasury how bad they had been, the result of some bitter disputes over the previous decade on exchange rate policy, debt management and bank regulation. For example, ten days into the job, on a bit of a whim, I asked Steve Robson, the civil servant in charge of financial services, to accompany me to lunch with Eddie George at the Bank. When we got there, Eddie's private secretary came down to say the Governor was very pleased to see me, but Mr Robson was not invited and not welcome. Steve took the news calmly and didn't even seem surprised.

And arguments over interest rates between Number Ten and Number Eleven also disappeared entirely as a potential point of tension. Nigel Lawson had ended up resigning because of Margaret Thatcher's attempts to influence his monetary and exchange rate policy, and John Major and Ken Clarke had strained discussions about interest rates. Not Tony Blair and Gordon Brown.

Crucially, what replaced that was an agreement around the fundamental duty of the Treasury to meet Labour's fiscal rules. When there were disputes between the Prime Minister and Chancellor, over public spending commitments or tax rises, we were able to warn how our decision could impact the Bank's next move on interest rates. 'Of course we'd like to be more generous,' we'd say, 'of course we'd like to spend more or tax less, but if the Bank of England think we're playing fast and loose with the level of the minimum wage or our spending on public services, the consequence will be that they'll make an offsetting increase in interest rates.'

That was always enough to persuade Tony Blair to change his mind, and we had to pull that trick many times over the years. So, any gullible journalist or historian who has written that Tony spent his later years as prime minister trying to rein in Gordon on public spending and the deficit is not only rewriting history but inventing it.

Following the success of Bank of England independence, the idea of handing over power and control to experts and suitable bodies took hold. The government would establish the objective, the structure and the rules for an institution, but hand over control to an independent arm's-length agency to make the case-by-case decisions, on the basis that they would be able to take a long-term, proactive approach, undeterred by short-term political pressures.

Straight after the 2001 election, we announced that we would follow the same model in competition policy: handing over decisions on mergers and big acquisitions to an independent Competition Commission to operate at arm's length from government. Then in 2005, we announced that the Office for National Statistics, already quasi-independent but still directed by ministers, would become fully independent, so as to enshrine the integrity of our national statistics in law.

When I became Education Secretary in 2007, I applied the same model to the issue of exam standards. The allegation that exams had been 'dumbed down' by interfering politicians trying to improve results had been a continual problem, and while my new civil servants were adamant there was no evidence for that, I felt that the allegation alone was deeply unfair to students working hard for their grades.

So I announced that responsibility for monitoring, checking and intervening on exam standards would be handed to a new independent body – the Office of Qualifications and Examinations Regulation, which became known as Ofqual. Unlike the Bank of England and the Competition Commission, Ofqual was a regulator rather than a decision-maker, but its creation came from the same devolutionary instinct I'd had in those cases.

And it was that same instinct, as Shadow Chancellor in 2012, that led me to propose the introduction of a new independent Infrastructure Commission which would take the big recommendations on the major infrastructure projects out of the control of ministers and finally put an end to short-term politics always blocking long-term infrastructure investment.

The irony is that for someone who championed the devolution of power in monetary policy, exam standards, statistics, competition policy and infrastructure, I was also often characterised in debates about public service reform as a centraliser rather than as a devolver – and with some truth. Because just as there are limits to markets and in the delivery of public services, so there are limits to decentralisation and devolution.

In all the cases I championed, there were clear and simple decisions which would apply universally across the country – the level of interest rates being a case in point. That kind of devolution doesn't work so well where the needs, characteristics and challenges vary hugely from area to area, where the decision-making levers are not so simple, or where the outcomes are difficult and politically controversial.

That's why, for example, you could never devolve the setting of tax rates to an independent agency without forcing them to make hugely subjective decisions about where the tax burden should fall, and thereby dragging that agency into the political lobbying process.

Different but equally important considerations act as a check on aspects of devolution to local authorities. Of course, the case for devolving responsibility for children's services or transport is clear. The circumstances are different in different parts of the country, and locally elected politicians are much closer to the ground and better able to make the right decisions for their area.

But that can only work within a very clear framework of national accountability. The fact that a child protection issue could arise in one London borough wouldn't make parents in Hull or Blackpool any less alarmed and horrified about what had happened, and want to know what would be done to stop it happening again.

In our parliamentary democracy, local leadership and delivery in an area like children's services can only command public confidence if it's done in the framework of clear national standards for training and delivery, national inspection and with the ability of ministers to intervene when things go wrong.

As I remarked many times while I was working there, the Department for Children, Schools and Families could not run 150 separate child protection services in 150 areas in the country. But we could set the standards for them all. Being told that children's services are excellent in Bristol isn't much compensation if you live in an area where they're not, so it is the job of national government to ensure that there is a baseline of quality in every part of the country.

In other policy areas the positives and negatives are not as easy to weigh up.

Going on to work as employment minister from his previous post as schools minister, my good friend Jim Knight remarked to me how big a contrast education policy was from benefits policy. In the latter job, he could order a change in policy and it would take effect instantly in benefit offices, affecting millions of people up and down the country.

But with well over 20,000 schools, each with its own head teacher, its own governing body, its own history, values and principles, whatever you try to instruct from the centre will only actually happen if those individual autonomous schools really believe it's the right thing to do, and get on with enthusiasm to implement it – a reality which will only become worse if the current government revives its attempts at 'forced academisation' and effectively strips local authorities from any monitoring role.

That's why, as Secretary of State, I spent so much time going to speak and listen at head-teacher and teacher conferences, trying to win their hearts and minds and convince them that we had a shared vision and that my job was essentially to support the mission and values of their schools.

There can never be any one-size-fits-all approach to devolution and centralisation. What you need instead are a set of models that fit the different challenges the government faces across all its areas of responsibility, from managing inflation to protecting vulnerable children.

If anyone ever tells you they believe in handing over control and devolving power in all circumstances, or holding power at the centre no matter what, one thing is for sure: either they'll change their mind pretty quickly once they're in government, or they won't be there for long.

II

Decisions

─────────────

Our decision on the euro showed that good economics makes good politics – should that be the golden rule of politics?

'Are you still the Chancellor?' I asked Gordon as he burst into the ground-floor study in 11 Downing Street. 'I genuinely don't know,' he replied, slumping into one of the luxurious armchairs. 'I don't know whether Tony's sacked me, or whether I've resigned, or whether we just carry on.' Fifty yards down the corridor in the prime minister's office, I was sure Tony Blair was in exactly the same state of uncertainty.

It was April 2003, and the Treasury's assessment of the 'five economic tests' to decide whether Britain should join the single currency had just been completed. Two days before, we had gone over to present the results to Tony in his office, with the unequivocal recommendation that it was not in the national interest for Britain to give up the pound and join the euro. It had not gone well.

But this was a decision we had to control, and a battle we had to win, and if Gordon had needed to resign to make that happen, I'm sure he would have done and so would I.

In politics, as in life, you think of your biggest achievements as being the things you create: Harold Wilson establishing the Open University; Nye Bevan launching the National Health Service; Gordon Brown making the Bank of England independent; Tony Blair introducing the national minimum wage.

However, sometimes in politics a decision not to do something can be just as significant – and there is no doubt that, for Britain, the decision not to join the single currency has been the most successful economic decision of the last thirty years.

As a young journalist at the *Financial Times* witnessing the ignominy of Black Wednesday and Britain's exit from the Exchange Rate Mechanism in September 1992, I was already convinced that any attempt by Britain to join the single currency would end equally badly. As far as I was concerned, the euro was economically and politically misconceived. Rather than trying to join up, the next Labour government should instead be putting in place our own domestic economic policy underpinned by an independent Bank of England.

For me, it was essential that the judgement on the euro had to be made on economic grounds; short-term political concerns should not be allowed to interfere. The great irony is that the politician at the time who was most associated with that viewpoint wasn't Gordon Brown, it was the then Chancellor of the Exchequer, Ken Clarke. Ken famously used to say that he had learned over the years that good economics is good politics and taking tough, difficult or controversial decisions on the economy always ends up being better for your political fortunes than ducking those decisions and letting your economic problems mount up.

I think he was, and is, absolutely right. Which made it so odd that on the one issue which, to me, proves that rule better than any other, Ken Clarke had a blind spot. He saw the euro not as an economic issue but as a political issue; a test of his pro-Europeanism.

When I confronted the euro issue, I was also very conscious of another rule: learn the lessons of history but don't assume that history will always repeat itself. If you do the latter, there's always the terrible danger that you're constantly fighting the last war.

At the Kennedy School back in 1988, I took a course taught by Professor Richard Neustadt entitled 'Uses of History for Policy Analysis'. It explained how the lessons of history can inform and assist objective policymaking, but also demonstrated how the personal history of each individual shapes their viewpoint and adds some unconscious subjectivity in how they respond to policy challenges.

I learned from that course that when you meet a

politician, a leader or a counterpart in any walk of life, it's always an easy but terrible mistake to project into their head what's in your own; in fact, to truly understand them, you have to start from their view of the world and the events which have shaped their thinking over the years.

With Ken Clarke – born at the start of the Second World War, growing up in a time when rations were still in place – I suspect that the importance of the European Union to maintain peace and prosperity has always been paramount, and any sense of Britain drawing away from the EU has been anathema to him.

So I could understand his motivations, but it also helped me appreciate that even his great political brain could be getting the decision on the euro fundamentally wrong. So after we had made the Bank of England independent, I did my most intense historical research since my days as a student, going over all the major economic failures in the United Kingdom during the twentieth century, and looking at why they each occurred.

I looked at the return to the gold standard in 1925, a catastrophe which led to a deep recession, industrial unrest and crippling poverty; the delays to devaluation at the end of the Second World War; Harold Wilson's decision not to devalue in 1964, only to have his hand forced in 1967; and then the decision by the Thatcher government in 1990 to join the Exchange Rate Mechanism with a punishingly strong link to the Deutschmark.

In every one of those past cases, there was a clear mainstream political consensus each time that it was right thing to do. And on every occasion, the economic voices who said

'This won't work, it will be dangerous, the risks are too high' were ignored. Keynes was ignored in 1925, Wilson's new economic advisers were ignored in 1964, and many voices on the ERM were ignored by John Major and Margaret Thatcher in the autumn of 1990.

And it was easy for them to ignore the economists because the political consensus was so wide. Take that ERM decision, which was supported by Neil Kinnock and John Smith, by the CBI, by the TUC, and by many newspapers at the time. They overestimated the importance of political momentum and underestimated the power of economic events and economic realities.

And my view was that we had to make sure that we didn't make the same mistake again: that we didn't let the politics railroad us into a binding economic relationship with our European partners which just couldn't be sustained.

As the 1997 general election approached, the euro debate was causing huge splits – not for Labour but in the Tory Party, with Ken Clarke refusing to bow to pressure from the Foreign Secretary Malcolm Rifkind and others to rule out joining the single currency in the first wave in the next Parliament.

Tony Blair, far from his later image as a committed Europhile agitating to join the single currency, was in fact worried that Labour keeping open the option was going to damage us politically. By contrast, it was Gordon who was concerned about the political signal it would send to our European partners and to the wider world if Tony succumbed to pressure and said we weren't going to join, just on the basis of the politics of the election.

Tony's rationale was very simple: British voters would hate the idea of giving up the pound. Gordon, having never confronted an argument he thought he couldn't win, believed that was facile. He was no dogmatist about the need to join the single currency but I think he considered it as semi-inevitable and perhaps even desirable from an economic point of view, and was dead set against having it ruled out before we were even in government.

Over the previous year, Gordon and I had travelled to Bonn and Paris to meet with the German and French finance ministers and central bank governors. We had reassured them that our decision on the euro would be made on the basis of long-term economics not short-term political considerations. And on those trips, as we discussed the differences between the UK and European economies in terms of convergence, flexibility and patterns of trade and investment, the famous 'five economic tests' for euro entry were born.

In the run-up to the election, Gordon was under increasing pressure from Tony to say something cautionary about Britain joining the euro. The crunch came on a trip to New York in February 1997. Gordon was due to speak to the American European Community Association and we'd brought the BBC's John Sergeant to New York with the idea of doing an interview, against the backdrop of the speech.

The plan was for Gordon to say that while in principle we saw the benefits, there were 'formidable obstacles' to joining the single currency. That was exactly the phrase which Tony wanted him to use, and John Sergeant knew it was a head-line waiting to happen. The problem was, as so often happened with Gordon when he wasn't mentally committed to the strategy behind the rhetoric, he just couldn't bring himself to use those words. So after forty minutes of sitting in a New York hotel room with John asking him again and again his views on the euro, and Gordon repeatedly saying anything other than the key words, John eventually threw his hands up in the air, turned off the tape, and said: 'That's it, I've had enough, I can't take this anymore.'

Sitting through Gordon's speech afterwards on the Upper East Side, I knew we needed to do something to take control of the situation, and avoid Tony's cautionary instincts leading to a premature, panicky and purely political decision. In the yellow cab afterwards, heading across Manhattan, Gordon and I talked through the options, then – with his blessing – I rang Robert Peston, the *Financial Times*'s polit-ical editor, who immediately knew this was a big story. It's been said many times that the five tests were invented in the back of a New York taxi. That wasn't correct, but it was in the back of that taxi, via the front page of the FT, that the world came to hear about them.

People look back and say the five tests were our way of trying to stop Britain joining the euro. In fact, in that frantic pre-election period, they were designed to prevent us ruling out joining the euro on political grounds and instead to say this was a decision to be made on the basis of the national economic interest, and one that would be controlled by the Treasury.

But for me, while I certainly saw the five tests as a way of locating the decision on economics rather than politics, I also knew they would help me in my task to persuade Gordon Brown that joining the single currency was a bad idea, and should not become the litmus test of whether he was sufficiently modernising, progressive and pro-European. The great irony, in retrospect, was that back in 1997 my strongest ally in that effort was Tony Blair.

After the election victory, we immediately began work on the analytical work which would inform the assessment of the five tests, ably assisted by Nigel Wicks, the Treasury's senior civil servant in charge of international finance.

We didn't get off to a great start. In my very first meeting with the team responsible, its manager Melanie Dawes patiently explained that they'd looked into it and concluded that there weren't really five tests. She said the final one ('Will joining EMU promote higher growth, stability and a lasting increase in jobs?') was too broad and difficult to measure, and it would be better to drop it and announce that we had just the four tests instead – convergence, flexibility and the impact on investment and on financial services.

Rather politely, I said we had to have five. That was what I'd told Robert Peston, that was what was in the election manifesto, so that's what we had to deliver. Savvy soul that she is, Melanie nodded and said with a smile that she understood.

Throughout those months there was continual speculation across Europe about whether the euro project would actually go ahead. If the German government had succumbed to pressure from the deeply sceptical Bundesbank, our problem would have been solved. In July we were called over to Number Ten for a meeting, apparently to discuss whether or not we should rule out joining in the first wave of the single currency, assuming it went ahead. But Tony Blair had other ideas. He told the meeting he didn't think the single currency was a great idea full stop and wasn't convinced it was really going to go ahead. He proposed ringing German Chancellor Helmut Kohl to persuade him the whole thing should be postponed. I said I thought that was an excellent idea. Nigel Wicks just went white.

We were in a bizarre situation for several months of that year where those of us speaking to Tony Blair knew how sceptical he was about the single currency, but the media – perhaps unduly swayed by conversations with Peter Mandelson, who was much more persuaded of the case for joining – were convinced there was a growing fissure between Gordon and Tony on the issue.

We were all worried that this speculation was damaging the government – we had all seen how the Margaret Thatcher 'wait and see' approach to the ERM had fractured her relationship with her Chancellor, Nigel Lawson. So in an interview with Phil Webster of *The Times* in October 1997, Gordon definitively ruled out Britain joining in the first wave later that year and also made clear that it was highly unlikely that we would join in the whole of that first Parliament.

The idea of the interview had been agreed with Tony. Indeed, Alastair Campbell was aware of what Phil was going to write and had spoken to him early that morning, even before Gordon or I had talked to him. But for some reason, the first Tony knew about the detail of *The Times* interview was via complaints from Peter and others after the story broke that night. And when Tony asked the Number Ten switchboard to contact Gordon or one of his staff to find out exactly what had been said, the only person they could track down was Charlie Whelan in the Red Lion pub, not exactly the most diplomatic when it came to handling the PM.

The interview in *The Times* not only destabilised some of our political colleagues but also parts of the business community. We tried to correct the balance somewhat when it came to the formal statement on our policy to Parliament a week later, showing more commitment to the principle of joining the euro by announcing a National Changeover Plan, a Standing Committee on euro preparations, and so on, while presenting the policy as one of 'prepare and decide'.

The official line was that 'barring unforeseen circumstances', we weren't going to join in the first Parliament, a sop to Peter Mandelson and some key figures in the business community so they could claim it hadn't been definitively ruled out. The *Sun* editorial complained the next day that Tony Blair should rein in his Europhile Chancellor – they certainly thought Tony was cooler on the issue – while other papers were briefed that the option to join in that Parliament was still alive. We didn't mind that too much in the circumstances, but at the same time, I was worried that the certainty we had been seeking had been diluted somewhat.

I had lunch a few months afterwards with the *Guardian*'s economics editor, Larry Elliott, at El Vino's on New Bridge Street. He asked me teasingly whether I could foresee any of these unforeseen circumstances occurring, and I said flatly

'No', which was, of course, literally true. In the febrile atmosphere of those days, that was enough for Larry to splash the *Guardian* a couple of days later, saying the Treasury was clear that Britain would not join the single currency this Parliament.

The timing couldn't have been worse. It came on the same day Gordon and Tony had scheduled breakfast with Ken Clarke and Michael Heseltine to reassure them that the government had not permanently taken against the euro. Once I'd accepted responsibility for Larry's story, Gordon gruffly replied: 'Well, I had a lot of explaining to do this morning.'

Things didn't really change publicly on the euro until after the 2001 election when the phoney war between Number Ten and the Treasury began in earnest. By then Tony's attitude to the euro had changed radically from four years before – he was much more wedded to the 'European project' and appeared to be coming to believe that the UK joining the euro was necessary, especially once the new currency became a reality after the millennium. That was certainly the Foreign Office view too.

Whereas Gordon's experiences in Brussels watching eurozone finance ministers' dysfunctional attempts to make the Stability and Growth Pact work had definitely hardened his scepticism, Tony's experiences as leader made him more convinced he needed to bolster his Europhile credentials. At that level, there is more of a sense that you are collectively responsible for driving the European project, and your commitment to it cannot be in doubt. So while I never saw any evidence that Tony Blair was really a big enthusiast for joining the single currency, he absolutely did not want to be seen by his European partners, or anyone else, as being someone who had ruled out joining or who wasn't an enthusiast.

The first clear sign of Tony's shift in thinking came the day after the 2001 election, with an extensive and very well-briefed story by Andy Grice in the *Independent*, saying that Tony had resolved that his second term would be defined by his campaign to take Britain into the single currency. Yes, it would happen on the basis of the assessment of the economic tests, but this was a campaign to secure Britain's pro-European destiny, and he would launch it in his speech to the TUC in September.

No one knew then that Tony's TUC speech would instead be remembered for his reaction to al-Qaeda's attack on the World Trade Center, with the issue of the single currency and the euro totally overshadowed by the consequences of 9/11.

I was with Gordon in his study that early afternoon in September, when we heard the commotion in the outer office from Gordon's staff reacting to the TV news of the first plane hitting the towers. We'd barely turned back to the study when we heard their shocked reaction to the second. Like everyone else, Gordon and I started thinking about friends and colleagues in New York and worrying whether they were safe, and then – as we were told the Treasury was in lockdown – wondering if London was going to be next. It was a very tense atmosphere in Whitehall that afternoon, as the

Civil Service briefed us in detail, for the first time, about emergency procedures in the event of an attack.

As we sat together that afternoon, Gordon said to me: 'This will change everything. Things will never be the same again. Everything will be about security and foreign policy.' He didn't know how America would react, but he knew that it was an absolutely life-changing event. For us in the Treasury, though, the subsequent action in Afghanistan and then Iraq consumed little of our time, other than finding the extra money to pay for it. It may seem strange in retrospect that Iraq was not a bigger deal given how that conflict now defines the Blair years, but that was the reality. The NHS and the euro were our main focus.

And for Tony, as he found himself at loggerheads with other EU leaders over the military response to 9/11, his public support for the euro was his way of continuing to assert his status as a 'good European', while blaming Gordon for standing in the way – just like his incautious approach to the budgetary implications of EU enlargement a few years later. That was certainly the message conveyed by Blairite outriders like Stephen Byers and Alan Milburn, apparently authorised by Tony to make regular interventions calling for Britain to join the euro.

Behind the scenes, though, an alternative truth would occasionally emerge. I remember waiting in Tony's office with Gordon and Jeremy Heywood for a Budget discussion. Tony came in from the Cabinet Room, where he'd been having a meeting with the former prime minister and financial treasurer of Australia, Paul Keating, who was something of a hero for both Tony Blair and Gordon Brown.

Tony told us how Keating had praised Bank of England

independence and said we'd done the right thing on the minimum wage, and various other policy issues. But at the end of the meeting he had said: 'Oh, but Tony, one thing, just to be clear – whatever you do, don't join that fucking euro.' It was the huge smile on Tony's face as he told the story that was revealing to me.

There has been a lot of talk – then and since – about secret deals between Tony Blair and Gordon Brown, where Tony would give up the leadership before the 2005 election if Gordon gave him the answer he wanted on the euro.

But I always took this talk of deals with a pinch of salt, even when I received those signals myself from people close to Tony: there was no way we were ever going to pass the five tests; Gordon would have treated it as putting the poison in his own chalice; and I don't think Tony – when he looked at the hard polling numbers – would have really thought it would be possible to win a referendum. In reality, I think the wider political world believed Tony wanted to join the euro, thought he needed to do that before he left, and assumed Gordon would take over. So they put two and two together and got to five or six.

It's certainly the case, though, that John Prescott, who saw his role as holding Gordon and Tony together, worked tirelessly on the euro issue, thinking that finding a compromise with which both men would be happy was the key to making the transition work. One memorable Sunday morning in 2002, John asked me to drive over to Hull to meet him, and launched into a lengthy discussion about the eurozone's Stability and Growth Pact. He was convinced that if I could design a reform plan for the pact, and sell it to Gordon and to Tony, then they could make it the precondition for joining the euro.

I nodded and talked John through the issues with the pact, but also made clear that – while it was a big deal – it wasn't the biggest problem we faced when it came to passing the five tests. After an hour and a half, I thanked John and was driving out of Hull when I saw behind me a Jaguar madly flashing its lights, so I pulled over onto the side of the road.

The Jaguar pulled up behind me and John emerged, in a rather breathless state. After our conversation, he'd turned on the radio, heard a discussion on *The World This Weekend* about the pact and had immediately tried to catch me up to tell me what had been discussed and ask whether it changed my view. So we stood by the side of the road and talked for another twenty minutes before heading our separate ways. It said everything about John that he tried to become an expert on one of the most dysfunctional parts of eurozone bureaucracy simply to try and deliver for Tony and Gordon.

Looking back, it seems pretty extraordinary that we were even having that debate, now that the consensus has become so fully established across all parties that it would have been a mistake to join the euro.

The fact that this new consensus is so entrenched means

that the euro debate has become a less important part of the history of the last Labour government, and the decision not to join is rarely listed among our achievements. Indeed, by the time George Osborne made a big deal in 2010 of abolishing the Treasury's Euro Preparations Unit, the unit by that stage was staffed by one man and a dog, and even the dog was working on other things.

But back in 2002–3, it was a very big deal. A political momentum was being built. There was much urging of the case from business, the media and parts of the trade union movement, as well as on both sides of politics. Tony's team in Downing Street certainly believed he was determined to join. And at times, as we were completing the assessment of the five tests, we did feel rather isolated and under pressure. With clear echoes in the recent European debate thirteen years later, there was a concerted effort to present those who wanted to join the euro as modern, worldly and business-like, and sceptics as backward-looking, Little Englanders and out of touch.

But in the Treasury, we just carried on with what we had dubbed the 'technical and preliminary work' – eighteen background studies on every conceivable economic issue, all designed to keep the focus squarely on the economics rather than the politics.

In April 2003, when the debate came to a head and we presented the Treasury's economic assessment, Tony and his team were furious that, rather than even debate the conclusions, we had just got a Treasury messenger to walk over the 300-page assessment document, and present it to them. In retrospect, it was one of the more heavy-handed and un-collegiate things that I was ever involved in, but it was a difficult time, and we weren't in the mood to compromise.

Their anger was expressed to Gordon, to me and to the rest of the Treasury in pretty forceful terms, first in a meeting with the senior Downing Street team and then, two days later, at that crunch meeting in Tony Blair's office. The meeting quickly descended into angry recriminations again and Jeremy, Jonathan Powell and I were ordered out.

Tony and Gordon continued arguing behind closed doors, and as often happened between them, they broke up not quite clear what had been agreed. Either Gordon had said he was considering his position, or Tony had asked him to. That afternoon, we sat for half an hour in the Number Eleven study not knowing what was going to happen next.

Then Tony blinked. A call came through from Number Ten saying the PM would like me and Jeremy to sit down, go through the text, and find some ways in which the language could be improved. Not only was Gordon still the Chancellor, but the issue was settled – the debate on the euro was comprehensively won.

If it hadn't been for 9/11, who knows what would have happened on the euro. Tony Blair was a missionary politician – and the events of September 2001 certainly defined the second half of his premiership, first over Iraq and then more widely in trying to tackle Islamic extremism. It is quite possible that, absent that mission, joining the euro and cementing Britain at the heart of Europe might have provided Tony Blair's defining purpose. Gordon certainly feared it might.

But even without the huge shift of focus by the prime

minister to foreign affairs, I've never been totally persuaded that Tony Blair really wanted to fight the euro campaign even if the economic case was 'clear and unambiguous', which it was never going to be.

We stuck to our guns because we'd learned the lessons of history, we knew decisions not to do things are just as important as the things you decide to do, and we agreed with Ken Clarke that good economics would be good politics. It's just a pity that Ken didn't agree with himself.

12

Identity

Britain is set to leave the EU after forty years of membership —
so why did we lose the referendum?

An hour after the EU referendum poll closed on 23 June 2016, Yvette set off to do an early morning ITV interview on Westminster's College Green. It was still too early for any results to be declared, but the financial markets had been calm all day anticipating a Yes vote, the Remain camp was upbeat and Nigel Farage had just conceded defeat. So I decided to get a couple of hours' sleep.

I was awoken by the clunk of the front door as Yvette returned, and I grabbed for my iPhone to look at my Twitter feed, always the fastest way to get the latest news. Shocked post after shocked post reacted to the results from the North-East of England. I went downstairs and we sat together in silence, watching the TV coverage late into the night as the probability of a Leave win went from likely to certain. Faced with a choice of staying in to fight for reform, and leaving to chart a different course, a majority of people had voted to end our forty-year marriage with the European Union and sue for divorce.

The referendum was always going to be desperately close. Two weeks before the vote, seeing the huge support for Leave in her Yorkshire constituency, Yvette was convinced Remain would lose. But in the final days of the campaign, after the tragic murder of Jo Cox and the unveiling of Nigel Farage's appalling refugee poster, I had thought, as in the Scottish referendum, that the vote for the status quo would harden up and Remain would just do it. I was wrong. But while I certainly felt shocked to see such a revolution happening, I wasn't altogether surprised.

I had sensed this parting of the ways coming sixteen years previously in an encounter at a European summit – not with some obscure Brussels minion but with the man who would go on to become the President of the European Commission by the time Britain finally voted to leave.

I first met Jean-Claude Juncker – the man the UK tabloids dubbed 'the most dangerous man in Europe' – back when he was the humble finance minister of Luxembourg, although, given their constitution, it also made him that country's less than humble prime minister. We were in a small meeting room in Portugal in the summer of 2000, as the battle over Germany's proposal to introduce an EU-wide savings tax was reaching its climax. In attendance were Gordon, Jean-Claude, the German finance minister Hans Eichel, as well as myself and a few other key aides.

For at least the previous five years, an argument had raged among Europe's finance ministers over the German proposal, designed to stop German taxpayers depositing their savings in Luxembourg bank accounts to avoid paying tax in Germany.

Jean-Claude had decided he was happy to go along with the plan as long as the tax rate wasn't so high as to deter German savers from coming, but high enough that Hans Eichel could claim to have won Germany's long battle to do 'something' on this issue, and recover a little bit of the money it was losing.

So Germany had a problem. It wanted an EU-wide solution. The 'solution' it came up with was not actually going to solve the problem. But it would allow Germany to claim 'victory', and for them that's ultimately what mattered. If that doesn't sum up how dysfunctional European decision-making could sometimes be, I don't know what does.

But when we arrived at the Treasury in 1997, the UK financial services community made it clear they were deeply opposed to an EU-wide withholding tax imposed by Brussels with all the damage that would do to London's savings business. You could almost see the glint in Gordon's eye as we took up the cudgels. He knew that it was a proposal that required unanimous agreement among the then fifteen Member States, and quickly made it clear to his rather startled EU officials that he was happy to take on the other fourteen for as long as it took.

However, we weren't just planning to block the proposal. What we developed instead was an alternative plan for a free flow of information among Member States. Luxembourg could tell Germany about German citizens saving in Luxembourg, and then the German tax authorities could decide what taxes they wanted to levy on those individuals. Every country could make their own decisions on what to do with the information they received, without the need for a Europe-wide tax.

This plan was very popular in the City, but caused some tensions with other Member States; and of course it alarmed tax havens like the Cayman Islands, Guernsey and Jersey – and also Switzerland – because if the exchange of information worked in the EU, it would raise the pressure to apply it on a global basis.

In his usual dogged fashion, Gordon made the argument that our plan was the best way to preserve the national sovereignty of individual tax authorities to levy the tax they chose on their own citizens, and he made it again and again, time after time, for two solid years. He wore his counterparts down not just by his force of will, but by the force of argument.

By the time we got to the summit in June 2000, we had pretty much everyone on our side, with the exception of Luxembourg. For Luxembourg, the tax advantage it offered savers was not only one of its only industries, but one of its only attractions, so its tourist trade relied on it too. Once a German saver knew they would pay the same tax whether they saved in Germany or in Luxembourg, they might as well stay at home and save themselves the petrol.

So in that small anteroom, with all the other European finance ministers waiting outside in the large open-plan meeting room, Brown and Eichel tried to put the screws on Juncker. 'Jean-Claude,' the German said, 'there is a consensus around the table that we should move forward not on our savings tax proposal, but on Gordon's exchange of information.'

Juncker said: 'But, Hans, this would be a terrible outcome for Luxembourg, it would be hugely damaging to our economy. It's not something that I can accept.' For perhaps the 150th time, Gordon then made his usual argument that his was a better system for Europe, but Juncker was unmoved. Then Eichel looked him in the eye and said: 'Jean-Claude, there is a consensus here, but we need your support for it to be agreed. You must do it for Europe.'

Juncker paused for a moment, held Eichel's gaze and said: 'Hans, you're right, this is very difficult for our country, but we will do this for the good of Europe.' He then walked out the door, marched straight to the waiting international press, and issued a statement that Luxembourg would support the exchange of information proposal. It was a great victory for Gordon's tenacious negotiating style. It was a victory for Germany who solved its tax problem. And it was a big defeat for Luxembourg, only delivered because its prime minister had put Europe's interests before his own country's.

As I sat in the room watching that extraordinary episode unfold, I thought: 'No British prime minister or finance minister could ever do that. And if they did, they wouldn't be in the job a week later. They wouldn't even bother getting the plane home.'

Back then, and subsequently, the starting assumption of the UK media – and an increasing body of the public – was that anything proposed in Europe had to automatically be against our national interest, and therefore the only way to protect Britain was to disagree and stand isolated.

So at every European Union summit a British prime minister has attended since we joined the EU in the early 1970s, the question has always been whether, in reaching an agreement with our European partners, British interests will be compromised. As we found with the savings tax, the only agreement trusted by the UK press was one that we'd proposed ourselves and had to fight to push through.

This has been the reality of the past forty years: a continual struggle to show the British public that joining the European Union did not mean putting the interests of the British people second. And in some ways, that was a good thing: it meant if we wanted change in Europe, we normally had to lead from the front, whether it was Gordon and the savings tax, or Margaret Thatcher and the reform of the single market.

People forget it was also Margaret Thatcher who proposed moving to Qualified Majority Voting so that no one country could veto important single market reforms. But she was constantly able to drive change and reach agreements in Europe because she was seen to embody the British national interest, not least in the epic struggle over the EU Budget and the UK rebate.

From the outset in 1997, Tony Blair and Gordon Brown tried to emulate that model, showing we were willing to fight to protect Britain's national interests, but also that we were going to actively lead the march towards greater co-operation and reform to make Europe more open, fair, dynamic and competitive. Though, like Margaret Thatcher before them, they were not averse to playing the nationalist and isolationist card when it suited them.

In his first few months in the Treasury, having announced to the UK press that his top priority was to implement Labour's manifesto commitment to cut VAT on domestic gas and electricity from 8 per cent to 5 per cent, Gordon would regularly head out to European summits and tell the media he would fight tooth and nail against any attempt by Brussels to stop him. Each time we'd arrive, there would be an air of bemusement, not just amongst our European finance minister partners, but also the Brussels press and our UK Rep officials, about the headlines they'd seen in the British papers. Counterparts would come to us to ask: 'Who is trying to stop you cutting the VAT? You can do what you like!'

But Gordon saw it – perhaps wrongly in retrospect – as a fairly harmless way of demonstrating his credibility to the British people in terms of fighting for their interests in Brussels, if not his credibility on the finer points of EC VAT law. We did much the same a few years later by turning a routine review of the functioning of VAT reduced rates across Europe into an all-out assault on our right to keep Britain's zero rates on food and children's clothes.

In the late summer of 2000, we faced another crisis. It was the height of the fuel protests in Britain and across Europe, when the combination of previous tax hikes with a sudden unexpected surge in oil prices had put pump prices up to record levels. That triggered mass public and media campaigns for tax cuts, combined with British truckers blockading our oil refineries in Britain and French farmers shutting down the Channel ports.

The social and economic consequences started to look very serious, with the roads gridlocked, fuel supplies running low, people unable to get to work, food stocks dwindling in the supermarkets, and the NHS ambulance fleet facing paralysis. Every finance minister in Europe was in the same dilemma as we met that September, and each one repeated the same mantra: 'We have to maintain fiscal discipline, we cannot give in to short-term political pressures, and we cannot cut our fuel taxes in the face of these demonstrations.'

The chair of the finance ministers' meeting said: 'Colleagues, it is clear that there is a unanimous view on this point, so we must issue a joint declaration from this meeting that Europe has decided that its finance ministers will not cut fuel taxes.' Gordon immediately interjected: 'Hold on, hold on, if you issue that statement, then I will have to cut fuel duties. Europe cannot tell the British Chancellor what to do.' But other finance ministers round the table said: 'But it's the opposite for me, I need to go back to my capital today and say I wanted to cut fuel duties but Europe has decided against it, therefore I can't.' Still, the idea of the joint press release was dropped. And a few weeks later we introduced a duty cut.

However, there were also times when that kind of straw man was much more dubious and harmful. At the height of preparation for the Iraq War in 2003, with the 'coalition of the willing' assembled and ready to invade, there was huge pressure to agree a second resolution at the United Nations to give unquestionable legal authority and international legitimacy to the action.

But when it became clear that too many countries were opposed to a second resolution, it put huge pressure on Tony

Blair, especially with a vote in Parliament coming up. Even though we rarely had anything to do with Number Ten's political planning on Iraq, somehow Gordon and I found ourselves in Downing Street talking strategy with Jonathan Powell and Alastair Campbell.

I don't remember whose idea it was first, but the others were moving quickly to the idea that someone had to be blamed for blocking the second resolution. The obvious scapegoat was the French president, Jacques Chirac, even though France was only one of the many countries who didn't believe the case had been made. Rather than the 'We don't have the backing of the UN' narrative, Tony Blair could instead say: 'We will not have our decisions on national security dictated by France.' I never got involved in foreign affairs outside of the economy, but I did respond a bit incredulously. 'Are we really sure we want to end decades of foreign policy cooperation with France just to get us a better headline?' The others looked at me with disbelief and said: 'Of course we do; that's the whole point!'

As well as my doubts about demonising the French, I felt deeply uncomfortable about the Number Ten strategy of cosying up to the Bush White House, to the extent that none of us were able to raise concerns with them about the American strategy of Iraq, or the extent to which we seemed hitched to it. That continued even into the period after Saddam had fallen.

I was with Gordon when he met his US counterpart John Snow in autumn 2003, over dinner in Washington. Gordon raised concern after concern about de-Ba'athification, the lack of efforts to institute local democracy and decision-making, the feeling of many ordinary Iraqis that they had no stake in the country's reconstruction, and the rising tide of sectarian violence.

Every issue he raised was dismissed by Snow with a broad smile. 'Gordon,' he said, 'as soon as we get the oil flowing, everything will be fine. That's the priority.' Even then, thirteen years before Chilcot, that seemed an extremely complacent approach to post-war planning, and Gordon was deeply frustrated and worried in our car afterwards.

It's part of the British character to want to stand apart, except – as with the Empire – when it's on our own terms and in our own interest. That is an attitude that stretches back many centuries, well before the decisions not to join the Iron and Steel Community by Labour and Conservative governments alike straight after the Second World War.

And while we have many times in our history chosen to cooperate with other countries for collective goals, in times of war and in times of peace, on issues of foreign policy and also of economics, we have always been insistent on doing so as an independent sovereign nation, and often one punching above its weight, in terms of our size and population.

Our membership of the European Union, and agreeing to the disciplines and strictures and the collective responsibility which came as part of that membership, while hugely important in terms of jobs, investment and trade, was a challenge to that vital trait in the national character, and a resulting dilemma for British politicians.

When I think back to the opinion polling that we did as

we were considering whether to join the single currency in the early 2000s, there was always a minority of voters – generally older, generally living away from the big cities in rural areas and industrial towns – who didn't care about the five tests or the national economic interest; for them, keeping the pound was an issue of identity; if we lost the pound we lost who we were.

And I genuinely think that, in the last decade or so, that minority view has grown considerably, it has become younger, it has seeped into parts of the big cities too, and most importantly, its views have become even more entrenched.

Not joining the euro was a hugely significant decision, because it changed the nature of Britain's relationship with our European partners. For the first time we were clearly not joining a central drive for European integration. It meant that when it came to decisions in the Eurogroup about economic matters, even during the financial crisis, we were not in the room, even though we were driving the response almost everywhere else in the world.

On a very simple level, anything which reinforces the 'them and us' feeling percolates into the public mood. Gordon saw that coming as far back as 1998, when he fought for Britain to be represented in the Eurogroup and, rarely for him, lost a Brussels battle.

That 'outsider' mindset has been reinforced by the subsequent failure of the euro as an economic project. And I stress 'economic failure', because – in many ways – the degree of commitment we have seen from the populations of Greece, Spain, Portugal and Ireland to stick with the politics of the project, despite the huge pain it has caused them, has been staggering to see, and in marked contrast with how the British public would have reacted in similar circumstances.

But the failure in economic terms has been clear: stagnating growth, higher unemployment, and the total inadequacy of Europe's institutions in fiscal policy or in banking policy to take the kind of decisive actions that have been needed both to deal with the aftermath of the 2008 financial crisis and to prevent the next.

When I was Shadow Chancellor, I regularly said that Britain would not join the euro in my political lifetime – and since May 2015, I've had to drop the word 'political'. There was and is no likely prospect of the euro becoming a cohesive economic project without a deepening of political integration and that is something the British people would never accept. But the failure of the euro to flourish and support prosperity in the way that was promised – and in the way people warned we would miss out on – undoubtedly tarnished the British people's view of the European Union.

But the other massive issue that has soured our relationship with Europe is immigration. When Tony Blair and Gordon Brown became leader of the Labour Party and Shadow Chancellor in the mid-1990s they often talked about the need to solve global problems as one of the driving reasons for Labour to modernise. Their pitch, even to Labour traditionalists, was that in an era of globalisation we couldn't achieve social justice either in Britain or around the world unless we embraced international cooperation.

But back then, they saw it in terms of the globalisation of capital and trade – of finance and goods moving freely around the world – which offered opportunities we needed to harness and risks we needed to manage. On both counts, we had to be global leaders and demonstrate the benefits of openness and free trade.

The one aspect of globalisation which Tony and Gordon didn't foresee was the extent to which it would result in the movement of people across borders looking for work. When the original Treaty of Rome was signed in 1957 founding what became the EU, 'free movement' applied to only a handful of countries, and the expectation was that only the elites and students would actually move. But today's EU is a much bigger and more complex beast.

After the diplomatic shock of Britain not joining the euro, the Foreign Office and Number Ten definitely saw Britain turning down the opportunity to have transitional controls on the movement of workers from the new EU entrants – Poland, the Czech Republic and the rest – as a way to signal our continued commitment to the European project. It was a terrible mistake.

The fact is that the Home Office, the Treasury and the Foreign Office never expected migration within the European Union on the scale that subsequently occurred in the second half of the last decade. It was a failure of forecasting, of fore-sight, of politics and understanding. And as the opinion polls have shown very clearly in the last ten years, the reality of migration and people's concerns about it have given rocket boosters to scepticism and hostility towards the EU.

In my former constituency of Morley & Outwood, I was very conscious of the political challenge of that miscalculation before I was elected. I started writing letters and holding public meetings on migration from 2008 onwards, as did Jon

Cruddas, my Labour colleague. Faced with the largest BNP membership in the country, I felt I had no choice. Having walked through a local election count and seen groups of tall, bulky men in suits and dark glasses, standing menacingly over the tables as the BNP votes were counted, I knew this was not an issue I or the country could afford to ignore.

But what became really clear to me in the many meetings I had on immigration was that people's concerns are much more thoughtful and nuanced than the popular debate often allows. With fifty to a hundred people in the room, there would always be two or three people who, Nigel Farage style, wanted to shut the borders, isolate our economy and go it alone. And there would be an equally small number who took a very liberal view – who thought that migration was unequivocally good for our economy, that it was a part of our identity: we were a nation of immigrants and we should be proud of it.

But the vast majority of people were in what I'd call the pragmatic centre: they certainly knew we needed skilled workers to come in; and they were content to see young Polish workers working hard behind the Costa Coffee counter in a motorway service station, or behind the bar in their local pub. They also knew that British people had gone to work in other parts of the European Union for decades. The culture of *Auf Wiedersehen, Pet* was still embedded in the memory of many of the people at my public meetings.

But they also felt that things had been happening too fast, that there was a lack of control on the numbers coming in, and that it was having a damaging impact on the wages and working conditions of British people. They were at best cynical and at worst very angry about politicians who claimed there was not an issue, or falsely claimed they could fix it overnight, as David Cameron did when he came into office and promised to reduce net migration to the tens of thousands.

Those constituents weren't remotely racist, and they didn't subscribe to the beliefs of the newspapers that were whipping up a frenzy on immigration. But they were concerned that politicians weren't getting a grip, and that the rules of the game weren't fair. They wanted something done. And an ever-expanding European 'free movement' free-for-all certainly wasn't it.

When I wrote an article for the *Observer* during the 2010 Labour leadership election, setting out my pro-European credentials but arguing that we had to accept that 'free movement' of labour could not work in an enlarged Europe of twenty-eight or more countries and that we needed more controls, I was setting out arguments I knew were needed to persuade my constituents to stick with Europe. I saw the writing on the wall.

This is the context in which the 2016 referendum was held. In 2011, David Cameron, George Osborne, Ed Miliband and I walked through the same voting lobby in the House of Commons, casting our votes against an EU referendum on the rapid timetable put forward by a Tory backbencher. But it became increasingly clear that David Cameron's position was unsustainable. Having posed as a Eurosceptic to win the Tory leadership and originally attacked the Labour government's decision not to hold a referendum on the Lisbon

Treaty, he came under intense pressure to agree one himself to calm the mutinous feeling on his own backbenches and to ward off the threat from UKIP.

Boxed in by his own backbenchers, David Cameron decided he had to concede. And while I was wrongly portrayed by some as believing that Labour should follow suit and commit to a referendum on the same terms as David Cameron, it's certainly true that I was also deeply worried that Ed Miliband was going to set our face against a referendum in principle. For many voters, the denial of a referendum on EU member- ship was a denial of the legitimacy of their views and concerns, and we risked feeding the same impression that people had of us before 2010, that we were elitist, out of touch, and in denial about immigration.

But it was clear from the outset that David Cameron's strategy was incredibly reckless and dangerous. I did not think it was remotely sensible to promise to renegotiate the terms of Britain's membership and hold a referendum by 2017, an arbitrary timetable set before he could know what appetite there was for reform across Europe. And then, to make matters worse, he announced that he would only decide whether to recommend a 'Remain' vote once he saw what reforms he could deliver. This caused two prob- lems. When the vote finally came, it became a referendum on him and his judgement. And in the meantime it prevented him and anyone else in his government from making the positive case to an increasingly sceptical public. He left the field clear for the Eurosceptics and they made hay.

Personally, it was easy to know that I would vote for 'Remain' in the 2016 referendum, regardless of Cameron's renegotiation, and it was based on the same economic reasoning that had pitched me against Britain joining the euro in the previous decade.

I had listened so many times from 1994 onwards to people saying that Britain had to join the single currency because if we stayed out our influence would be undermined. But the view I took was that the damage joining the euro would do to our economy and our prosperity would undermine our influence and standing in the world far more than leaving our seat at the table empty.

But for me, maintaining our membership of the European Union was never a trade-off between influence and prosperity. I believed, and still do, that walking away will undermine the influence we wield on the biggest issues facing our world, from managing the global economy to tackling shared security threats and trying to reverse climate change. It will risk destroying the prosperity which came from being part of this enormous single market, and jeopardise all the jobs and trade that rely on our place within that market.

The status quo was far from perfect, but I thought we should stay in and fight for a better deal for Britain. So when, early on in the campaign, I was asked by David Cameron's private secretary to appear at a joint event with George Osborne and Vince Cable to make the case for staying in, I immediately agreed. In the final weeks of the referendum campaign, I received a regular flow of texts and phone calls from the Remain campaign, the Prime Minister's office and George Osborne about how the campaign was going and what needed to be done.

But, in retrospect, the referendum was lost months before

when the Prime Minister, without any consultation with people outside his inner circle and certainly not with any Labour or SNP figures, decided to do his renegotiation at breakneck speed, focus solely on persuading Tory voters and critics, bring forward the referendum to 2016 and then try to make the whole thing his personal battle and victory.

In the final days before he concluded his renegotiation, it was clear that, while David Cameron had made some good progress on a number of issues, he wasn't getting the break-through he needed on immigration controls, his so-called 'emergency brake'. I wrote an article for the *Wall Street Journal* saying that these reforms were a good start but that we needed to keep reform of free movement on the table.

But then, to my horror, David Cameron returned from the summit declaring he had won, that he had 'reset' Britain's relationship with Europe and that this was to be the basis of his campaign to stay in, with him at the forefront. From then on, things began to spiral out of control. First, the renego-tiation was ridiculed by senior figures in his own party and the media, and within days the campaign became a personal fight between David Cameron and Boris Johnson, which both alienated and ignored Labour voters.

Then the Remain campaign became a defender of the status quo. Rather than saying 'the status quo is not good enough but this is no time to walk away, we should stay and fight for a better deal', the Remain campaign instead said that now David Cameron had reformed Britain's relation-ship with Europe, the status quo was good for Britain and we should not jeopardise it by leaving. The problem was that, outside the cities, many people thought the status quo was what needed to end. And when the Leave campaign promised to 'take back control', that struck a deep chord.

David Cameron drew the wrong conclusion from Scotland and from the general election that followed. He concluded that a campaign based on fear and defending the status quo was enough to win the vote, whatever the longer-term implications. That forgot what actually happened with the Scottish vote. In the weeks approaching the referendum, the nationalists had the initiative, they were for change and optimism and national self-determination, and on the other side was an unpopular Tory leadership in Westminster, remote from the reality of people's lives in Scotland.

But ironically, given his name was on it, Cameron ignored what happened at that point of the Scottish campaign. In the final days before that poll, with the SNP enjoying all the momentum, all the UK political leaders made a public vow to the Scottish people that they would deliver more devolution – that there was more on offer than simply the status quo. At the time, while I agreed with the politics of the vow, I was deeply worried that devolution of income tax would ultimately lead to the collapse of the union by making the UK-wide Budget process unsustainable, and that we would 'win the battle and lose the war'. George Osborne told me that we should worry about that afterwards.

But in the later stages of the EU referendum, when Yvette and I both called for a similar vow-like statement that the UK would continue to push for more reform of free movement, we were told by the Remain campaign that our interventions were unhelpful and not to rock the boat. Deputy Leader Tom Watson and key figures in the Labour and Remain campaigns knew something had to be done. I believe – based on our conversations at Ryanair and subsequently – that George Osborne did too. But David Cameron refused to budge from his view that his renegotiation was sufficient. And then when Jeremy Corbyn appeared on television the weekend before the poll to declare that free movement was non-negotiable and there could be no upper limit to immigration, the argument was lost.

So now, the future. Britain faces a huge and vital task, not simply to negotiate Britain's exit from the European Union, but to establish a new economic and political relationship with our neighbour and biggest trading partner. Whether we get this right will have a great bearing not only on our access to the single market, for jobs, investment and the future of UK manufacturing and financial services; it will also determine what kind of country we are to become.

We have to decide whether to maintain access to the single market on good terms for Britain, or reject any compromise and retreat entirely; whether to remain an open and internationalist trading nation, or choose protectionism and isolation; and whether to stay open to ideas and talent and creativity from around the world, or to turn in on ourselves and cut Britain off from the world.

Theresa May, the Conservative party's new leader, and the prime minister who will have to conduct these negotiations, has a great responsibility and a big choice to make. She will need to think hard about what kind of Britain she wants us to become and learn the right lessons from Britain's chequered history of negotiations with Europe.

She must understand that pandering to the emotional centre of party members and setting aside pragmatism and economics would be a disaster for Britain. What we badly need in Britain is a return to the sort of leadership exemplified by Margaret Thatcher as Prime Minister and Gordon Brown as Chancellor; someone who can persuade the British public that it is possible to secure the national interest while also working with neighbours to advance our national interests and the common good.

What Thatcher and Brown both showed is that you've always got to be in the negotiation room fighting for the national interest and to reach an agreement. When David Cameron walked out of a summit in 2013, blocking Europe's agreement on a treaty change for the Eurozone on the grounds that he couldn't secure protections for the City of London from excessive regulation, he saw it as an act in the mould of Margaret Thatcher; in reality, it was the total opposite.

His failure to secure any truly historic, significant reforms in the run-up to the referendum was a huge setback for that style of leadership, and if he is succeeded by someone who would always rather be outside the room, rattling their sabre than inside securing the best deal for Britain, then our country will be on a steady slide to economic isolation and irrelevance.

You may win popular acclaim from the newspapers by walking out, but it does huge long-term damage to your negotiating hand. My experience was always that our European partners were willing to accommodate Britain so long as they believed we were genuinely trying to find a cooperative way forward. With Britain now leaving, it will be harder to persuade them to cooperate. Winning the argument with our European partners that restrictions on free movement are necessary for Europe and not just for Britain will be infinitely harder.

It will be a huge task of leadership to find a new economic relationship that works for Britain and which our European partners will agree to. But it will be possible if our new British Prime Minister stays in the room, builds alliances and is seen to be both tough and reasonable. Britain was never going to follow Jean-Claude Juncker and sacrifice our national interest for the good of the European project. In the end, that is why we are leaving. But we are never going to tackle the huge problems we and the world face by cutting ourselves off from cooperation with our European allies.

Instead, we need leaders and negotiators who accept that there is plenty of middle ground between capitulation and walking out – people who stay in the room as long as it takes, and win the argument for Britain.

13

Mission

Every Child Matters – everyone can agree on that, so why couldn't I persuade the Tories to sign up to it?

I was being interviewed by BBC Radio Leeds at 7.30 a.m. from our house in London in June 2007, when the call came through.

I'd forgotten to put my mobile on silent and – given he'd just been asking me what job I expected to get in that day's reshuffle – the interviewer excitedly asked whether it was Number Ten on the phone. I glanced down to the screen, saw 'GB (Mobile)', but said I didn't know who was calling. The phone stopped ringing. 'You've missed your chance!' the interviewer laughed.

I was fairly sure I hadn't though. Even by Gordon's standards, that would have been a tad impatient. A short while later, I spoke to him and immediately afterwards I got a text message from my new office at the newly formed Department for Children, Schools and Families, asking where to send the car to pick me up.

I was taken to Great Smith Street, where waiting for me were my private secretary, Mela Watts, and the Permanent Secretary, David Bell. We shook hands, and they ushered me in, taking me up in the lift to the Secretary of State's rather large office overlooking Westminster Abbey, which I'd only seen once before at a meeting with Charles Clarke five years previously.

Mela, the epitome of the efficient, authoritative and insightful civil servant, came into my office to start my introductions, when a bell rang. She said: 'That's the division bell, you have to go and vote.' So I rushed downstairs and out to the front where the car was again waiting to whisk me round to the House of Commons. I arrived with just a minute to spare. Voting on reshuffle day is always a difficult experience. You end up bumping into people with new jobs, people with the same jobs, people who are still hoping for a phone call and, most unhappily, people who've just lost their jobs. You could always tell from people's faces who was in which camp.

I jumped back in the car, returned to the department, said hello to the security guards for a second time, got into the lifts and then realised that I had absolutely no idea which floor my office was on. I hadn't clocked it when I'd arrived half an hour ago, and the last time with Charles Clarke so many glasses of wine were consumed I barely knew which building I was in, let alone what floor.

I went back to the security guards. 'I'm terribly sorry,' I

said, 'I'm the new Secretary of State but I've no idea which floor my office is on.' They escorted me to the lift and pressed the right button with only mild smiles on their faces. It was not a hugely auspicious start to my Cabinet career.

The next twenty-four hours were a whirlwind of meetings and phone calls: a procession of civil servants from different sections introducing themselves; a relay of calls to the leaders of all the teaching unions; several exchanges with Gordon about who would be in my ministerial team; and my first trip to Buckingham Palace to be sworn in as a privy councillor.

The next day, David Bell suggested that I give a few short words of welcome to staff in the department, which would also be beamed by live video to our sites in Sheffield, Darlington and Runcorn.

It was my job in the welcoming speech to be clear, enthusiastic and passionate about the new department, to say we weren't just changing the name on the door, but also expanding the mission everyone came to work each day to deliver and to communicate what that mission was. In truth, though, I was still trying to work out what our new purpose really was. We were no longer solely a department of education, but of wider children's and family policy too. But what did that actually mean? I was excited at the challenge; I knew that we could achieve something remarkable. The scale of my new responsibilities weighed heavily. I had to deliver.

I found it a very difficult speech to make. It went down fine but, in retrospect, I should have told David that it was too premature. It was the moment when I learned properly that, as someone in a leadership position, it's very hard to say what any other human being would – that you're new and you've got a lot to learn.

Once I did sit down with my officials to work things out, it was apparent what a big and important opportunity we had in the new department. Our first meetings revealed a shared vision: to break down every barrier to learning so that every child could make the most of their abilities.

That didn't just refer to what happened in the classroom – after all children are only at school 15 per cent of the time; it included their health, well-being, safety, happiness and family circumstances; and it meant having integrated but specially tailored strategies for different children with different needs and special challenges. We decided to call it the 'Children's Plan' and to dub the DCSF the 'Every Child Matters' department.

The process of drawing up the Children's Plan over the next six months, the consultation that we did with experts, and also with parents and teachers in half-day meetings on Saturdays around the country, helped me to understand the potential in this area and also to build a sense of common purpose. Everyone involved – parents, the 'partnership' of teaching unions and school leaders, social workers, child health professionals, the children themselves – was bound together by a desire to help every child succeed. Our job was to support them.

A couple of weeks into the job, I arranged to do an

unannounced all-day visit to a secondary school. John Dunford, chair of the Association of School and College Leaders, suggested a school in Banbury where I met an excellent head teacher who took me to the morning staff meeting and then around the school.

In one class, an English teacher was using sherbet lemons, one for each pupil, getting them to use the taste and sensation of the sweet as an inspiration to write using metaphors and similes. It was a lower-set class, and it was amazing to feel how enthused they were, and see the lesson she was teaching sink in.

The head teacher told me how many children in the school arrived with what were called 'behavioural problems', but which turned out to be unidentified learning difficulties such as dyslexia and – close to my heart – interiorised stammers, which had led them to become selectively mute. It was clearly crucial to identify such conditions early to help those children learn better, and to ensure specialist support was available to help teachers cope.

We also talked about the extent to which problems outside school could affect a child's ability to learn. Innovations like breakfast clubs might seem like a simple convenience for parents – dropping the kids off on the way to work – but at least some children are guaranteed a proper breakfast, which they otherwise wouldn't have, and that puts them in a calm and positive mood for the day.

If the teachers and children's professionals I spoke to were enthusiastic and full of ideas about the Children's Plan, I found it harder at the beginning to engage the Civil Service in the process. I'd inherited an exceptional group of civil servants at the DCSF, but they seemed unaccustomed to leading an agenda or expressing a point of view.

The previous Department for Education was, I think, used to being pushed and pulled by competing agendas from Downing Street and the Treasury, which is never conducive to the civil servants feeling empowered and in control. I was clear that we were not going to be told what to do by Number Ten or Number Eleven, and that I wanted our agenda to be shaped by what my civil servants told me, not me simply issuing or passing on instructions.

I wanted them to tell me what they thought, give me their ideas, and help us reach a collective view. We got there in the end, but it took weeks of me saying to senior civil servants: 'Stop asking me what I think and start telling me what you think, because that's what matters to me.' And when we decided to face down those parts of the teaching establishment who wanted to abolish compulsory tests for eleven-year-olds – the SATs tests – it wasn't only because as a parent I thought those tests were important, or that as a Labour politician I was so frustrated when primary head teachers in low-income areas told me their test results were poor because 'that's the best you can expect from kids round here'; it was also because my civil servant advisers were passionate that the tests were vital to raising standards for all children and that they must stay.

I took a similar approach with my ministerial team. What I'd learned from Gordon was that while he was good at devolving issues to his ministers – at least those he respected and trusted – he tended to only hand over the issues he didn't care so much about or, on occasion, didn't want to touch with a bargepole. I tried to build a more collegiate approach to working through all the big issues we were facing, and I was lucky to have such a talented group with me.

Many other departmental teams treat preparation for their parliamentary questions sessions as a bit of an administrative chore, but for us, it became an important way of keeping a strategic grip on where the department was going. We'd divide the questions between us, work out the areas where we wanted to push forward our message, and also the areas where we had vulnerabilities, making sure that we improved our lines and had better policy responses.

As well as my ministerial team, I was blessed with a brilliant team of officials in my private office. They were my eyes and ears into the department and would regularly tell me whether I was getting various relationships and issues right.

Their big frustration was that all my meetings overran, so I was perpetually late. Timekeeping was never my greatest strength, but not out of laziness – there were always just too many important things to talk about, and too little time.

As my stammer changed my speaking style, my speechwriter, Richard Winson, was a key part of my team – as were my political advisers: Francine Bates, Caroline Abrahams, Richard Brooks and former Treasury civil servant Jo-Anne Daniels; and on the media side Balshen Izzet and Alex Belardinelli. The best team I could ever have hoped for.

Francine's role was particularly important in the new department. A campaigner for better services for disabled children, who knew everyone in the children's policy world, she had worked with me when I was a backbench MP and held hearings in Parliament so parents of disabled children could explain how tough things were and what extra help they needed. Just a few years later, we were working together in a new Children's Department to provide short breaks and extra specialist support for disabled children and their families – ensuring 'Every Child Matters' properly included disabled children too.

By the time we got to publishing the Children's Plan in December 2007, and announcing the new resources to go with it, the department seemed really enthused about what we were doing. I got a real buzz out of walking into the building with the foyer and the walls of the lifts decked out in all the new rainbow branding that we'd developed for the launch.

But when I returned after Christmas it had all been taken down. 'What's happened to all the Children's Plan stuff?' I said. 'Well, I guess they think we've launched it now,' Mela said. My old Treasury head would have thought: 'Yep, now we move on to the next big thing.' But my new DCSF head thought: 'No, this isn't just an announcement, it's our mission. Everything we do needs to be about this.'

I said we couldn't risk people thinking it was back to business as usual so we needed not just to put the branding back up but also make sure that every email, press release and document that came out of the department from that point on fitted with the Children's Plan objectives and messaging, and that it was truly embedded in every aspect of the department's work. I was determined that the changes we made would really stick.

I had quickly learned the importance of having the right people around me. We could not have achieved what we did without the help and input of every member of the department. It took me a little longer, however, to learn how to work with my new bosses.

For any Cabinet minister, the relationship with Number Ten is hugely important, whether discussing big announcements with the policy unit or handling problems with the media team. I worked hard at establishing a partnership with Downing Street, but made clear that I saw it as our job and our job alone to set the strategic direction or issue public lines. We were not there simply to take orders.

For me, it was made more complicated by the inevitable change in my relationship with Gordon. I was used to talking to him in person or in a rather relaxed and discursive way on our mobiles, but with him at Number Ten suddenly surrounded by a vast operation and a hundred things to do, and me similarly busy in a different department, the conversations we had ended up being much more functional and business-like, and neither of us got out of them what we were accustomed to. Nor was sitting with Gordon in the back of an armoured Jaguar in the middle of a police convoy, crawling through central London on the way to a school visit, conducive to relaxed conversation.

And then there was the relationship with the opposition. I wish I'd tried harder to engage the Conservatives and make them part of our mission as well. But Michael Gove was never an easy Shadow to deal with and he ensured our exchanges in the House of Commons were always confrontational. Although we had regular discussions, he never embraced the idea of the Children's Department, and clearly wanted a return to a department focused solely on education, a narrower 1950s-style curriculum and a rigorous focus on a top-down imposition of teaching practices.

Immediately after he became the Education Secretary in 2010, the department's name changed back, and the Children's Plan and all the strategies and objectives it contained were consigned to the dustbin. It was no great surprise but it was still very hard to take that all the work and effort the entire education and children's community had put into that plan was being deliberately erased.

My other big disappointment at the DCSF – compared to the Treasury – was that as well as failing to secure lasting change and consensus around our reforms, I wasn't able to change the culture. It was far too easy and natural for the Civil Service there to slip back into the old habits of being told what to do by a domineering minister, like Michael Gove, who almost certainly had little time for their opinions, and publicly referred to them as 'The Blob'. And once Michael Gove became so unpopular with parents and teachers that he had to be removed, the department went back to business as usual with the Education Department once again having policy on academies dictated to them by Number Ten and the Treasury.

Yet some of the effects of my time at the DCSF have been more lasting. Even six years later, I regularly meet teachers, head teachers and directors of children's services who say: 'We're still doing "Every Child Matters".' It might not be official policy any more, but many of the changes that we implemented are still there in the daily lives of schools and children around the country.

And the experience did change my thinking about issues like these. It just seems wrong that the education and welfare of small children – and the schools that look after them – should so regularly be turned upside down just because a new government or minister comes in and wants to put their own stamp on things.

We need to work harder to establish a cross-party and public consensus on children's policy, along with other issues like social care of the elderly, and agree plans that will last for ten years or more, not just until the next election or reshuffle. At least then the civil servants, the school leaders, the teachers and, most importantly, the children would have a bit of stability and certainty.

Perhaps in retrospect, when I thought about the mission of my new department, I should have realised that, and worked harder to make children's policy more independent of short-term politics, including my own. Sometimes the best way to demonstrate leadership is by accepting you need to give it away.

14

Ambition

———————————

Every politician wants to get on — but does it really matter how high you can climb up the greasy pole?

My first brush with political death came in 1994, when my career had barely begun.

Shortly after I left the FT to join Labour and soon after Tony Blair became leader, we organised a big economic conference to launch what we called Labour's 'New Policies for the Global Economy'. It went pretty well, with one glitch – the media bashing Gordon received for using my phrase 'post-neoclassical endogenous growth theory' in his speech. He was pretty annoyed at me, which was somewhat unfair as Ed Miliband and I had cut the offending sentence from the final draft and Gordon had scribbled in the margin 'put back the theory'.

Nevertheless, I'd got the blame publicly, and Gordon's

annoyance reached a peak when Michael Heseltine mocked the phrase in his Tory Party conference speech, accompanied by the famous line: 'It's not Brown's, it's Balls'.'

As Heseltine delivered his line, I was accompanying Gordon on a visit to the US Federal Reserve in Washington, and as we walked up its famous sweeping steps, I got a call to say the Heseltine quote was going to lead the BBC six o'clock news. When I told him, Gordon gave me a look which roughly translated as: 'Why have I employed this idiot?'

Half an hour later, when we were sitting in Alan Greenspan's office, my head was 3,700 miles away wondering how bad 'The Six' was, when I suddenly heard Gordon say, 'Ed, tell Alan about the work you've been doing on this.' I stared at them both in horror and had to confess I didn't know what 'this' they were talking about. Gordon didn't bother to enlighten me, just gave me a subtle yet infinitely more menacing variation of his earlier look.

In retrospect, I probably served up for Michael Heseltine one of the media highlights of his career. Alongside Rab Butler, and perhaps David Miliband, Heseltine has come to define the 'nearly man' politician, who always desperately wanted the top job and had many of the qualifications, but never fulfilled his own ambitions. That ambition in many ways diminishes everything he did achieve and his excellence as a retail politician, who knew how to press his party's buttons and give the media their banner headlines.

But if you'd told me back then that Gordon would ever consider making me his Chancellor, I'd have said you'd lost your marbles or assumed he had.

★

Don't get me wrong – it felt like I'd been preparing for the role of Chancellor for most of my life. From the time I started my A levels in 1983, with unemployment rising above three million, the country riven with industrial strife and monetarism already beginning to fracture, I was fascinated by economics. Even then, as I joined the Labour Party, I was convinced that all fundamental issues in politics came down to economics. Throughout university, throughout my early career in journalism, I was gripped with a growing frustration. I didn't just want to observe and write about politics, I wanted to do it. And that for me meant being in the Treasury and, perhaps, some day getting the chance to become the Chancellor myself. Certainly, as a 27-year-old joining Gordon's Treasury team in 1994, that was not only my bold ambition, it was my tentative hope.

When Gordon became prime minister in the summer of 2007, I'd by that stage worked for him in opposition for three years, then as chief economic adviser at the Treasury for seven years, and then as a Treasury minister for a year. Given the extent to which I knew the ropes, there was inevitably a lot of speculation about whether Gordon would make me Chancellor in his first Cabinet. But I was sceptical. I wanted a job in the Cabinet, I felt ready and qualified; but becoming Chancellor, and the youngest ever at that, seemed like far too big a jump. So about six weeks before Tony Blair was due to step down, I was interviewed by Alex Brummer, economics editor of the *Daily Mail*, and said that I wasn't expecting to be Chancellor and I wasn't going to be – it was too early for me and I didn't feel ready.

I thought that would knock it on the head, but still the

speculation continued that Gordon was having to choose between me and Alistair Darling. When we finally got round to talking about jobs, Gordon's main preoccupation was his own Number Ten operation, and the need for a strong unit of people around him. He asked if I would consider a joint role as the Treasury Chief Secretary and lead minister in the Cabinet Office.

I thought this was a doubly bad idea. Firstly, because people would inevitably conclude I was being placed in the Treasury to keep the new Chancellor in check. Secondly, we'd always both believed that the Treasury played an important constitutional role in balancing against Number Ten, especially in a government with a majority. That's why we'd fended off Tony Blair's attempt in 2005 to create some hybrid of the Treasury and the Cabinet Office. Having held that position for the previous decade, it would be illogical and unprincipled to try and fudge the divide just because Gordon was now the PM.

In Manchester, on the Sunday when Gordon became Labour leader, just three days before he went into Number Ten, he grabbed my arm as we were walking out of the hall following his acceptance speech. He said: 'I need an urgent word,' and pulled me through a set of swing doors off the corridor.

Neither of us had any idea where the doors led, and we found ourselves in an empty kitchen, with the lights off, surrounded by pots and pans. Gordon said: 'I've been thinking hard and I've decided to be bold. I'm going to make

David Miliband Foreign Secretary, Jacqui Smith Home Secretary and I'm going to make you Chancellor. The only way for me to do this job is to make big decisions from the beginning, and that's what I'm going to do.'

I said: 'Well, it's good you're making David Foreign Secretary, but you know you're under no obligation to make me Chancellor at all. You've read my interview in the *Mail*. I don't think I'm ready. And what about the others?' I thought both Jack Straw and Alistair Darling would have their noses put out of joint if I got the job ahead of them. He said: 'It's got to be done, and the only thing I want you to do for the next forty-eight hours is work out who you want as Chief Secretary.'

Yvette and I drove back to London, me feeling worried, excited and daunted in equal measure, her telling me that it would be fine, I had been preparing for this day for years, and I had to do it. So, as Gordon had asked, I started thinking about the job and the challenges ahead.

The next day was strange, as reshuffles always are for a minister. You go through the motions of an ordinary working day, but your officials treat it all like it's a waste of time, clearly desperate to know what's really going on. You try your best not to act the same, even though that's exactly what you're feeling. All I could do was establish an uneasy truce, where my office staff kept the phones clear, and I promised them that – if the call came – they'd be the first to know the outcome. We waited and waited. But the phone didn't ring.

Eventually, later that night, Gordon called me on my mobile. He said: 'It's got more complicated, it's difficult. I need to talk to you in person. Can we meet tomorrow?' I arrived at his office the next day, and he immediately steered me into his small private office, strewn as ever with piles of books and papers. 'Look,' he said, 'I can't do it, it's too difficult.'

I wasn't at all surprised, and actually I felt rather relieved. I went over my arguments again for why it might be too early for me to take such a big, pivotal job, and told him he shouldn't worry. He looked torn. 'It's terrible, I can't do it, it's too difficult, they'll try to destroy you if I make you Chancellor.' I didn't ask who 'they' were.

He then pointed towards a large whiteboard in the room, which had every government department with lists of names written on board magnets underneath them. 'Which job do you want?' I said: 'Well, you're going to be prime minister, that's your decision.' He said: 'Do you want to be Home Secretary?' I paused. 'Aren't you making Jacqui Smith Home Secretary? That's what you told me on Sunday.' 'Yes,' he said, 'but if you want it you can have it.' There was no way I was going to take a job that someone else had been promised.

I looked at the board and said: 'I'd like Children, Schools and Families,' the new department which he was establishing and which I and all my Treasury colleagues were very enthusiastic about. He said: 'Fine, done, that's it.' I walked out of the Chancellor's office, not knowing that was the closest I would ever come to occupying it myself. Perhaps if I had done, I'd have argued the toss, but at the time it felt like a reprieve.

I wanted my first job in the Cabinet to be one where I could learn the trade. I also knew that I was still struggling with my media and parliamentary appearances, even if at that stage I still didn't know why. The job of Chancellor is so exposed and unforgiving, especially on the big parliamentary occasions, especially if you're grappling with the demands of public speaking.

After six months at the Department of Children, Schools and Families, the Children's Plan was due to be published in the second week of December, with the key announcements trailed in the Sunday papers, and an interview on *The Andrew Marr Show*. It was only my second appearance on the programme, and it was a stressful prospect.

I was in my ministerial office on the Saturday, working on my Commons statement, thinking about the TV programme, and contemplating my biggest week so far as a minister, when I had a call from Number Ten that Gordon wanted to speak. I took the call, and he said he was coming in from Chequers to see me personally. He asked me to meet him in Downing Street at 5 p.m. He wouldn't tell me what it was about, but I could only think it had something to do with my statement or the *Marr* programme appearance.

I finished up my statement as best I could, and went over. Both of my guesses were wrong. Gordon told me he needed more support in Number Ten, and had decided I should give up my job as Children's Secretary immediately, and come over to the Cabinet Office to act as Chief of Staff and run his office – just like I had for years in the Treasury.

I said that I couldn't do it, that I wanted to be in the job I was doing, because I was enjoying it and it was important, and I was only at the beginning of the role. In any case, I said, me coming into Number Ten wouldn't solve his problems there in the wake of the 'election that never was', because I would just become a stick for his internal party critics to beat him with. Nevertheless, with Gordon, you can never quite say 'No', so I said I would think about it.

I spent the next two weeks trying to find a solution to Gordon's problem that wasn't me, attempting to persuade Jeremy Heywood to move from his Cabinet Office strategy role to be the Prime Minister's principal private secretary. What I didn't realise was that Gordon was simultaneously offering a new political 'Number Ten Chief of Staff' job to a senior Brunswick lobbyist called Stephen Carter. Fortunately, Jeremy accepted. And so did Stephen.

The speculation about the Chancellorship resumed in the late summer of 2008, after David Miliband's abortive coup against Gordon and Alistair Darling's doom-laden interview about the prospects for the British economy. A few weeks earlier, Gordon had asked me to break my August holiday and come up to Scotland because he said he had a big plan he wanted my views on.

I travelled up and he explained that the 'big plan' was bringing Alastair Campbell into the government as sports minister. I was rather perplexed. I said I thought Alastair would be an excellent sports minister, and that it presented no problem for me. But I knew Gordon well enough to know that couldn't really be the 'big plan' – it felt more like he was testing me. Three weeks later, he said: 'Listen, the other idea I have is to bring Peter Mandelson back from Brussels to be in the Cabinet.'

Peter and I had always got on better than anybody realised, even if it had been a bit difficult at certain times. He had been very influential in persuading me to leave the FT in 1994. And, unusually in politics, we've managed to maintain our friendship, through government and opposition, right up to the present day. But back then, with Gordon's premiership under huge pressure, I wasn't sure how Peter and Gordon would work together, or how destabilising it was going to be.

So I asked if he was sure, and he replied: 'I will not make this decision unless you agree with it.' That seemed a ludicrous thing to say, but as time passed, it made an increasing amount of sense. Gordon was just feeling embarrassed that he was planning to make bold, controversial appointments in his reshuffle, but couldn't go as far as making me Chancellor. I was fine with that – with the financial crisis raging, this was no time to start destabilising the Treasury, but Gordon still wanted to know he had me on board.

Sure enough, when the day came, Gordon told me bringing Peter back was a big gamble designed to unify the party after a fractious summer, and he didn't think he could couple that with a divisive change of Chancellor. I said: 'That's fine, I'm not looking to move. I'm happy to wait for the right time.' But of course, the right time never came.

The Chancellorship became a spectre which haunted my Cabinet career. On three more occasions, Gordon called me in to say he wanted to make the move – even offering to put his commitment in writing, an offer I refused – but every time the crunch came, he found he couldn't.

In June 2009, as the local and European elections approached, there was a fever pitch of speculation that Gordon would be having a reshuffle, and that Alistair Darling would be replaced. This provoked the usual furious but anonymous reaction from Alistair's camp, which just stoked the fires further. The whole thing looked a mess, and I was worried I'd come out looking like I'd wielded the knife. I told Gordon: 'Drop this, it's a bad idea, and it's too late.' I rang everyone I trusted in Downing Street to give them the same message, and I told key contacts in the parliamentary press lobby to stop their speculation, because I didn't want the job.

Gordon persevered. He sent Peter to visit Alistair on the day before the local elections to ask him to move. Alistair refused. But Peter told me Gordon was going to do it anyway. Then, in the wake of the terrible election results that Thursday night, James Purnell resigned, triggering rumours of a fresh coup attempt against Gordon, and forcing him to sue for peace with his internal critics. Replacing Alistair was never going to be a part of that truce.

As always happened when Gordon had to withdraw the Chancellor offer to me, he replaced it with a demand that I come in and run Downing Street instead. In retrospect, I often wonder whether I should have agreed, and feel some degree of guilt that I said no. But it never seemed right at the time, and I was always focused on what I was trying to do in my own department.

In 2009 and on every other occasion, I felt more irritation at the process than at the outcome. It was an important distinction because it meant that I didn't dwell on what hadn't happened, but just got on with the job I was doing. By contrast, when Gordon had similar experiences being thwarted over the planned handover of the premiership by Tony Blair, I could see the disappointment eat away at him a little more every time, and the look of frustration about the next routine Treasury meeting or speech he'd have to do.

Whenever he was fulminating about how long Tony was going to stay in the job, I would say: 'You're the most un-assailable Chancellor for decades, presiding over huge changes for which you are responsible. Bank of England independence. Keeping Britain out of the euro. All the millions of people we've lifted out of poverty. All the extra funding for schools and hospitals. Can't you see these are great things? Stop thinking about that job, and just enjoy this job for a minute.'

But it never made a difference – because for a highly driven person like Gordon, who wanted to achieve great changes for the country and in the world, once you've decided the only way to achieve those ambitions is by becoming prime minister, it's hard to think of anything else.

So when I look back at the historic things Gordon and I did together at the Treasury, I probably do so even more proudly than him, although I'm sure he takes pride in the way he steered the world through the financial crisis in 2008–9 as PM. Yes, I wanted to be Chancellor. But with the benefit of hindsight, while I never got that job, I know that in my nine years at the Treasury I achieved the kinds of things I dreamed about as a teenager and as a young reporter at the

FT, regardless of what my job title was. And I achieved equally important things as Children's Secretary.

It's now a tired old cliché to say 'politics should be about the job you do, not the title you hold', partly because we forced Gordon to say it so many times in his interviews and conference speeches. But it's such an important lesson to learn. Go back to Michael Heseltine. He probably ended his political career feeling he failed: he never held any of the great offices of state, and he never achieved his great ambition of becoming prime minister.

Yet Heseltine will be remembered for truly great political achievements: the regeneration of our cities; leading internal Tory opposition to the poll tax; and trying to stop the Tory Party's slide towards a British exit from Europe. As well as more than a few ingenious conference jokes.

Could he have done even more if he had spent less time chasing his own political ambitions, especially by choosing to leave the Cabinet for four years? Undoubtedly yes. Could Gordon have done even more as Chancellor if he'd stayed entirely focused on that job as long as he was doing it? Yes again.

I had five separate opportunities to flounce out of Gordon's Cabinet over my own thwarted ambitions, but despite my frustration, the thought never occurred to me. You cannot achieve anything sulking in your tent.

I'm so glad in retrospect that was my instinct. Because now, at the seeming end of my political career, I can look back with pride at the important things I did, and I know they will matter to me infinitely more in the years to come than the list of job titles on my Wikipedia page.

15

Image

Image matters in politics — but is there any other profession where it can be so distorting?

One of the best-liked MPs in the Labour Party is Alan Johnson. Having worked his way up from a very deprived background to postman to trade union leader to a successful Cabinet minister, he was a viable candidate to stand against Gordon for the Labour leadership in 2007. When he decided to stand for deputy instead, it was both a relief for Gordon as well as a potential opportunity to have such a popular figure as his number two.

But Spencer Livermore, Gordon's pollster, conducted some focus groups and the results that came back were astonishing. He showed people footage of Alan speaking, and what they said was: 'I don't like his shiny suit'; 'He talks like some cockney wide boy'; 'He looks like a used-car salesman'. They didn't care what he was saying, they weren't even interested in listening, and they certainly didn't want to know about his 'backstory'. They had built an immediate impression of him just based on what he was wearing and the sound of his voice.

Alan went on to be a respected Home Secretary before writing acclaimed memoirs which have won him both great accolades and widespread public affection. Along the way, he's also stopped wearing those shiny suits.

Which all just illustrates the absurdity of modern politics. A politician who lacks experience, wisdom and vision can win the public's admiration and attention just because they appear to mean what they say, and come across as genuine. Conversely, a politician can have all those things and be successful at their job but still be dismissed by a section of the population simply because of how they look or talk.

Is there any other profession in the world where image matters so much and can be so distorting?

The truth is it is really hard to alter people's first impressions of you. For me, my public image starts with my name. By some considerable distance, the biggest issue that people would raise when asked about me in focus groups was the fact that I am called 'Balls'. With the name I have, they wondered whether I could really be taken seriously.

One Labour Party conference, I had agreed to answer readers' questions in the Monday morning's *Independent* newspaper. The questions were always a mixture of serious, quirky and funny, and you needed your answers to match. The final question was: 'How do you cope in politics with the surname Balls?' My reply was: 'If you think it's been bad for me, think what it's been like for my sister, Ophelia.'

That day I was having lunch with a group of journalists in the conference hotel, and as we sat down, the then editor of the *Independent* came over and said to me: 'Very good Q&A today, but did your parents really call your sister Ophelia?' I laughed and explained it was a joke. But I sensed surprise in his eyes. Perhaps he thought it odd for me to have a sense of humour about it.

The fact is that my name has helped to shape who I am. I was teased about it all the time I was at school, and have heard every conceivable insult you can imagine. The taunts didn't always come from my schoolmates, however: I could take all the kids laughing every time my name was read out at the beginning of a football match, but when all the parents on the sideline laughed as well, it was a little tougher to deal with. I think it explains why I've always had to be willing to lead with my chin. It's also why, of all the insults that have been thrown my way by fellow politicians and the media over the years, the only one that makes me flare up is 'bully'. When you've spent your childhood facing down bullies, it's the worst thing to be called one.

By the time I was a politician, though, I realised that my surname had changed from a burden to an asset. There's nothing more difficult in politics than not to be noticed or recognised. But when Yvette and I would walk through the streets in our constituencies, I could always count on every group of kids we'd walk by yelling out in unison: 'Ed Balls!'

As Yvette used to say, I had to be one of the best-known politicians among teenagers in the country.

My name recognition went to a new level after I mistakenly tweeted my own name, giving birth to 'Ed Balls Day' every 28 April. It was a silly mistake that is seemingly celebrated around the world with thousands of people ritually retweeting my original mistaken tweet. Every so often on those mad days, I'll see someone from the US or elsewhere tweet: 'Is there really a politician called "Balls"?' and I'll just sigh and think: yes, that is my name. I can't change it, and I wouldn't want to. Like my stammer, it's just part of who I am.

Once people have got past my name, the next thing they notice – before I've even opened my mouth – is my frame. I've always looked more of a prop forward than a speedy winger. The *Sun* once asked YouGov to run a poll asking voters who would be most likely to win a fight in the House of Commons, and I came top with 23 per cent of the vote, for no other reason than I look the part – politics loves a cartoon. And when a story appeared in 2008 claiming I'd had an argument with Jack Straw and nearly hit him, it gained traction only because I looked like the kind of person who might enjoy a punch-up. The reality is I don't think Jack Straw and I have ever exchanged a cross word in our lives.

On the football pitch, I was actually a rather pacy striker, but when, in the annual football match between MPs and journalists, I accidentally elbowed *Northern Echo* reporter Rob Merrick and he ended up going off to hospital for stitches, I fear the newspaper coverage of his blood-spattered face and shirt rather reinforced my 'bruiser' image. There are times when that label has bothered me, but ultimately you have to accept that how you come across to people is probably never going to change – and I've certainly done a few things in my time, both on and off the pitch, to reinforce that image.

The worst thing you can ever do in politics is start trying to change who you really are to create a different image in people's minds. I found that out when I appeared in March 2016 on a special edition of *The Great British Bake Off* for Sport Relief. I've never played a game or entered a competition without trying to win. It's just who I am. But everyone told me beforehand: 'It's for charity, for goodness' sake, so don't be competitive.' And in my head, I tried really hard not to come across that way. But there was no concealing the truth, and in some ways, I'm glad; I think it would have been much worse if people had said: 'Look at him trying to pretend he doesn't want to win.'

In an age when there is such inbuilt distrust of politicians – people are almost waiting for you to be exposed as a 'fake', so the last thing you should do is actively tempt that fate by doing and saying things you know aren't real.

After all, when politicians are caught out being dishonest or disingenuous, it usually taps into some existing public scepticism about them. When David Cameron was discovered by the *Daily Mirror* riding his bike to work with a chauffeur driving behind him, carrying his papers, shoes and suit, it only confirmed the suspicion in many people's minds that his statements on the environment were just spin.

Similarly, when Cameron told an audience he was a

supporter of West Ham rather than his supposed childhood team, Aston Villa, and then tried to explain that it was because they wore the same colour shirt, it merely reinforced what most people already thought – that he'd only invented his Villa support in the first place to try and make himself look like 'one of the lads'.

Gordon Brown, of course, had the ultimate moment of inauthenticity, describing a voter as a 'bigoted woman' seconds after promising to look into the issues she'd raised and cheerily wishing her goodbye; it went to the heart of the doubts that people already had about Labour's stance on immigration, and their view of the people who were concerned about it.

But the times when Gordon was most authentic was when he revealed who he really was. The football fan talking passionately about his love of the game. Or even when he and I went on a school visit and – after I handed him a tennis racket – I saw him bash the ball down the court in suit and tie with real intensity and ferocity, regardless of how the pictures would look, because he really wanted to win the point.

The fact is you can't go through your whole political career projecting an image which is at odds with who you really are. You'll end up lying to yourself as well as the public. If you want people to listen to you, they've got to identify with who you are. The only way to do that is to be yourself. If they don't like you, then you've probably picked the wrong career. But the chances are, in my experience, if you are true to yourself, and present that clearly and openly, you will at least be respected for it.

★

Of course, just being yourself in politics is easier said than done. One of the great challenges of politics is that the public very rarely gets the chance to see the real, authentic you.

Those times on *The Agenda*, ITV's Monday-night topical chat show, or an extended interview during the lunch break on *Test Match Special* – interviews outside the normal political realm – are gold dust in politics because there's a time and space to talk about a range of issues and reveal who you are, and what really matters to you.

The House of Commons dispatch box or the *Newsnight* studio don't offer the same opportunities. On those occasions, in a confrontational environment where pictures speak louder than words, your public caricature is liable to take over. David Cameron becomes Flashman. I become Jake LaMotta. People just see the image they already have of you, and everything you do reinforces the caricature.

For those politicians whose main trademark is 'authenticity', there is an opposite danger. Boris Johnson, Nigel Farage and Donald Trump have all carved out celebrity status as politicians because they come across as real, unvarnished, and happy to speak off the cuff. And it does tell you what a low ebb trust in politics and politicians has got to when Trump, Farage and Johnson can pose as outsiders – 'not the usual kind of establishment politician' – and get away with saying things that from the mouth of anyone else would be seen as racist, sexist, misogynist and often deeply dangerous.

But politicians who trade on authenticity can destroy their reputations with one ill-judged decision or one telling revelation. For that reason, Boris Johnson's decision to back the Leave campaign in the EU referendum, which looked like political calculation rather than an act of principle, was one fraught with danger. It has cost him the Tory leadership as a result, because his colleagues and the public saw it as cynical or underhand, two characterisations totally at odds with the image that he had successfully portrayed to date and leaving him wide open to be knifed by Michael Gove.

That was the problem Ed Miliband always faced: he'd present himself as a different kind of politician, 'Mr Nice Guy', but the public always saw him as the man who'd stabbed his brother in the back to get the job; someone who would put power ahead of his family. I thought the only way for Ed to deal with that was – as I always have – to lead with the chin, and say: 'Yes I took my brother on, because much as I love him, I think he's the wrong man to lead this party and this country, and I told him that to his face.' But Ed never wanted to address the issue, and when asked, he'd pretend that everything was hunky-dory between them, something no one believed.

In September 2015, Labour elected Jeremy Corbyn who – like Boris Johnson and Nigel Farage – had, back then at least, authenticity as his chief selling point; some critics would argue his only selling point.

Can that be enough, in this age of deep cynicism and hostility towards politicians, to win an election? Have we all grown so tired of politicians who aren't authentic, or, even worse, who fool no one by pretending to be, that the public would treat a character like Jeremy Corbyn as the breath of fresh air we need, and sweep him into Downing Street?

In my opinion, probably not. Which isn't to say that those people can't win elections if their opponents badly mess things up. But are traits like authenticity, integrity and honesty ever enough on their own? No – because just like the estate agent who trades on authenticity, you might believe every word they say, but if the house they're selling turns out to have dry rot up every wall, then you're not going to buy.

Authenticity may help you personally, but if your party is divided, if your policies are outside the mainstream of British public opinion, if your economic message lacks credibility and if you yourself are not seen as prime ministerial, then you cannot win an election. You can only hope that the other side loses it.

Authenticity may be a vital asset, but it only goes so far. For the rest, you need good policies, good communications and good politics.

16

Clowns

_____

Politicians are no comedians – so why is humour such a vital part of the job?

'Have you got any jokes?' It's a question guaranteed to cause a pall of gloom to descend over any gathering of political advisers.

It's a great irony that one of the most miserable parts of a job in politics is the hours spent sitting around a meeting table trying desperately to think of a line that will make the audience at a speech laugh politely, or make your side of the House of Commons erupt in pantomime mirth at the other lot's expense.

And yet, it remains a vital part of the craft of politics. Done well, humour, self-deprecation or mockery of your opponents can get an audience going, establish a connection, or – in Parliament – ram home a point. But the actual process of coming up with jokes, lines and anecdotes is extremely tortured, time-consuming and stressful – and certainly no laughing matter.

Clowns may not be in much demand these days, but you'll find plenty of them in politics, miserably rehearsing their familiar routine of squirting flowers, riding unicycles and throwing custard pies in the hope of getting a cheap laugh out in the circus ring, and always on the lookout for something to freshen up the act.

Of course, not every politician is good at it. I'm sure Prime Minister Clement Attlee was not a great joke-cracker and Margaret Thatcher found it notoriously difficult. But woe betide any young politician who thinks it's some unnecessary frippery. Indeed, I've witnessed some of them on the Labour side, who attend a constituency fundraising event, make a perfectly solid and earnest speech, and then wonder afterwards why the audience seemed so flat and unappreciative, and why they never get invited back. They soon learn.

And the truth is the bar is pretty low for politicians. People expect to be bored by your speeches, so showing just a bit of effort to entertain or enthuse the audience is normally all it takes to get them onside. Whisper it quietly, but almost none of the jokes we tell are actually, well, funny.

Take Gordon's conference speech in 2002, made two days after it was revealed that Edwina Currie and John Major had conducted an affair while he was prime minister. Gordon had to make some kind of joke about it, but was also very prudish about saying anything too salacious. We agonised over what he should say and worked through literally hundreds of options, finally deciding that he would start his speech with the simple exclamation: 'The Tories! What will they get up to next?' It brought the house down. Like I say, the humour bar is pretty low.

The amount of time spent searching for the right joke for the right occasion was one of the biggest surprises for me when I first entered politics back in 1994, and it was especially surprising to me that as substantial and serious a figure as Gordon Brown would spend so much time thinking about punchlines.

On my very first day, I was due to meet him for breakfast in the Atrium restaurant to talk about our work plan for the period ahead. But when I arrived, it turned out I was his second breakfast meeting of the day. His first was with the then little-known author and scriptwriter John O'Farrell and his colleague John Langdon, who had been tasked with working out topical joke lines for an upcoming speech.

I was taken aback that the Shadow Chancellor should have as part of his wider advisory team not just economists, political advisers and spin doctors, but also professional comic writers. But they were a godsend. Before any speaking event Gordon would write down five or six thoughts and fax them off. A day or so later a long list of lines would arrive. Some of them totally unusable, some of them not particularly funny, but one or two absolutely golden. And as a politician, that's usually all you need.

★

In politics, humour plays a number of roles, depending on the situation you're in – a business speech, a party conference audience, a House of Commons debate or a small political gathering.

When making a business speech, what you're trying to do is just convey an impression of yourself – relaxed, self-deprecating, with a good sense of humour – and make a connection with your audience. I learned my craft by watching Gordon Brown speaking to business audiences in the mid-1990s, when building bridges was vital in his job as a modernising Shadow Chancellor. The ice-breaking wisecracks Gordon would tell almost became more important than whatever pro-enterprise rhetoric he was planning to say.

The first joke I ever heard him tell was a real old stalwart of the after-dinner speaking circuit. He thanked the chair for the very kind introduction and then said it was in marked contrast to a week ago, where that night's chair had turned to him and said: 'Would you like to speak now or shall we let them enjoy themselves a little bit longer?' It raised a smile, was nicely self-deprecating, lowered expectations for the rest of the speech, and away he went.

He had a similar ice-breaker where he'd say he hoped to be brief, and would not make the mistake he'd made as a newly elected MP when the chair at a pensioners' lunch had asked him to speak for 'forty-five minutes' on the subject of pensions and the economy, something he had found a bit of a stretch but succeeded in doing, even if the audience looked rather bored by the end. The chair turned to him as he finally took his seat and rasped: 'What part of four to five minutes did you not understand?'

As a devotee of American politics, Gordon had a neat habit of pinching well-established jokes from the US Congressional circuit which British audiences probably wouldn't have heard before. When he was in a pre-speech tizzy about not having any jokes to open with, we'd just say as a default: 'Do your "Alexander Haig" . . . then your "Ronald Reagan" . . . then your "Henry Ford".' That shorthand would give him five minutes' material at the start of a speech.

His favourite was 'The Texas Oilman', the made-up story supposedly told by a speaker who had come onstage in the session before Gordon at an American conference, and had been introduced as a man who had made a million dollars from the oil industry in Texas. The man got to his feet, thanked the chair, but said: 'Just to clarify, it wasn't Texas, it was Oklahoma; it wasn't oil, it was gas; it wasn't me, it was my brother; and he didn't make it, he lost it.'

As I say, it wouldn't win any Perrier Awards – even the best political jokes don't read well on the page – but it was absolutely guaranteed to get two good laughs every time, and if even a few people at the CBI or the Institute of Directors thought that Gordon actually was sharing stages in America with oil moguls, it wasn't the worst impression to leave with them.

When speaking to Labour audiences, both the subject and intention of Gordon's jokes were very different. They all seemed to revolve around Donald Dewar and various stalwarts of the Scottish trade union movement, usually engaged in comical but borderline criminal activities or reflecting on the deprivation of their youth, and – while Gordon never touched blue jokes – were always a little risqué.

Again, there was something very smart about Gordon's

choice of jokes. Speaking to English Labour or union audiences, those Scottish anecdotes served two purposes: first, the audience wouldn't have heard them before, so were more likely to laugh; and second, they'd see Gordon as steeped in Labour traditions and folklore, at one with some of the legends of past battles against the Tories.

So I had a lot of time to study Gordon's great successes – and struggles – with political humour before I embarked on my own. However, my very first after-dinner speech was a bit of a nightmare, a black-tie event at the local Chamber of Commerce. I had some long-forgotten joke about Tony Blair and Sven-Göran Eriksson in a phone box, which got absolutely no response and in retrospect was probably a bit overambitious.

One thing I learned that night, though, is if what you think is your best joke doesn't work, for goodness' sake don't persevere with numbers two and three; just get on to the serious stuff and get offstage. The audience then sat in silence throughout my long and typewritten speech on 'Full Employment and the Regional Economy of West Yorkshire', and gave me a brief round of polite applause when I sat down. However, what followed was even worse: a proper 'comedian' who told a stream of offensive jokes which left the audience appalled. And while sitting there wondering whether to walk out, it dawned on me that I could use this story to my advantage in future, especially as events delivered me a good 'after-line'.

As we sat at the top table towards the end of the evening, I said to the comedian: 'Tough audience tonight,' and taking a long drag from his cigarette, he said: 'Tough? I've been doing this gig for fifteen years, and that's the hardest it's ever been.'

'Sorry about that,' I said. 'I wasn't exactly the best warm-up act.' To which he replied with a withering look: 'Sonny, after you, they should have laughed at anything.'

I've told that story many times since at the start of my speeches, coupled with a small invention: 'I knew it was going really badly for the comedian when one of the business folk shouted out from the back of the room: "Bring back Ed Balls."'

Like Gordon, I tried to build up a strong stable of reliable jokes for business and Labour audiences, and after a while, my advisers would be able to say to me the same kind of thing I'd say to him in the past: 'Do "The Economist" . . . then "Frank McGinty" . . . then "Bob Nipple".'

Indeed, after a few years as the compère for the annual Cooperative Party reception at the Labour Party Conference, my willingness to tell my old jokes on more than one occasion reached such renown that people would call out requests for their favourites, and then announce the punchline along with me.

Of course, there are experts on joke writing and humour who can tell you exactly why some jokes work and others don't, and what characteristics you need for a good line. I'm afraid I've never had quite that degree of sophisticated understanding, but I knew the key was building up suspense and tension so the audience laughs out of relief as much as anything. I would like to think I'm good at recognising a funny line when I hear one and able to deliver one too.

To that end, nothing beat having my own experience – something confusing or embarrassing or straight-up funny – that would become my own original and, most importantly, new joke. Some people collect stamps or butterflies; politicians collect jokes, and the most prized item is something both original and unique.

One of those came out of a real-life experience at the twentieth-anniversary dinner for the Chief Rabbi. HRH the Prince of Wales was the lead speaker and Vernon Coaker, Jim Murphy, Caroline Flint, Yvette and I were all seated at one table to represent the Shadow Cabinet.

But next to Yvette was a man none of us recognised, who engaged her in intense conversation for the duration of the dinner. 'Who was that guy?' I asked her afterwards. She said it was Prince Charles' royal protection officer, and they'd been going round the houses for the last hour about how to tackle terrorism and the impact of the courts on policing.

Towards the end of their chat, he'd said: 'You seem very up on these issues, but if you don't mind me asking – who are you? And why are you here?' Yvette said that she was the Shadow Home Secretary. The security officer said, 'Oh, I see, so you're all politicians?' and then, pointing at me, said: 'Yes, I *thought* I recognised Nick Griffin.'

Once Yvette told the protection officer who I was, she also pointed out that Nick Griffin was unlikely to be invited to a dinner in honour of the Chief Rabbi. When she told me that story, I knew it was going to be gold dust for me on the speech circuit, and it's gone down well ever since.

★

If there was one area where Gordon failed to use humour effectively, it was – unfortunately – at Prime Minister's Questions in the House of Commons, where it is such a powerful and important weapon. Obviously, it's easier for the opposition in PMQs. Standing in as acting party leader, Vince Cable had his 'from Stalin to Mr Bean' jibe at Gordon ready for a week, and expecting Gordon to come up with something equally funny and cutting on the spot was nigh on impossible.

The alternative way he attempted to deal with those jibes – by trying to rise above them and remain serious – is incredibly hard, especially when you're the subject of such derision and hilarity, but he found it difficult to do anything else. It was partly a question of atmosphere and noise. He was much more effective at using humour in his outings at Treasury Questions and in debates as Shadow Chancellor and Chancellor, but as I know myself, when you've got hundreds of MPs baying and howling at you, any ability to 'think on your feet' and have a lightness of touch can go out the window.

I worked hard on introducing humour into my House of Commons appearances. The most enjoyable were the extended debates that followed Budget statements, where I could easily be on my feet for thirty or forty minutes if I took lots of interventions from the Tory benches. The trick was to have a central theme to my retorts to the Tory MPs, but personalised to every one of them, and have them ready to deploy as they each took their turn. I think the other side actually enjoyed the effort I'd gone to, and there were times when you could see them relishing the chance to make an intervention just so they could see what line I'd prepared for them.

One such occasion came after the 2015 Budget speech when George Osborne referenced Shakespeare as he announced funding to celebrate the anniversary of Agincourt. I did a section of my speech using quotes from Shakespeare to characterise the Budget and George Osborne's 'vaulting ambition', and – as expected – some of the Tory MPs took the bait.

Erudite souls that they are, they intervened quoting Shakespeare in Osborne's defence or in criticism of me, but I had a number of retorts at my fingertips befitting each type of MP who might speak – 'People say that empty vessels make the loudest noise' and the like – so I got a good laugh all round whenever I came back at them, apparently spontaneously.

One genuinely spontaneous exchange came in another Budget debate when Matthew Hancock – the Tory MP for West Suffolk – invited me, as a fan of Norwich City, to welcome a government road-building project which would make access to Norwich easier.

I stood up and roared back, with mock indignation, that he'd got the name wrong. 'It's *Premiership* Norwich City . . . which is more than can be said for any team from *Suffolk*' – the county home of our rivals Ipswich Town spat out as if it were a post-watershed swear word. 'Premiership' got a mild cheer, but 'Suffolk' got a big belly laugh, even from Hancock, and I think what people especially liked about it was that we'd gone from a relatively sober debate about fiscal policy to a full-blown explosion of football rivalry in the space of ten seconds.

But in the House of Commons, the best moments – the equivalent of that Nick Griffin story – are when you can use humour to get to the heart of a live political issue, in a way that not only makes people laugh but makes headlines, Vince Cable's 'Mr Bean' jibe being a prime example.

I had one when I was Education Secretary and Michael Gove had been mocking some of the publicly available GCSE exam questions for being too easy. So I hit back using the same exam papers to ask him a series of science and maths questions and goading him over why he wouldn't stand up and answer them. The many thousands of hits that exchange got on YouTube suggests I made my point.

After the 2012 Budget, which had been stupidly trailed in advance by the Liberal Democrats as a 'Robin Hood Budget' despite it announcing the new 'granny tax' and cuts to tax credits, at the same time the 50p tax rate was cut, I was able to demonstrate it was the exact opposite, concluding my analysis with the lines: 'The Chancellor is not Robin Hood, he's the Sheriff of Nottingham. And as for jobs and growth, he couldn't give a Friar Tuck.'

I had to rehearse that several times to make sure the intonation of 'Friar Tuck' was exactly right, which meant that lots of MPs and journalists in the Chamber only half listening at that point reacted in quite a startled way: 'Did he just say what I think he said?'

It made the opening segment of the 10 p.m. news on ITV and summed up exactly the message I wanted to get across about the Budget, so I was chuffed, but my favourite aspect of it was looking across the dispatch box to see Vince Cable head down trying to hide his smile, while George Osborne looked plaintively up at the deputy Speaker, like a boxer appealing to the ref after catching a punch below the belt.

★

Besides external speeches, party events and the House of Commons, jokes and funny anecdotes also play a crucial and underrated role in binding together the members of a political team.

As a Cabinet minister and then Shadow Chancellor, I always made sure we had good Christmas parties for my ministerial team, my advisers and campaign staff, so we could all laugh at the old jokes, along with some karaoke. It was an important binding ritual that I had learned almost twenty years earlier.

From before 1997, it was my job to organise the annual Christmas party for Gordon and his inner circle of political advisers in a Westminster restaurant or later up in the Downing Street flat, sometimes the one time in the whole year where he'd stop and thank all of us collectively for the punishing and occasionally painful hours we put in.

As well as dinner and Secret Santa, and the handing out of presents from Gordon and Sarah, and from Sue Nye – usually lurid but fashionable ties – there were also certain customs that became established over the years, most sacred of all the singing of 'Jerusalem' (twice) complete with the elaborate acting-out of the lyrics – shooting arrows, wielding spears, and so on.

If that sounds awful, it at least served as the best possible induction into the team for relative newcomers. You lost your inhibitions pretty quickly when Ian Austin was shouting at you: 'What the hell do you call that? You're supposed to be riding a chariot!'

But after the singing came the best part of the evening: the telling of all our favourite old Gordon Brown jokes, which – after a bit of cajoling and begging from the rest of us – he would finally agree to perform. 'Japanese Admiral', 'Donald Dewar's car radio', 'George Brown and the Papal Nuncio'. Jokes he'd told a hundred times, but at the Christmas party, a combination of our heckling and his hysterics usually meant he'd fluff the punchlines, which was far funnier than if he'd got them right.

Those were always very happy nights – probably the only times I routinely saw Gordon over the years when he didn't have another care in the world, no issue that 'I need to talk to you about', as he'd always say. But the humour and the jokes were also needed on much less happy occasions.

In the final hour of his premiership in Downing Street, we'd all been gathered by Sue to be there at what looked likely to be the end. Gordon was due to speak to a dithering Nick Clegg before deciding to go to Buckingham Palace to resign.

Gathered in the room were Sarah, Sue, Ed Miliband, myself, Alastair Campbell, Andrew Adonis, Peter Mandelson, Stewart Wood, and some of Gordon's newer political advisers. And as we sat waiting for Nick Clegg to call, I thought we should fill the time not with long silences and slack conversation, but by going back to what we knew best.

So we spent a good chunk of that final hour retelling some of the old Gordon Brown stories. We told the old jokes and laughed uproariously, Gordon took the call from Clegg, and then we stood in the private office as he thanked his team, and left Downing Street for the final time with Sarah and the boys.

In a place where Gordon's voice had bounced off the walls for thirteen years – usually booming, arguing or barking instructions – the last it heard from him was his great guffaw of laughter.

PART THREE
Learning The Hard Way

In life and politics you often learn more from the mistakes you make or observe than from successes. These chapters look at the lessons I learned from some of the toughest issues and toughest times I faced in politics.

17

Assumptions

_____

*Things rarely turn out as you expect – so how do you challenge
yourself to challenge the consensus?*

If you ever doubt that policy decisions taken in Whitehall
can change the course of people's lives, take a look at the
fallout from the infamous 75p increase in the state pension,
which caused us so much political grief back in 1999.

In 1990, the average income of a pensioner in Britain was
30 per cent lower than that of a non-pensioner. Today, it is
higher – a truly remarkable shift, and one which goes against
all historical convention.

There are many factors which have driven that change,
including long-term stagnation in wages for working people;
but very high on that list is the way in which successive
governments have fled in the opposite direction, having seen
the mess we got into over pensions in 1999.

And that shift sums up for me one of the most important lessons I learned during my time in politics: many of the long-term assumptions you have will almost certainly be proved wrong.

The 'decision' itself was a complete accident. Our policy was simply that the pension would rise in line with inflation each year. We never sat around debating whether 75p was an acceptable amount. But when the annual inflation figures emerged in September that year, the figure of 1.1 per cent dictated a miserly rise the following April, which pensioner groups leapt on with understandable outrage.

Going ahead with such a small rise was a mistake, but not one any of us knew we were making at the time. It came as a particular shock to Tony and Gordon. I would regularly see the self-appointed pensioners' champion, Dame Barbara Castle, wrap them round her little finger in side meetings at party conference. And they were both in awe of Jack Jones, the former trade union leader and by then head of the National Pensioners Convention. So to incur the wrath of not just one but two of their beloved grandees was a night-mare for Tony and Gordon, and they were equally baffled as to how they had got themselves into such a mess.

What's followed has been fifteen years of ever more generous state benefits being given to pensioners and, alongside that, a morbid fear passed from Gordon Brown to Alistair Darling to George Osborne of making another 75p mistake – hence the immunity of pensioner benefits from any of the cost-cutting that has come from the financial crisis.

The cumulative impact of those policies over twenty-five years has turned median incomes around to the extent that the average pensioner now has a higher annual income than the average working-age person, even though many of them will be at a stage of life where the kids have left home and the mortgage is paid off.

Back in the early 1990s, I would never have believed that the rise in pensioner incomes would be one of the trends of our time. In fact, I assumed the exact opposite – that, because of the ageing population, we would be in a continuous battle against rising pensioner poverty.

In 2015, I returned to the Kennedy School at Harvard, twenty-five years after taking my master's degree there, and it was really instructive to recall the assumptions we made back then and to realise quite how many of them had proved to be wrong.

Take security: in the early 1990s, the assumption was that the great security threat of our age would be other former Soviet bloc countries following Yugoslavia into violent separation, a process made more dangerous by the continuing disintegration of Russia's power and the risk of its nuclear weapons falling into the hands of rogue states and separatist movements.

We would also have anticipated escalating conflicts with power-hungry, tyrannical regimes in Iraq, Iran, Libya, Syria and elsewhere, with state-sponsored terrorism expected to remain the main threat from the Middle East and North Africa. A quarter of a century on, the main security threats we face actually come from a newly emboldened Russia, and the rise of Daesh exploiting power vacuums in Iraq, Libya and Syria, with Iran one of our most important allies against them.

Back then, one clear economic assumption we all had was that Japan was and would remain the biggest threat to America's global economic superiority. In 1989, I took a class with 150 other Kennedy School students taught by Robert Reich, a Democrat economist and thinker who later became Bill Clinton's Secretary of Labor. He asked us which outcome we'd prefer for the next twenty years: America growing by 3 per cent per year and Japan growing by 4 per cent, or both economies growing by 2 per cent. The vast majority of the class voted for the latter, judging that falling behind Japan was a worse outcome than having lower growth. I was in the minority, and was rather shocked that the largely American group of students would rather be worse off than see Japan pull ahead.

The point is, of course, that no one was thinking or talking about China at all as an economic superpower. And since then things have reversed. Japan is stuck in its second decade of stagnation, and faces severe long-term challenges over its shrinking working-age population, while China quickly emerged in the years after I left the Kennedy School as America's main economic rival – much to everyone's surprise.

At that time, we were also just beginning to debate the impact of globalisation. The assumption I and others made then was that globalisation would result in a huge increase in trade, with goods for our markets being increasingly produced more cheaply overseas, alongside free movement of capital, with investment that might have been made in British factories going instead to Brazil or Hong Kong.

Those were predictable trends we were right to worry about, but what no one foresaw was the extent to which globalisation would also become about the movement of people – the wealthy, professional super-rich hopping from city to city, and the brave, working poor searching for a better life – and that debates about immigration would become so critical and divisive on both sides of the Atlantic.

Put simply, the basic assumption about globalisation was that British people would risk losing their jobs to cheaper competition from overseas, not that they would feel threatened by competition from immigrants for jobs in this country. That was badly wrong, and until as recently as 2004 and the expansion of the European Union, we didn't see it.

A related assumption was that increasing advances in technology would impact the wages and jobs mainly of unskilled workers. What we didn't see was that the squeeze on wages and jobs would affect skilled workers too, that technology would pose as much of a challenge to the jobs and wages of the middle classes as the working classes, and perhaps more so. Think about modern banks or airlines: they still need security guards, cleaners and drivers, but they need far fewer old-fashioned clerks doing the sophisticated work that computers can do.

Looking at what has happened to the number of skilled and unskilled jobs in the UK over the past two decades, you observe an absolute decline in the number of middle-skilled jobs, while there's been an absolute increase in the number of high-skilled and low-skilled jobs, something that helps to explain the slowdown in the growth of median wages across many developed economies, and the current political anger about the status quo and today's politicians across Middle England and Middle America alike.

One other economic assumption I made that turned out completely wrong was about the nature of the threat to economic stability. Twenty-five years ago, I believed that the biggest threat had been, and would continue to be, governments getting it wrong on inflation. It was a key driver behind our push to make the Bank of England independent in 1997, and give it policy control over interest rates.

When the 2008 financial crisis hit, inflation was low and stable in Britain and all over the world. That wasn't the problem; it was a total failure of adequate regulation and control of the world's banks, and specifically the health of their investments. Back in the early 1990s, we were shocked to discover that banks could be brought down by the desperate actions of one rogue trader; we never thought that the whole banking system would go into meltdown as a result of sober decisions taken around a boardroom table to invest, often off-balance sheet, in the US subprime housing market.

And then there are the media and politics. I assumed back then that newspapers would continue to be the most important drivers of the political agenda, and that – for a politician – the key challenges each day were to influence the papers and news programmes, and shape the way that a story was told on the *Today* programme or the ten o'clock news.

I had no idea how 24-hour news and social media would change the dynamics of how stories would reach the public, and that actually the challenge for the politician would become not just getting their decisions right and getting their lines out there, but doing all that as quickly as possible, and never allowing themselves to get behind the curve.

And then there is politics itself: by the beginning of the 1990s we assumed that the Militant Tendency had been permanently rooted out of the Labour Party as a result of Neil Kinnock's leadership, and by the end of the 1990s we assumed that New Labour was here to stay.

Ed Miliband was the first Labour leader since Michael Foot to believe that Labour's route to power was to move to the left; but even as late as 2013 when the calamitous changes to the method of electing the Labour leader were enacted, even so-called Blairites backed the changes, believing that weakening the role of MPs and handing the decision over to party members would move the party towards the centre ground. How naive that looks in retrospect.

Of all those assumptions I got wrong – the nature of the future security threat, the rise of China and the dangerous dependence of the world economy on its demand, the migratory effects of globalisation, the impact of technology advances on middle-income workers, the pace of the news cycle, and Labour's lurch back to the left – none are close to being resolved.

While some of those things were inescapable trends, those of us with any influence could have prepared better for them if they had been anticipated earlier, and in some cases – such as the rise of Daesh, uncontrolled immigration from the EU accession countries, or the election of Jeremy Corbyn – avoided them entirely.

That makes it all the more important for politicians to challenge their own assumptions. When they ask themselves 'What if I'm wrong?', it is not an indication of wobbling or weakness; it is a sign they are prepared to properly think through the consequences of their decisions before making them – an essential quality in any leader.

That's also why it's important for politicians to have people around them who are capable of challenging their thinking, and who require them to explain the views under-pinning their decisions. Sometimes it's exactly what you need to bring your own doubts to the fore, and it's why I always insisted on any major decisions being taken not on paper but round a table, to prompt those discussions. That was how I managed the Budget process for my first seven years in the Treasury, and also how I ran the Department for Children, Schools and Families, once I persuaded the civil servants that I genuinely wanted to hear what they thought.

Ironically, if there is one body you would have expected to have those kinds of honest, open debates about the direction of policy and the assumptions underpinning it, it was the

Cabinet. But while it was a huge honour to be a Cabinet minister, the meetings were, in retrospect, often a waste of time, and a huge drag, particularly when Yvette and I had to rush to get the children dressed, fed and out of the house. I am sure there were many mornings when we looked a little bedraggled as we walked up Downing Street.

The meetings usually featured one Cabinet minister – occasionally me – talking at length about a very important but, probably on that day, second-order issue. There was no real discussion or deliberation – that tended to come in Cabinet subcommittees with only the affected ministers present – and in an age of texting and BlackBerries, lots of people present were clearly more focused on going through their inbox than they were on listening to what was being said. If you wanted the active support of Cabinet colleagues for something, you had to ring them all personally outside of the weekly meeting.

I often wondered why Gordon, who couldn't abide wasting time in pointless meetings, didn't impose more control on Cabinet discussions and ensure that the key issues of the day were properly debated, rather than just presiding over what seemed to be a series of fairly meaningless presentations. But even Gordon treated Cabinet meetings almost as an orchestrated chore to get through; like meeting foreign dignitaries, it was perhaps one of the occasions where he felt required to act out the role of prime minister, rather than get on with the job.

Even worse, Cabinet didn't just fail to debate prospective policies properly; it also stayed silent when we'd clearly got something wrong, instead of working out collectively what to do about it. And that wasn't only Gordon's failing; that's also how it was back when Tony was at the centre of the table, and the 75p pension row was going on.

When I look back to that debate, I recall right at the outset hearing the 'media lines to take': we were simply following the inflation-linked policy, and would not deviate from that policy purely on the basis of one month's inflation figures. Even while nodding along, I remember feeling queasy, and worrying whether we were getting ourselves into unnecessary trouble. In that situation we needed someone in the room asking: 'What if we're just wrong on this?' In retrospect, I know I should have been asking that question myself, not waiting for others to do so.

When I returned to Harvard shortly after the general election in 2015 that was one of the lessons I tried to teach. I told my students how many of the guiding assumptions I had made at their age had been wrong, and challenged them to reflect on their own most strongly held assumptions about the world and economy.

There were many interesting responses, and you could sense the chill in the room as these young people shared things which they knew to be 'true', and then asked themselves inwardly 'What if I'm wrong?', no more so than when one student said: 'None of us in this room will ever have to fight in a world war like our grandfathers did.' Let's hope he's right.

18

Risks

Sometimes leadership is about boldness, sometimes caution – so what does taking the plunge really mean?

I always felt guilty hearing about the dawn phone calls other people had to take from Gordon Brown. I learned very early on that the only way to ensure a manageable start to the day was to leave my phone and pager as far away as possible from my bedroom.

The one call I do vividly remember taking was on a Friday morning in October 2007. It was the Friday following the Tory Party conference, and decision day for Gordon on whether or not to call a snap election, only a few months after becoming prime minister. He was in London, but I was up in Yorkshire, hoping to get some extra photographs for my leaflets, which I needed to have ready for what by then looked pretty certain to be an imminent general election.

I'd decided on an early start, and planned to drive around my constituency with a photographer and a bundle of different clothes and ties in the back of the car, taking pictures in different locations and meeting different people. Back then it was a necessary part of the process: no politician could spend five years walking around with a professional photographer in tow, and, in the pre-iPhone era, the pictures your staff took every week for the website didn't usually pass the 'professional' test.

While I was getting ready at six thirty, I got a call from Gordon. I was heartened to hear him say: 'I've thought hard, and we're going to go for it.' I said that at this point there really was no choice. It was not only the right thing to do, but we'd marched so far up the hill, there was no taking the party, the media and, most importantly, the public all the way down again.

By then, it seemed pretty clear to me: the 'risk' of going for an early general election was nowhere near as risky as deciding not to.

The election march had really started a month before that phone call. In early September, Gordon summoned me, Ed Miliband and Douglas Alexander to meet with Spencer Livermore and Bob Shrum at Chequers to discuss his upcoming conference speech, his first as party leader. We were all in buoyant moods. Gordon was having a really good start as leader, from handling the Glasgow airport terrorist attack and a foiled car bomb in his first week, to managing the

latest foot-and-mouth outbreak with huge skill and attention to detail.

He was not only proving his leadership skills, but was also
benefiting greatly from the presentational contrast with
David Cameron, who was at that point floundering around
fighting with his own party on grammar schools, and
getting into difficulties with his depiction of a 'broken
society' at a time when national feeling was on the up.

Going into September, Labour had a double-digit opinion
poll lead, and Gordon's first conference speech was a chance
to really put his stamp on the country. We thought that
the speech was the purpose of the meeting at Chequers, but
the conversation quickly took a different turn.

Spencer and Bob asked in a roundabout way whether we
should discuss going for an early general election. After all,
there was rampant speculation in the press that he would be
mad not to, given the poll lead and the opportunity to seek his
own mandate. It wasn't clear if that was the sole reason the
media were speculating – given the split in the Conservatives
at the time, an early election would have given the Tory rebels
a reason to get rid of Cameron at the earliest opportunity.

Despite the speculation, the conversation at Chequers still
came as a surprise. Gordon personally had shown no appetite
for election talk in his early period in the job, and the people I
was closest to in his inner circle had never mentioned it.

The truth was, he'd been head down in the job, and I think
it came out of the blue for him as well. He reacted rather
testily, arguing that if 'you guys' wanted an early election,
we ought to have got onto the appropriate war footing in
August, rather than disappearing on holiday – which was

rather a Gordonesque thing to say, especially as he'd been on holiday himself for only a day before returning to deal with foot-and-mouth. While he was in the Treasury and Number Ten, he always saw holidays as morally slightly reprehensible, other than for maybe a maximum of two or three days at a time. But the fact was that we had come out of August with a big opinion poll lead and that frankly meant we were already on the right footing.

Ed Miliband and I were cautious about the idea as we weren't sure that Gordon had really got his pitch quite right. The presentation was fine, but we hadn't broken through on the substance yet or set out any kind of proper vision. Spencer and Bob were much more enthusiastic and Douglas was keen to keep the option open. So it was agreed to commission some more detailed opinion poll work in the marginal constituencies where any election would be decided; and then we got on to talking about the speech.

By the time we arrived at the Labour Party conference a fortnight later, the speculation about an early election was at fever pitch. The opinion poll lead was strengthening and Douglas did an interview for the *Guardian*, from which the story became 'Labour on election footing'. As head of election campaigning, he certainly wanted to be ready if the election was called, but the headline just fuelled the fire.

Inadvertently, I ended up doing the same the following day. I was up to do the interview on *The World This Weekend*, following Gordon's Sunday interview on *Marr* where he had batted away the speculation about whether an announcement was coming in a rather stern way. When asked about his response, I said the key issue was setting out the divide on the choice of policy between a Labour future and a Conservative future, and we would be doing that work and setting out our ideas in the coming weeks and months.

Immediately, the words 'and months' – combined with Gordon's interview – were seized on by the media as a clear signal that an early election was off. But because they knew it was very much top of the internal agenda, Gordon's media team spent the afternoon explaining that hadn't been the intention of the two interviews, that the option was still open and that no decisions had been taken. It felt either chaotic or as if we were all playing games.

In truth, I went into the conference still cautious about whether or not an early election was the right thing to do. But that week, I gradually became persuaded. Politics is about momentum and, at that point, we were on a runaway train; and I was also becoming increasingly worried that this was as good as it was going to get.

Over a series of breakfasts, lunches and dinners with journalists during the week, I could sense a residual hostility to Gordon and to Labour, not least in the wake of Northern Rock's collapse, but also from those pushing for an election to secure a new Tory leader. From their point of view, Gordon's media honeymoon was a means to an end: let him win his mandate; let him exhaust his burst of popularity; and then let David Davis, Liam Fox or whoever else they had in mind destroy him.

It started to infect my thinking and bleed into my

conversations and interviews with the media. On the eve of my first party conference speech as a member of the Cabinet, I was at a drinks reception with Nick Robinson, then the BBC's political editor, and he asked me whether Gordon would take the risk of going for an early election. Shaped by the lunches and dinners of recent days, I said: 'The interesting question now is whether it is more risky to go for an early election or more risky to play things long and hope that things strengthen rather than become more difficult.'

Just a few hours later, I was in a poky hotel room being interviewed by Sarah Montague for the *Today* programme, and – whether she'd had a tip from Nick I don't know – she asked me exactly the same question: would Gordon 'gamble on an early election?' And I said words to a similar effect – the issue is where the risk really lies. It was loose of me to turn a conversation over a drink into a soundbite on the radio, and the media interpreted this as yet another signal, and in my case a shift, of Labour's thinking. If they weren't writing hard stories about an early election before, they certainly were afterwards – and Gordon's office weren't correcting them this time.

Reports began to circulate of money being raised, leaflets commissioned and election agents and regional directors being briefed to be ready to go. Like every other Labour MP, I certainly took the message that I should be prepared, and driving back from the conference that day, I rang my constituency team up in Yorkshire to say that we needed to get on with planning our leaflets and recruiting volunteers because they were going to be needed sooner rather than later.

The following day, we had a message that Gordon wanted

everyone to come again to Chequers to talk through the decision – with the same core group, plus others from his close circle like Ian Austin, Sue Nye and Damian McBride. The idea was to have a discussion round the table about whether to call the early election. But it wasn't a debate – it was a planning session. Douglas explained in detail the work he was doing to get things ready, and the conversation he was having with the unions about being ready for a quick mail drop. Despite my enthusiasm, I decided to play devil's advocate, given no one else was doing so, raising some of the reasons why it might be a good idea to delay. I was conscious that Gordon – rather ominously – seemed the least convinced person there and said he wanted to wait and see the polling.

The next day, George Osborne pulled a rabbit out of the hat, with his announcement at the Tory conference in Manchester to raise the inheritance tax threshold to £1 million. It was an issue Gordon had been very worried about for some time, but – based on the polling we'd done – I wasn't convinced it was enough to turn the outcome of the election; not so long as we continued to demonstrate we too were on the side of aspiration and people getting on in life, but targeted our measures at the vast majority of voters, rather than the minority who would benefit from an inheritance tax cut.

Nevertheless, there's no doubt that the positive headlines the announcement received spooked things within Labour and Gordon's inner circle that week. And things were made worse when Gordon made a visit to Iraq to see the troops that same week and got a media roasting for the implication that he was trying to undermine the Tory conference.

Despite all of that, the opinion polling remained relatively strong and the early election had become an assumption. Osborne's announcement wasn't seen as a masterstroke at the time and no one remotely thought the Tories were in a fit state to fight an early general election. All it seemed he had done was announce one of his key manifesto pledges, unify a Tory Party that had been ready to tear itself apart in Manchester, and given the Tories a much needed polling boost which at least indicated the election wouldn't be a complete walkover. But it didn't fundamentally change things, and needn't have done so, which was why I was reassured to get a 6.30 a.m. phone call that Friday telling me we were going for it. But as I made my way around my constituency, I began to receive a number of text messages from London saying things were rapidly changing, and, eventually, that I should speak to Gordon as a matter of urgency.

I got back to our house in Yorkshire in the middle of the afternoon and rang him. He said: 'It's off, we're not going for it.' He explained that the marginal-seat opinion polling that had been done earlier in the week had been much more negative than the polling experts had expected. While it suggested we would keep our majority, it might come down from the high sixties to the high thirties. And the general feeling he said was that this was too big a risk.

He kept saying: 'They've changed their minds. They're telling me we shouldn't go for it now.' He sounded in agony. I argued with him, saying it was too difficult to change course now, expectations were too high, everyone was ready to go, and the inheritance tax thing wasn't so strong. But faced with Gordon telling me that all of his other closest political advisers were taking a different view, and swayed as he always was by the pollsters, I folded, saying: 'Well, OK, if that's what you've decided.' He said yes, and asked if I'd come back down to London the following day to help with the announcement.

In retrospect, I should have said: 'I'll come down to London, and let me talk to you and the others face-to-face before we make a final decision.' But part of me felt I was paying the price for becoming slightly semi-detached since having my own department to run; I didn't feel like I'd be able to turn everyone around. I just said I'd be there in the morning.

I travelled down early the next day with a growing sense of foreboding. My mood only darkened when I got to Downing Street. The meeting was like a wake held by a particularly acrimonious family – simultaneously mournful and suspicious. In between moments of blaming himself, Gordon was lashing out at Spencer simply for doing his job as a pollster and Damian for trying and failing to keep a confused and restless media onside. The atmosphere inside Number Ten was poisonous. Everyone was watching their back, fearing they were going to get the blame for one of the biggest disasters in modern political history. And the easiest way to avoid blame in that situation is to make sure it's shifted to others.

As a result, the next twenty-four hours were a hugely damaging mess. Gordon's pre-recorded interview with Andrew Marr leaked out on the Saturday afternoon, the other broadcasters were furious they had not been given the story properly, the Sunday newspapers were full of anonymous briefings about who was to blame, and when the Marr interview finally played on the Sunday morning, Gordon's claim that he hadn't looked at the polls in deciding whether to call the election was not remotely credible.

Damian has since admitted failing to properly handle the way the announcement came out, but I felt Spencer was very harshly treated. He had simply told the truth at every stage to Gordon about what the polls were saying and whether it was the right or wrong time to go for it. The way he was dealt with on that day, and subsequently sidelined, was deeply unfair.

And while I won't add my suspicions as to who did what to all the other versions that are out there, I can only say that I categorically never told anyone to brief on my behalf or against anyone else, and did no such briefing myself. Nor did I give anyone nods and winks encouraging them to do so. Apart from anything, I was utterly confident no blame could be attached to me, so I felt outside and rather appalled by the frenzy of back-stabbing and score-settling that followed in the Sunday papers.

But if there's one important lesson those twenty-four hours taught me, it's that the press feeds off paranoia, and anyone who gives in to the fear that everyone's out to get them is actually doing themselves in. If you're that kind of politician or adviser, a journalist calls you up and says: 'The knives are out for you.' 'Whose knives?' 'I can't reveal my sources.' 'Right, well, let me tell you a thing or two.' And so the vicious circle begins.

On the most frenzied of days, the jackals in the media find it easy to pick off the weaker members of the herd, and that's what happened that dismal day in October, a day from which Gordon's premiership and the togetherness and trust of his closest advisers and confidants never recovered.

It's always important for any leader to take a range of advice from a range of people, and when it came to the election decision, Gordon certainly did that. But in the end, as a leader, you can't take the advice and follow the consensus; you have to hear a range of views and then decide for yourself what you really want to do. In Gordon's case, that probably meant killing the speculation as soon as it started, because I never believed he thought it was the right course.

That's the lesson for leaders, but there's a lesson for advisers as well. I was always seen as a cautionary influence around Gordon when we were at the Treasury, as was Ed Miliband. The then Permanent Secretary, Sir Andrew Turnbull, gave an interview to Larry Elliott early on in our time in the Treasury in which he said there were two types of advisers: amplifiers and absorbers. And the reason why the Treasury worked well in those years was that both Ed and I were absorbers who would not wind Gordon up but hold him back, make certain he was sure, get the evidence, test every issue.

But it's also important at times to say: 'You've got to act, you can't sit on this any longer, you've got to decide.' Our mistake was not to have said that sooner over the election in 2007, probably at that first Chequers meeting in September: 'Decide now. Go for it or shut it down.'

And in the end, my mistake was not saying to him more forcefully on the Friday afternoon what I'd said to Nick Robinson in Bournemouth: 'It's too late, the risks have switched.' Being an absorber may be about being cautious and careful, but you have to realise when delay and inaction are infinitely more dangerous than decision and boldness.

There's one period in my career where I faced the same sort of dilemma. For me it was important, but for the nation and the party much less so. It came three years later, following our general election defeat and Gordon's immediate resignation, when I put myself forward as a candidate to be the leader of the Labour Party.

I'd gone into the leadership election with my eyes open. I knew that I was well behind David Miliband, and that I would be seen as a continuation of the Gordon Brown era, which had just lost the election.

Indeed, when Yvette and I had discussed which one of us should run straight after the 2010 election – not in a Costa Coffee shop, as I joked at the time, but around our kitchen table – I was clear that if she wanted to go for it, then I would take a back seat. I knew it was a difficult time for me. But Yvette didn't want to run, she felt the children were too young and she wasn't ready. She agonised but she was clear: it was my turn this time, her turn next.

With me in the race, David was likely to get more traction as the agent of change, even if it was a change back to the leadership and politics of Tony Blair. What we didn't anticipate was that Ed Miliband would enter the race and take on his brother. It shifted the dynamic dramatically: I was the Brownite choice, and David was still the Blairite choice, but Ed was standing apart and presenting himself as the candidate for real change.

It simultaneously amused and annoyed me when Ed distanced himself by claiming that he was never part of New Labour. But it deeply angered me when, via his advisers, he briefed the media that I was responsible for a Brownite culture of spin, bullying and – ironically – anonymous media knifings that he wanted to escape from.

By the end of July, with Ed enjoying the momentum and his duel with David dominating the election narrative, it was clear that my campaign was going nowhere, even though I thought I was doing far more than either of them to roast the Tories in Parliament on the cancellation of Building Schools for the Future, and the increase in VAT.

But in media interviews, every question I was asked was about Gordon Brown, Tony Blair and the past. I'd been deserted by most of the unions who I'd hoped would support me. When the news came through at the end of July that Unison were backing Ed Miliband as well, and there were polls showing that I was headed for fifth place behind Andy Burnham and Diane Abbott, I was at my lowest ebb.

I did what Gordon did back in 2007, and consulted my friends and allies. Tom Watson, who had backed me, was clearly of the view that I should pull out and throw my weight behind Ed to stop David winning. My long-time friend Ian Austin was of the opposite view: he wanted me to pull out, but in order to support David.

Both of them made the same argument: that to struggle on and come last would be disastrous for my reputation and career, whereas pulling out and potentially delivering victory for the winner through my endorsement would put me in good stead for the future. It was the cautious, sensible option.

I talked to newly elected MP Michael Dugher and a number of others who said the same and, no surprise, a story soon appeared in the *Sunday Telegraph* and the *Sunday Mirror* claiming that close friends of mine were urging me to pull out, and that was what I was minded to do. The briefing was understandable. Even my closest allies wanted to smooth the path for me to pull out so I – and they – could be free to switch to other candidates.

There were others who felt differently. Charlie Whelan told me to stay in and fight, as did Damian, two loyal friends who went through life with their hands taped up and could never accept defeat. Yvette did what I should have done at the outset with Gordon and just asked me what I thought was right. And then there was my dad. I spoke to him the morning the *Sunday Telegraph* story broke. He said to me he was surprised to read it. He'd never known me pull out of anything before and he assumed that I wasn't going to do it this time either.

And as I weighed things up that Sunday morning, I looked at what was supposed to be the cautious move – withdrawing, admitting defeat, disappointing my team, my supporters, my friends and my dad – and thought: 'This isn't cautious at all, this is the riskiest thing I could possibly do.' Whereas the supposedly reckless and brave option – being myself, sticking to my guns and doing my best – was not only the right thing to do, it was less dangerous. I asked myself that basic question: 'Where does the risk really lie?' and there was only one answer. I went on Radio 4's *The World This Weekend* to say that the report of me pulling out was all nonsense, and that I was definitely carrying on because I had an important argument to make.

The next day we flew out for a short family holiday in America. And there – urged on by my campaign chief, Jim Knight, to get working on a 'big speech' – I thought: 'Right, you've decided to stay in – now show people why.' And while I was there, driving our camper van round New England, I constructed the words in my head that I'd deliver on my return – what became known as my Bloomberg speech.

It was easy enough to write. I argued that none of the fundamental problems in the world economy had been fixed, that George Osborne's premature decision to launch an austerity programme would backfire, and that we needed Labour to set out a radical economic alternative, not just go along with slightly diluted versions of the Tory position.

It was a defining moment for my leadership campaign, and for my political career. For the first time, it changed the media dynamic – which had been stuck in my past with Gordon – into a future where people asked: Is this the man to take on Osborne? When people commented afterwards that it was less a pitch for the leadership than a pitch to be Shadow Chancellor, I didn't mind a bit.

The speech took on a life of its own. It summed up the

unease that many economists felt about how quickly the major world economies were trying to pretend that the financial crisis hadn't happened. I even received overtures from intermediaries in both Miliband campaigns suggesting they might offer me the Shadow Chancellor job in return for me pulling out, though there were no formal offers, and I dismissed them as new versions of the risk I'd already rejected.

And when I came third in the leadership contest, behind the Miliband brothers, whose rivalry had dominated the contest, I felt vindicated, whether I eventually got the Shadow Chancellor job or not. A bronze medal feels infinitely better than stepping off the track. We'd lost, but I'd emerged stronger, and had moved on from the caricature that Ed Miliband's advisers had tried to paint. And I was very conscious I'd put into practice the lesson I learned from Gordon's calamitous decision in 2007 not to 'risk' an early election.

Sometimes, leadership is about being decisive; sometimes, it's about being careful. But you must never equate those terms with action and inaction. Whenever a big decision is required, never assume that one option is cautious and the other is bold. Ask yourself instead: 'Where does the risk really lie?'

19

Spin

_____

The media writes the first draft of history – so how do you stop them getting it wrong?

In February 2009, I awoke to a front page of the *Sun* saying that a twelve-year-old boy named Alfie had fathered a child with a fifteen-year-old girl. His cherubic face holding his supposed three-month-old daughter became an international sensation.

In terms of domestic politics, it was yet more evidence for those who were arguing that Britain's society was broken. David Cameron – aided at that time by his communications chief, Andy Coulson – was so eager to pile into that debate that he already had a comment piece lined up on this latest example of Britain's moral disintegration, which ran in the same edition of the *Sun* that carried the story.

'Looking into his bewildered eyes,' he said, 'I was both

heartbroken and deeply concerned . . . I applaud the *Sun* for bringing this to public attention. I've said for years that strengthening our society is the central mission of our party. Maybe that way we can help ensure that Alfie isn't a grand-dad before he's 30.'

Of course, so 'deeply concerned' was David Cameron when he was shown the pictures of Alfie that his first reaction was to write an article about him for the *Sun*, as opposed to – for example – checking that the story was actually true. The reality was the Tories didn't care. Cameron had achieved his aim: exploiting the story to further his narrative, achieving valuable banner headlines as a result. What appeared in the 'corrections column' of those papers three weeks later was none of his concern.

Whether it was the *Washington Post*'s legendary Philip Graham or someone else who originally said that the press writes the first draft of history, the phrase has always resonated with me, both in my short career as a journalist and even more so in my longer career in politics.

It's tempting in an era of falling newspaper circulations, declining ratings for broadcast news, and the proliferation of online and social media sources of information and debate, to say that the mainstream media doesn't matter anymore, and that the world has moved on.

But from 1994, when I first saw how much newspapers and broadcasters mattered to the political process, to the present day, one fundamental truth has endured: when the media assert something as the truth, it is incredibly hard to shift that perception in the public's mind, regardless of the facts.

Of course, making that judgement requires you to establish what the facts actually are. Which is why, when the Alfie story broke, my reaction on being asked for a comment, first by the media and then by the ever-agitated press team around Gordon Brown, probably with him in their ear, was that I would not be saying anything – and nor should anyone in the government – until we had asked the local authority's Director of Children's Services to look into what had actually happened.

But before the truth could be established, what I regard as the crucial thing in modern news took place: the story leapt from the front page of the tabloids to the bulletins of the BBC. In some ways, that is a reflection of how the BBC has changed over the years: I couldn't imagine them running that story twenty years ago, but in an era of rolling news programmes and 5 Live radio phone-ins, they need to reflect what the nation is talking about, even if it's a rather questionable story.

What hasn't changed in the last two decades is that the broadcasters still have much greater power and sway than the papers, not only because they have much bigger audiences but also because the public are more likely to believe them and take what they say more seriously. And rightly so. The BBC operates in a fast-moving, deeply political media world, and their reporters and interviewers face more scrutiny than anyone else over supposed bias. It's no overstatement that they are required to be more professional and objective than any other journalists in Britain, and their commitment to that task keeps our politics sane and fair.

But that power comes with a great responsibility. And things sometimes go badly awry. In the case of young Alfie, when people saw the story on the BBC and heard debates about Broken Britain on 5 Live and News 24, whatever scepticism they may have had about the story probably disappeared.

Surprise, surprise, Alfie's local authority soon reported back to my department that he wasn't the father at all; it turned out that a close family member had been touting the idea of the boy-turned-father round the newspapers, correctly if distastefully realising there was potential money to be made out of the lie and the shocking photographs.

The truth never got widely reported because the local authority slapped an injunction on the press – quite rightly – to protect a vulnerable twelve-year-old from further press intrusion, having had his face plastered across newspapers, TVs and computer screens all over the world, even though he'd done absolutely nothing.

Today, if you ask people on the street if they can recall the story of the twelve-year-old boy who fathered a child, it's surprising how many not only remember the story but also remember his name. The real truth did emerge, but it was barely heard. And in any case, the damage had already been done.

What does this story tell us? That often in politics the recalled 'truth' is what gets written down first. Yet if you're in any way a responsible politician, one of the most important lessons you learn when dealing with the press is never to

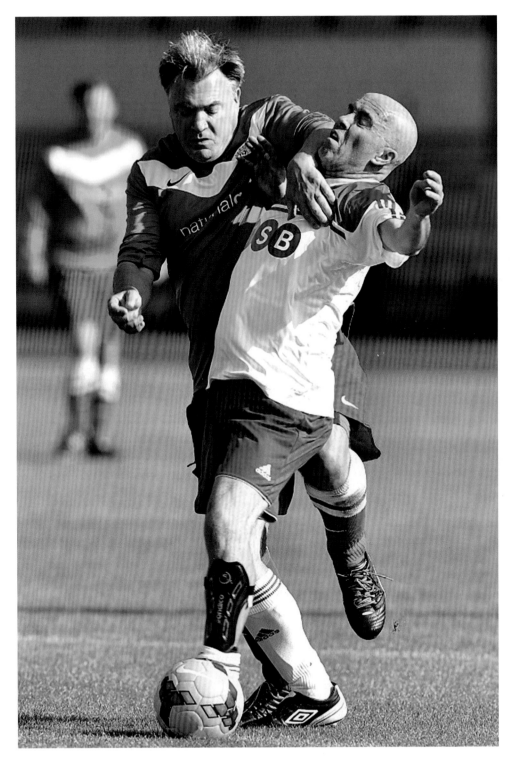

MPs v Press at the 2014 Labour conference – I was steadying to shoot when *Northern Echo* Westminster correspondent Rob Merrick threw himself, face first, at my elbow (*Spin, Image*).

Above: Behind the stage at the 2000 Labour conference in Brighton – Ian Austin and I are talking to the lobby about pensions following the Chancellor's speech (*Spin*).

Right: Yvette and I hated our rushed trips to No.10 on Cabinet mornings (*Emotion*).

This *FT* cartoon captures my message on financial stability: scan the horizon for global risks, but always keep one eye on what's happening at the end of your nose (*Crisis*).

Left: Campaigning against Michael Gove's abolition of the school building programme (BSF) with NASUWT's Chris Keates during the 2010 Labour leadership election (*Opposition*).

Below: Getting my 2010 *Spectator* Parliamentarian of the Year award from David Cameron (*Opposition*).

Above: Working for Gordon in opposition, circa 1995 (*Opposition*).

Key members of my team on the set of *Coronation Street*, during the Labour Party conference 2014. Left to right: Karim Palant, Alex Belardinelli, Balshen Izzet, Leo Haigh, EB, Jon Newton, Ellie Gellard. We are missing Jo Coles, Gary Follis and Julie McCandless (*Opposition*).

I was a strong supporter of SATs for 11-year olds – this *Private Eye* front cover appeared when the marking of the tests was badly delayed (*Mistakes/Mission*).

No comment (*Mistakes*).

On the platform at the end of my conference speech with Harriet and Ed (*Mistakes*).

Up close and personal: launching a Labour poster to mark the cut in the top rate of income tax from 50p to 45p in 2013 (*Civility*).

Nothing wound up David Cameron at PMQs like my (in)famous 'flat-lining' hand gesture (*Civility*).

I stood in for Santa ten years running at the Westminster Children's Christmas party (*Civility*).

26 miles is a long way . . . (*Hinterland*).

Playing Schumann at Kings Place in front of 500 people, and shaking like a leaf (*Hinterland*).

Delivering my Maiden Speech as a newly elected MP, 25 May 2005 (*Purpose*).

Celebrating bringing the breast-screening unit back to Morley – with Councillor Neil Dawson and ASDA's community champion Maxine (*Purpose*).

The new Norwich City Chairman and owner Delia Smith celebrate a goal (*Future*).

jump in when you're unsure of the facts and say something which turns out to be untrue.

If there's a story in the newspapers about your financial dealings or something your office is supposed to have done on your behalf, it can deeply offend your sense of integrity, but you can't afford to shoot back, and certainly not before you've established the full facts, until you're in a position to rebut the story without fear of contradiction.

It's why politicians sometimes need to take time to respond. Because issuing a denial that turns out to be false is disastrous, no matter if you believed it at the time. We can all remember occasions where senior politicians rushed to dismiss a story and were ruined by the subsequent proof that they 'lied'. On the other hand, when you absolutely know that a story is wrong, speed kills. The faster a story can be knocked down, the less likely it is to take off – by which I mean cross from one newspaper front page onto the BBC broadcast bulletins.

Sometimes, though, the act of knocking it down can also be what rocket-fuels the story. So when that fateful call comes through at 10 p.m. to say there is a problem in tomorrow's papers, you have to both establish the facts and decide whether to act. Sometimes, like the leak of a bunch of my private papers in 2011, it's a no-brainer – it's going to be a big story anyway so you have to respond. Other times, like the appearance of a stupid and embarrassing photo of me at a student union meeting aged twenty dressed as a Nazi commander – I guess the left caucus knew what they thought of me when they chose that Christmas meeting's fancy dress – it's just best to keep your head down, knowing any response will shift the story from inside a tabloid onto the broadcasters.

One particular dilemma I faced as Education Secretary occurred when the *Sunday Times* splashed that I was chairing an 'attack unit' in Downing Street which met weekly to plan smear operations against the government's opponents. This was not long after Damian McBride had resigned for plotting a smear operation against the Tories, and there was a fairly transparent attempt by some fairly transparent people inside Number Ten to try and move the story onto my supposed masterminding of his activities, all in anticipation of leadership battles to come.

The reality that no one knew at the time was that Gordon had asked me to go back into Downing Street to help keep his office focused and cohesive at a time when it was falling apart and, as a compromise, I had agreed to chair a weekly meeting. Attendees at the so-called 'attack' meeting included Jeremy Heywood, the principal private secretary, and Michael Ellam, the head of communications: two impeccably neutral civil servants to whom a smear operation meant organising people to butter the scones at a garden party.

The sourcing of that story always looked pretty doubtful, and the day it appeared the BBC didn't touch it; whereas if I'd gone on the warpath and issued a denial on the record, the BBC would have had the licence, and been much more likely, to cover both my denial and the original story. So, deeply frustrated, I just had to sit back while Alex told people it was all rubbish, and allow the drip, drip, drip of people reading the *Sunday Times* to draw their own conclusions.

Of course, these days you don't need people to buy one paper for that dripping effect to take place. If untrue stories are endlessly repeated on social media and political blogs, while you have to work extra hard to refute them, you often just end up trusting that the people reading those stories will take them with a pinch of salt, even if they're hearing them from their peers. And in this new world, a denial often means nothing. Many people who only get their political news from Twitter or Facebook assume that all politicians are liars, or don't really care what they say. Either way, the idea that you'll stop the social media mob making their collective mind up by telling them they're wrong is rather like waving a red flag in front of a runaway train.

Social media has undoubtedly changed the pace at which stories can run these days, but it has also changed the way in which the traditional media operate. In 1994, there was no Twitter, Sky News was in its infancy, and BBC TV had only two political outlets of significance – the 6 p.m. and 9 p.m. news. As a politician, you had time to think back then. How things have changed.

When David Cameron attacked me in an interview in the *Sunday Telegraph* in January 2012, saying sitting opposite me in the House of Commons was like dealing with 'someone with Tourette's', the story broke online at 8.30 p.m. on a Saturday night. By 9 p.m., I was receiving telephone calls from children's speech campaigners from across the charity world. A Twitter storm began.

By 9.30 p.m., one veteran disability campaigner was interviewed on Radio 5 Live, lambasting the Prime Minister for his poor choice of words. By midnight, the original *Sunday*

Telegraph headline had been changed to 'David Cameron apologises to Ed Balls for Tourette's syndrome jibe'. It was a Number Ten statement, which the PM was forced to repeat when he appeared on the *Marr* programme the next morning.

None of that could have happened in an age before social media and twenty-four-hour news coverage. And the boot was on the other foot a couple of years later when, in the 2015 general election, I unveiled a popular new Labour policy, stealing a march on George Osborne by reforming the taxation of 'non-doms' – generally quite wealthy and usually foreign citizens who live in the UK but don't pay full tax here.

The story started well in the newspapers, and we followed up with a good interview on *Today*. But I was on the train to Wales when things started to go badly wrong. A transcript appeared on Twitter of what purported to be a local BBC radio interview that I had done a few months back in which I appeared to contradict our new policy and agreed with the Tory line that it would not raise any money. This was clearly a disaster, but it didn't ring true.

Over the next forty-five minutes we managed to track down the actual interview, discover it had been selectively edited by the Conservative Central Office, and issue an outraged blog piece from me exposing this ruse and reaffirming our policy, which we then heavily tweeted. We scrambled a TV crew to greet me when I arrived in Wales and, while the lunchtime news was pretty messy, by the evening things were back on track. If I'd been on a plane rather than on a train, we could have been scuppered, but as it was, we killed the Tory attack.

★

As well as speed, the modern politician needs to have Goldi-locks skin when dealing with the media: not too thick, and not too thin. You cannot have skin so thick that you are unable to appreciate problems or criticism; you cannot have skin so thin that you take every reference to yourself as an act of aggression.

I would often say to Gordon that we should always remember that most things that happen in politics are a cock-up, but we should never forget that they might be a conspiracy. I think sometimes I was inclined to see too many cock-ups – and Gordon certainly saw too many conspiracies.

Take Charles Clarke. He's someone who – despite us working together for many years, and often seeing each other at Norwich City – would occasionally issue some very barbed words in my direction, or even call for me to be sacked. And usually I'd think 'That's just Charles being Charles', and take the criticism on the chin. Gordon, however, would do the opposite. His reactions to Charles' frequent complaints would consist of 'Who's put him up to this? What's the game here? Who's going to come out next? Do you think Tony knew he was planning this?'

It's almost certain that Charles was always acting alone, and had probably gone a bit rogue because of his mood on a particular day, so Gordon was wrong to be paranoid. But, equally, my instinct that every attack was only what it appeared, every mistake only a cock-up, may not have been right either.

What I learned to do over the years was discuss each suspect story with Yvette or my advisers, and ask the question: 'What do we think is going on here?' You look at who's written the story, which paper it's appeared in, how prominent it is, whether the quotes look crafted or off-the-cuff, and whether there appears to have been a follow-up briefing to broadcasters.

You weigh up the evidence that it's a deliberate act and the evidence that it's an accident, and you proceed accordingly. David Miliband's notorious *Guardian* article in August 2008 describing how Labour could win the next election – without mentioning Gordon – was a case in point. I looked at all the evidence, and told Gordon that without doubt, on this occasion, he was right: this was a conspiracy – although, as usual, not a very effective one – and he needed to get a grip of it.

It helps as a politician if you understand journalism and journalists. Because I'd come into politics straight from the FT, I think I was always more likely than most advisers and MPs to build good relationships and friendships with the economics and political editors I met over the years, while trying not to forget that they had a job to do.

In general, it has been my experience that most of those journalists act with honour and integrity. Of course, that is not a universal truth. Some journalists and editors were a total nightmare – and I might have felt differently about them in general if I'd been a tabloid celebrity. But it's important to differentiate between the sort of hacks who write celebrity stories and the kind that cover Threadneedle Street and Whitehall.

As a consequence of that innate respect for my media counterparts, I invariably took the view that, while mistakes should be corrected, to shout and scream at journalists, or to try and strong-arm them, would usually end up backfiring. And for the same reason, my instinct has always been on the side of protecting a free press and not wanting government or judges to be able to veto what the print media publish. Although, having seen the weak, pusillanimous Press Complaints Commission at first hand, there's no doubt that – even in the era of the Independent Press Standards Organisation – newspaper editors and proprietors still have a point to prove about their methods, and about their willingness to admit it and make amends when they get things wrong.

I also feel, even though this is not an issue of regulation, that the major print outlets are much more politicised today than at any time since the 1980s; and sadly, just like then, reporting standards risk falling when what matters to them above anything else is prosecuting a political agenda.

During the New Labour years, the newspapers were often politicised in a different way, and while it would not have been obvious to the general public, it was corrosive of trust between many Labour figures and their media counterparts.

The anonymous sniping between the factions around Blair and Brown – for which we were all to blame – was certainly unhealthy for the Labour government, but I believe it also turned many individual journalists into mere pawns who could be relied on to deliver the splashes and protect their sources, then come back for more. It didn't matter that if such-and-such a journalist wrote a heavy anti-Gordon story, we'd easily guess their source, because as long as the public were blithely unaware and it couldn't be proved, then it was no skin off their nose. But it wasn't great for the integrity and independence of the journalist.

Not that I was innocent in these matters myself. Most notoriously, it was in a Manchester restaurant, the night before the leader's conference speech, while having dinner with the *Sun's* editor, Rebekah Wade, that I came up with the line 'this is no time for a novice' to simultaneously characterise both David Cameron and David Miliband's challenges to Gordon Brown. It was her enthusiastic response, telling me this was exactly what Gordon should say in his speech the next day, that convinced me to go and persuade Gordon and Ed Miliband to make it happen.

The reality is that conspiring, whether it is thinking up lines for a speech or anonymous briefings, has always been deeply corrosive in our politics, something which frankly is easier to reflect on once you are out of it than when you are in the trenches day to day. As one who has been on the receiving end of a large number of stories based on unattributed comments and anonymous sources down the years, and blamed for a few too, the reliance on those kinds of briefings for even very serious and significant news stories is ultimately unhealthy, and not something that is tolerated in the United States precisely for that reason.

Back in 1997, we had highly experienced media operators in Alastair Campbell and Charlie Whelan, who had deep and long-standing media contacts and operated very effectively in the shadows. Although, when both of them eventually became the story, their media friends showed no mercy, as happened with Damian McBride a decade later. I can't deny I was often frustrated with Charlie, and furious at Damian for what he got involved in. But they were good at their jobs, became good friends and I have kept in touch with them ever since.

My job was to speak to the columnists. And most of the time when I got into trouble with briefing, it was by mistake rather than on purpose. I learned my lesson early on after the 1997 election when I agreed to have lunch with a well-known columnist. I assumed we were speaking on 'lobby terms', which means off the record and not for attribution, and I was talking fairly openly about the challenges we were facing in the transition, how difficult it was for the Treasury to deal with the Bank of England, and so on, just so she knew that what we were doing wasn't easy.

An hour after my lunch, I had a call from a close contact at her paper to say that the newspaper was planning to splash on 'Treasury and Bank at war', with quotes directly attributed to me. In a state of high alarm, I called foul and the story was downgraded to the business section without me being quoted by name.

When I moved into the Cabinet, I made a decision that everything I said would be on the record, that there would be no officially briefed stories or comments using the phrases 'advisers said' or 'sources close to', and when we were briefing an announcement, we would tell all the papers, not just a select few. I'd had briefings for which I'd not been responsible blamed on me many times, and I concluded that this was not the culture I wanted in my first department.

I'm proud to say that – with the help of the brilliant Alex Belardinelli and Balshen Izzet – we stuck to that policy pretty religiously for our three years together at Education, and – despite plenty of anonymous briefing from elsewhere in the Labour Party – five years in opposition.

I think it's proof that when people say you can't take that approach in modern politics and still maintain an active media profile, they're simply wrong. Just as when politicians say you have to give up on the mainstream media entirely and appeal straight to the public instead via the Internet or public meetings, they are – with all due respect – deluding themselves.

The media will always mediate the message and decide what the public hear. They will always write the first draft of history, as the Alfie case shows. That's why you've got to get your message to them quickly, that's why you have to get your facts right, and that's why – when you've got something to say – you should do it on the record.

20

Emotion

———————

When your head tells you one thing while your heart is urging the other – which one should you listen to?

The toughest jobs are those when you find your human emotions totally at odds with your professional obligations.

Certain roles encounter these kinds of dilemmas daily: doctors and nurses; soldiers and police officers; lawyers and teachers. But they know that managing those tensions is an essential part of their job. They are trained to cope.

Politicians don't receive that kind of training. And thankfully, for the most part, they don't need it. There are perhaps only a handful of positions in government where you have to face that kind of dilemma between head and heart. From 2007 to 2010, I had one of them.

★

By far the hardest thing I ever had to do as a politician was open the case file of Peter Connelly – known to the public as Baby P – and read it cover to cover: the details of the injuries inflicted by his mother and her boyfriend, the lengths they went to in order to cover it up and the repeated failures of social workers, health professionals and the police to see what was going on.

I can't bear to repeat the details of the brutal torture he suffered in his short seventeen months on this earth, but I will never get them out of my mind. Sitting alone in my office, I was repulsed, horrified, and unable to believe that anyone could do this to a tiny child in their care. It was an unspeakable tragedy, and one which millions of people across the country had to face in the coming weeks.

For many people, and for me, the first instinct was to look away – to hide our eyes and protect ourselves from the truth. But I had no choice. Before opening the file, I already knew it was going to be an extremely difficult case. For months, Peter had been monitored by local social services and health workers. Concerns about his welfare had frequently been raised. He had been seen at home by professionals. People who were tasked with keeping him safe failed to do so. The idea that Peter's abusers had been able to fool them by obscuring the cuts and bruises on his face with smeared chocolate was just grotesque.

But what made this case even more difficult was that it had happened in Haringey, the very London borough where young Victoria Climbié had lost her life in equally terrible circumstances less than a decade before. The Climbié case had rightly sparked a huge investigation and inquiry. An influential report by Lord Laming had at its heart the instruction to children's professionals to put all normal procedure and practice second to understanding the risk and danger from the eyes of the child.

Lord Laming had made vital recommendations which led to our integration of children's education and social services across the country, and the creation of a specialist position, 'Director of Children's Services', within each local authority, a position carrying the legal duty to make the safeguarding of children the highest priority. He said children's safety should certainly never be compromised by stand-offs between the health-care, police or social work professions.

But only a few years later it was clear, in the case of Baby P, that once again a child had been failed. And once again it was Haringey. Perhaps, if the Laming framework had been followed to the letter, Baby P would still be alive. But it clearly had not been. It was not as though professionals didn't know what to do or how to do it. Nevertheless the terrible fact was that the system had failed him.

I spoke at length with children's minister Beverley Hughes in the days before the court case was concluded and the reporting ban was lifted. We were expecting a Serious Case Review into the Baby P case to be published, prepared by the local Safeguarding Board. But we decided that we should also ask Lord Laming to return, in the light of the Baby P case, to assess whether the recommendations of his original report had been properly implemented in all areas, and whether further reforms were needed.

We were trying to be sensible, professional and calm in our response; but having read the case file, we knew that the level of anger that we felt would be replicated right across the country and the media. There would be a demand for those who had let Peter down to pay the price with their jobs.

Our initial priority was to reassure people that the Laming reforms were the right ones and that we would tackle any gaps and weaknesses in implementation. We wanted to make sure there were proper lessons learned from this tragedy in Haringey without throwing the whole child protection regime into chaos with another lengthy public inquiry.

The following week, the case concluded with the mother, her boyfriend and his lodger brother found guilty, and the public reaction was as strong as we had expected. Haringey's Director of Children's Services, Sharon Shoesmith, was handling the response to the judgement as the responsible local official, and she held a press conference in which, from where I was standing, she appeared not to understand or acknowledge the seriousness of her department's failings or to understand that it was important to establish why this had happened again in Haringey. On the other hand, our decision to commission Lord Laming to do a follow-up review was well received. We thought we'd managed a difficult situation as well as we could.

But the following day, things took a turn for the worse when David Cameron raised the case at Prime Minister's Questions, and published an article simultaneously in the *Evening Standard*, using it as an example of a broken and morally decaying society, condemning the manner in which the case was handled. By pointing the finger at Labour-controlled Haringey, and targeting Shoesmith, he was politicising the situation in a way which firmly turned the media spotlight onto the DCSF.

I left PMQs, and after a short conversation with a very agitated Gordon, I went back to the department. I assembled the leading experts in the department to discuss what had just happened, and how to respond. Cameron had correctly – and to Bev's and my surprise – highlighted at PMQs that the report absolving the local authority of blame had been chaired by the Director of Children's Services herself, so nobody was going to think that 'review' sufficient – a serious procedural weakness which we should have spotted.

I was very clear that the situation was now going to escalate, and that the Laming follow-up review would not be a sufficient response. We didn't want another drawn-out public inquiry, essentially to repeat what we already knew, but we recognised that it was now imperative to address the issue of why there had been this second major failure in Haringey.

The civil servants advised me that the best solution was for me to commission an immediate independent inspectors' report. We agreed that this should be led by Ofsted, who already oversaw children's services, but we would ask them to cover the role of the health professionals and police as well. I said that the review needed to be thorough – we had to establish the facts – but that it should be done as soon as was humanly possible. We agreed the strategy and at 5 p.m., Nick Robinson arrived in my office to conduct an interview for the BBC news, in which I was to formally announce the independent inspectors' report.

In that interview, I found myself saying in public what was

really going on inside my head. That as a parent, I was horrified that such terrible things had happened to such a small, vulnerable boy, and I felt angry that it had been allowed to happen. But as Secretary of State, my job was not to act as judge and jury; it was to set up this independent review to find out what had happened in Haringey and take any necessary action.

I knew I was walking a dangerous tightrope, reacting emotionally as a human being but also trying to be a responsible public official carefully assessing the facts, before deciding what needed to be done. As I expected, I felt the full onslaught of media and public reaction. Like David Cameron the day before, the *Sun* and many other newspapers demanded immediate action – the sacking of Shoesmith. A number of heads had to roll, they said, and I was privately warned by many senior media figures that if they didn't, mine would.

But I knew that I couldn't buckle. I kept repeating that no matter how angry people felt, we had to do things properly and wait for the independent inspectors' report. Anyone looking back at the media coverage that month would see constant criticism of me as to why it was all taking so long, and why I was standing behind Shoesmith, and repeated questions about why Ofsted had been tasked with doing the review since they'd given Haringey a clean bill of health just a few months before.

One newspaper editor in particular directly threatened me, saying that since I had the power to remove Shoesmith, their paper would come for me if I didn't. Another paper organised a petition calling for Shoesmith's removal, which ran into many tens of thousands of signatures, and tried to get me to receive the petition, which I refused to do. I said instead I would meet the political editor in my office. But then, for their own reasons, Number Ten allowed them to be photographed bringing the petition up Downing Street, a group of men in dark suits carrying sacks of readers' messages. It was one of the nastiest, most threatening images I've ever seen in British politics; an attempt to impose vigilante justice via the front page.

After what seemed like an endless three weeks, the inspectors' report finally arrived. I had steeled myself that if it repeated the conclusions of Haringey's own report and absolved the council of any responsibility, I was going to have to go out and defend them. I had defended the process; I would have to defend the outcome.

But as it turned out, the report was much more devastating about the failures in Haringey than any of us in the department were expecting, and was utterly damning about the failures of social care, health services and the police in Baby Peter's case. On the Sunday night when the Ofsted report arrived – they were only willing to give me a few hours' notice to read it before publishing it in the morning – I read it along with the Permanent Secretary in my office. We agreed that, while I would wait until the next day's meetings to make a final decision, the report was so critical that we could see no option but to use my powers in legislation to remove Shoesmith from the statutory position as Director of Children's Services – we were worried about the safety of other at-risk children in Haringey and knew we urgently needed new leadership there.

The next morning I met with the head of Ofsted, Christine Gilbert, and representatives of Haringey Council. They were very sombre meetings, with Christine Gilbert markedly more critical of leadership failings in the Haringey children's department than in her written report. Parliament wasn't sitting so I couldn't make a statement to the Commons, but I didn't feel I could just sit on the report or refuse to take questions. The only option was for Bev and me to hold a press conference.

As has been well documented since, that decision was challenged by Shoesmith at the High Court and upheld, but then overturned by the Court of Appeal. They judged that I should have allowed Shoesmith to put her case before making the final decision to remove her from her position as Director of Children's Services in order to ensure that she was not made a scapegoat. The independent report was so clear and unequivocal that I felt it would have made no difference at all to my decision, but there was a procedural mistake, and Shoesmith was eventually paid £680,000 in compensation.

At the time, I acted on what I thought was the proper legal advice from the department, but it was wrong. If I had met with Shoesmith, I wouldn't have reached any different conclusions, but it would have helped combat her claim for compensation. I can only say that – aside from ensuring Shoemith had a chance to put her case before removing her from her statutory position – I would do eveything the same again.

And even though this was a deeply emotional issue, it reinforced a basic lesson: it doesn't matter how you feel as a human being; as a minister you have to make your decisions in the right and proper way and be absolutely sure about that before you take action. I tried to do things by the book when it came to Haringey and Shoesmith. I tried to be as fair and objective as possible. Ultimately even that wasn't enough. But I do know that I never let my immediate emotional reaction dictate my judgement, because I don't think I could live with myself if I had.

If you allow your emotions to dictate the decisions you make in politics, you'll get things wrong. But at the same time you always have to understand and listen to your heart because it matters, and because you have to be ready to cope with the way others will feel.

It's your heart and your gut that will tell you when something is going to be a big political problem, even when your advisers and officials – and your own head – are probably busy trying to rationalise it and find a logical way to dismiss it. So you have to let your heart react to a problem, even if your head has to deal with it.

I can remember in 1997, when a backbench Labour rebellion was growing around Labour's cuts to lone-parent benefits, talking to Yvette, then a brand-new MP. I was rationally trying to explain why the decision we had made was the right one, and was important in terms of sticking to the Tory spending plans. But hearing her talk, seeing her emotional reaction, and listening to her describe the views of other colleagues, I got a wave of concern in the pit of my stomach that we'd got this wrong. And many times since I've learned that you ignore that feeling at your peril.

Yvette had a similar reaction in November 2007, when I

raised a dilemma with her. Bird flu was spreading round the world and we were trying to decide what to do in case the outbreak became a pandemic. The night before the key government-wide strategy meeting, I was going through the background reading at home. One significant decision to be made was what we would do about schools: should they stay open or be closed if a flu pandemic was under way?

On the one hand, closing schools would stop the flu being passed from child to child in the classroom; on the other, closing schools would cause enormous disruption – parents would be forced to stay at home to take care of their children, which could have a sizeable impact on essential services, most notably in health care. How would we cope if many doctors and nurses were at home looking after their kids?

As I read over the documents, I explained the dilemma to Yvette. Close the schools and stop the spread, or keep them open and keep the workers. She replied immediately: 'Whatever you decide in your committee tomorrow, you need to know: if there's a bird flu pandemic, our kids aren't going to school and that's the end of it.'

I said to the committee the next day that I knew from my own family, keeping the schools open was no guarantee that mums and dads would still go to work. We needed to plan our strategy around that reality.

Of course, sometimes the head and the heart clash in other ways. All too often the demands of politics come up against the emotional realities of life. Just imagine the appalling dilemma for Robin Cook, sitting at Heathrow with his wife, preparing to go on holiday, and being told by Alastair Campbell that a story about his affair was about to break. At that time he had to find a way to balance the need to protect his wife and family against the reality that he had to put out a public statement.

In the terrible days after the tragic death of Gordon and Sarah's first baby, Jennifer, I remember so well the anguish Gordon faced at having to deal with his and Sarah's deep emotional pain while simultaneously having to deal with political mundanities that no other parent would have to face in the same circumstances, like who would go and make a statement to the cameras outside the hospital, and how long we were going to have to delay the Budget.

Those of us around him tried to take much of that load on ourselves, but it was so hard when we were all struggling to cope with our own grief. One adviser, Ian Austin, was walking down Horse Guards Road with a director of communications from another department, who gave Ian his sympathies. They walked along in silence before his companion added: 'Mind you, it might be good for his image.' Ian said nothing and kept on walking. When he got back, he was seething. 'It took everything in me not to punch him there in the street,' he said. I just thought: 'You bloody should have.'

In an infinitely less significant way, Yvette and I have had to deal with that balancing act between head and heart all of our political lives. Married during her first year as a Member of Parliament, the first married couple ever to be in the

Cabinet, we have always had to balance our personal life with political reality.

And we knew before we became Cabinet ministers, even before the expenses scandal, that focus groups of voters responded to us very differently when they were presented with who we were as individuals than they did when they knew we were married. It was a strange thing to know. People thought well of us individually. But when they were informed we were married, their views changed. It made us a career couple, each so committed to politics that the only soulmate we could find in the world was another politician. People would say things like: 'God, are they going to bring up all their kids to be MPs as well?' And this was even before the popularity of the US version of *House of Cards*.

Journalists and other politicians were also often at risk of treating us as a couple rather than as individuals. Even though Yvette had been an MP for eight years longer than me, a minister and Cabinet minister too, the undercurrent of everyday sexism in our society meant that she was far more often referred to as Ed Balls' wife than I was as Yvette Cooper's husband. Some MPs warned Yvette she shouldn't run for the leadership in 2015 because she would be seen as my wife, but it was striking that this almost never came up during her campaign and was raised in only one media interview, ironically on *Woman's Hour*.

But that is just the reality of our lives, our love and our shared history. We are aware of it. We are careful not to appear together too often in public and have turned down all the offers to do joint 'his and hers' magazine interviews. It's why we resist the temptation to reveal every detail of our private lives, things which are personal and special to us, because they inevitably become less so when you talk about them in public.

In the end, being a politician occasionally requires you to walk a tightrope. You have to separate how you react emotionally to a situation as a human being from how you make decisions as a politician. But you also have to remember that you need both head and heart to succeed.

Usually in life, when someone says: 'What's your heart telling you? What's your head telling you?' there's an implied judgement about which one you should follow. In politics, they need to work in stereo, and it's only when you find yourself not listening at all to one or the other that you need to stop and retune.

21

Crisis

_____

The 2008 financial crisis was staring us in the face – so how did we miss it, and what are we missing today?

It was a Thursday afternoon in late 2006. Mervyn King, the Governor of the Bank of England, Callum McCarthy, the head of the Financial Services Authority, and I were being presented with a dangerous and fast-changing financial war-game scenario, designed by our officials at my request to test out our mechanisms for dealing with a future financial crisis should one arrive. This was the tripartite system for financial stability in action – the FSA, the Bank of England and the government working together to find a solution.

In that war game, a northern building society was on the verge of going bankrupt, having borrowed far too much. One of the largest British clearing banks was heavily exposed to that building society and now risked running out of money overnight. Unless we did something immediately to guarantee its deposits and provide emergency resources, there was a real danger the bank would have to cease trading. Its cash machines would empty, the doors of its branches would close. At best, public confidence in the banking system would be lost. At worst, there would be widespread panic.

We debated what to do. Mervyn was clear that bailing out the clearing bank risked what the economists call 'moral hazard', the idea that banks and their shareholders will be more emboldened to make risky investments if they think they are immune from the consequences.

Callum and I took a very different view, namely that a large bank going bust would hugely damage confidence in the UK economy, and in our war game I was clear that we had to make a public statement before the 6 p.m. news to calm the public's worries and reassure them that we would not let the financial system collapse. It was also obvious to Callum and me that the deposit insurance legislation safeguarding savers' money was out of date, so we decided we would immediately raise the amount we could guarantee to protect, with legislation to follow.

To shore up the fictional clearing bank, Callum proposed approaching international buyers but Mervyn was worried it might constitute a breach of EU state aid rules. My view was that we should take whatever action was needed and sort out the legalities afterwards, and that was our decision.

It was a frightening scenario, and one we struggled to resolve. Little did any of us know that just eight months later a crisis with eerie parallels would unfold in real life.

★

I left the Treasury in June 2007 to move into the Cabinet as Children's Secretary, and just a few weeks later in August, the credit crunch began: markets started to lose confidence in the American subprime mortgage market, and the scale of often disguised investment in that market from US and European banks started to emerge.

In August, on holiday in the south of France, Yvette, the kids and I visited Sue Nye and her husband, the economist Gavyn Davies, at their holiday home. While the children played in the pool, Gavyn and I discussed what was happening. We agreed that the financial markets looked as shaky as we'd known them, and it would be very important for Mervyn King to send a clear signal that the Bank of England would step in to provide support if needed.

As it turned out, and contradicting the conclusions reached during our war game, Mervyn did the opposite, informing the Treasury Committee just a few weeks later in early September that he did not think it was the Bank of England's job to bail out ailing financial institutions.

Two weeks on, with queues of savers waiting to get their money outside branches of the deeply troubled Northern Rock, the crisis became a reality for the public. It was the latest victim of what was becoming a global crisis, as mortgage providers were revealed to have made billions in loans which had no chance of being recovered, with major international banks left exposed to those losses as a result of their own bad investments in what became known as the subprime market.

And a year later, as the crisis in America grew, with two US investment banks effectively bankrupt and Northern

Rock nationalised to prevent its total collapse, the same questions loomed over RBS/NatWest, one of Britain's and the world's largest banks.

After Northern Rock's bankruptcy fears were exposed by Robert Peston on the 10 p.m. news, I was astonished to wake up the following morning to find there was still no government line on the 7 a.m. BBC bulletin explaining that things were under control and that people's deposits were safe.

It was one of the very rare times that I called the Downing Street switchboard and asked to speak to the Prime Minister urgently. Something needed to be said to reassure the public that the government was in control. Alarm bells must also have been ringing next door at 11 Downing Street and an hour later Alistair Darling was on the *Today* programme explaining that a plan was in place: the deposit insurance scheme was to be expanded, thereby protecting all savings.

But twenty-four hours later, walking through central Leeds with Yvette and the kids to go shopping, I could see unconvinced savers, desperate to withdraw their money, queueing outside the Northern Rock building society on the Briggate – I had never expected to see anything like it in Britain in my lifetime.

It is an uncomfortable truth that less than a year before this Northern Rock debacle, we acted out that 'war game' at the Treasury anticipating almost exactly this scenario, and rehearsing how the British financial authorities would respond. And yet, despite that effort, we were still taken totally by surprise and unprepared when the real crisis struck.

In 2008, there is no doubt that the UK Treasury led the

world in responding to the deepening financial crisis, with Gordon Brown cracking the whip from Number Ten. But that previous September, as the Northern Rock fiasco unfolded, the Treasury was badly behind the curve.

And there was a reason. Nine months earlier, at the end of our war game, Bank of England staff were tasked with working through the various recommendations we'd made, but with a twelve-month time frame. If we had known a real crisis was just around the corner, we would have acted with rather more urgency. But we didn't.

For all the talk now of Labour's championing of the City and supine reliance upon the banks to bring in tax revenues, the explicit task I was given when I became City minister in 2006 was to try to repair what had become very antagonistic relations between the banking industry, the City of London and the government.

Gordon Brown had never been a great fan of banks. When I joined Labour in 1994, senior figures like Gordon were still elected annually to the National Executive Committee in a poll in September. He and Robin Cook used to vie to top the poll – and they did so by essentially running the same campaign every year.

As industry spokesman, Robin Cook's campaign was always about saving Post Office branches, and resisting government attempts to privatise the Royal Mail. Gordon's campaign was always about the excessive profits of the banks and the need to make the banking industry work better for small businesses in the real economy, rather than just filling the pockets of executives.

A year after I arrived, as the scandal emerged of the excessive profits of the privatised utility companies and the share options of their bosses, Gordon switched focus away from bashing banks to utilities. But his reputation among the banking industry had already been established. And on assuming the Chancellorship in 1997, he commissioned Don Cruickshank, the former Telecoms regulator, to conduct a review into competition in the banking industry, something the banks definitely saw as an unfriendly act.

In retrospect, I look back now on our response to the Cruickshank report as bit of a damp squib. We eventually managed to make some of his recommended reforms to the payment systems and to curb the ability of banks to charge for using their cash machines, but we ducked the call for more competition on the basis of very heavy lobbying from the Department of Trade and Industry.

Cruickshank wasn't the only reason why the Treasury's relationship with the banks was rocky. The decision – alongside Bank of England independence – to move responsibility for banking regulation away from the Bank to a new statutory regulator, the Financial Services Authority, was seen as an attempt to get tougher on the banks, following the fiasco of Barings Bank's 'rogue trader' Nick Leeson.

In fact, both senior Treasury officials and the new Deputy Governor of the Bank, Mervyn King, wanted to go further and have a complete separation of the Bank of England from any oversight of the commercial banking system. But both I and the Governor, Eddie George, were determined that the

Bank of England should continue with an oversight role for the wider stability of the financial system, which obviously included the health of the banks. Mervyn would regularly complain to me that the financial stability wing of the Bank of England was much too overstaffed compared to monetary analysis. He was determined to rebalance the Bank's priorities when he took over as Governor.

Senior figures from the stability wing have subsequently told me that they felt unable to ask the FSA for the details of the capital health of individual banks. They felt that was the FSA's job, not the Bank of England's, and in retrospect, I understand how those kinds of turf wars can occur between institutions.

If anyone had ever come to me, as a Treasury adviser and then as a minister, to complain they weren't getting access to information, I would have immediately done something about it. But no one ever did, and I'm afraid neither the Bank of England nor the FSA were spotting what was going on, and post-hoc attempts to say 'We'd have spotted it if . . .' are rather too wise after the fact.

We look back now and think of the period as one of light regulation. The reality was that the financial services industry saw the establishment of the FSA as being a toughening of banking regulation. The reason why the Tories voted against the new legislation, the Financial Service and Markets Act, back in 2000, was because they argued that statutory regulation would hurt the City.

Even Tony Blair made a speech in 2005 criticising the FSA for being too heavy-handed in regulating the financial services industry and holding back this important part of the economy. It was quite something for a prime minister to make a speech criticising the regulatory structure his own government had established.

But what surprised me most when I became City minister was that the big debate on the contribution that banks made to the economy versus the regulation they operated under was not on anyone's agenda. In my round of introductory meetings with all the bank chief executives, I'd ask them what they wanted to discuss. It was always a very familiar list: one unfair burden after another, from providing basic bank accounts for benefits claimants and requiring more free cash machines in lower-income areas, to subjecting them to an Office of Fair Trading investigation into charges for overdrafts.

In my first speech at Bloomberg in 2006, it's true that I talked about the importance of London having light-touch regulation, and I did so to reassure the banks and wider financial services companies that I was aware of their complaints in this area, even if the only specifics they seemed interested in were the micro-issues raised in those early meetings.

The week after I made that speech, I was contacted by a concerned Callum McCarthy, who said to me that it's not about being light or heavy, it's about risk: we should be really heavy where there are big risks and much lighter where there are low risks, and that was the policy the FSA applied.

We were much too light on the big banks because we didn't see the risks that pertained to them, not because in principle we wanted to be light in our regulation. So in my one year as City minister, I found myself dealing with issue after issue which at the time seemed important or threatening to the banks. In reality, though, we were putting out small fires while missing the enormous powder keg.

We talked about the promotion of the City of London, and the importance of EU financial directives not discriminating against London. We talked about stopping the insurance industry ripping off Britons travelling on package holidays, and we wrestled with where regulation would sit if the UK Stock Exchange was bought by an American company. The big picture was nowhere to be seen.

However, I do remember one particular visit to an investment bank. I had a meeting with its executives lasting about an hour, and we then spent a while touring the large trading floor where the actual work was being done. And as we walked through, the London-based chief of this huge international firm turned to me and said: 'It's so complex what these guys are doing these days. All these special purpose vehicles. It's very hard for any of us to know what's really going on.'

He clearly meant it as a light-hearted remark, the kind of self-deprecating thing the chief executive of a major pharmaceutical company might say when passing the labs where his boffins were experimenting. But that exchange has haunted me ever since. The Treasury, the Bank and the FSA didn't know what was going on, because the chief executives and board members and risk managers of these banks didn't know what was going on either. And it wasn't the first time I had heard it said. When I look back, I now realise that I was ignoring one of the first rules every politician must learn:

always listen for echoes, and then – when you hear the same things said by, say, bankers in London and policymakers in Washington – ask, what is the common theme?

In retrospect, worse was to come when the issue arose as to whether RBS would be allowed to take over the Dutch Bank ABN AMRO, which it was competing to do against Barclays. I asked senior Treasury officials to give me their views and to get advice from the Bank of England and the FSA.

And the word back from all quarters was that the takeover was fine to proceed. The only word of caution was the Bank insisting that the merged entity had to be regulated out of London rather than the Netherlands because we didn't trust the Dutch regulator. At no stage did anyone raise even the slightest concerns about the state of ABN AMRO's balance sheet, or whether RBS/NatWest's balance sheet was strong enough to cope with the added stress. If we'd looked into those in anything like the detail required, we'd have seen that both of them were potentially in huge trouble.

But if you want a sign of how much that was off our radar, look back at our war game in late 2006, when the fictional UK clearing bank was in difficulties and the FSA suggested an international bank as a possible buyer. Who did they suggest? ABN AMRO. In hindsight, it's tragic.

But even if no government or regulator around the world saw the trouble on the horizon, one thing is absolutely clear: we were far better prepared than the Americans. Following our war game, we invited the US authorities to join us in a similar exercise by video link looking at a fictional transatlantic crisis.

This was a bigger exercise, which meant we had Gordon,

Mervyn King and Callum McCarthy all in the same room in the Treasury, plus me and the Permanent Secretary, Nick Macpherson, discussing the fictional situation we were facing, and able to come to swift conclusions about the action we would take.

When we relayed these to our American counterparts, we had to speak to four different TV screens: one for the regulators of the New York Fed; one for the Treasury Secretary in his Washington office; one for the head of the Securities Exchange Commission in a separate office in DC; and one for the head of the Federal Reserve, also in DC.

In the course of that discussion, it became abundantly clear that not only were they rarely in the same room as each other, they obviously didn't talk to each other much full stop. And while Gordon's leadership during the eventual crisis was hugely important, both domestically and around the globe, it at least helped that we'd worked through some of the issues in advance that the United States in particular had to deal with in real time.

So why didn't we see the crisis in advance? It wasn't because there was a Labour government, the Conservatives missed it too. And while Vince Cable warned often of booming prices at the top end of the UK housing market, that was not where the crisis hit – it began at the bottom end of the US housing market, with hundreds of thousands of families with no or even negative credit ratings being given mortgages that they could never afford to pay off.

Naturally the Tories have tried to pin the blame for the UK crisis on Labour, and therefore on the tripartite system we created. The reality is that these risks and problems were missed in America, Germany, France, Japan – countries all around the world – some of whom had central banks in charge of bank regulation, or independent regulators, or the finance departments themselves.

Talking to Mervyn a few years later, I asked him whether he worried that, only a few months before the financial crisis, none of us spotted the warning signals that the financial system was becoming too overextended. He replied that, in fact, the financial stability wing of the Bank of England had done some work in their annual report, led by the then Deputy Governor, John Gieve, which highlighted some of the risks.

But as I said to him then, the fact that we used to meet every month while I was the City minister to discuss the financial system, and not once did the Governor raise any of those concerns with me, indicates that they were clearly not at the forefront of his or anyone else's mind at the time, except perhaps John Gieve's.

My year as City minister now looks very different to me, and to others too. I look back and agonise about whether I should have done more, worried more or probed more. The fact that no one was ringing alarm bells in the Bank of England, the Federal Reserve or the European Central Bank isn't really any comfort. We should have asked more questions, and we didn't.

The big conclusion I draw from that is that in terms of the global markets, it's usually the most obvious assumptions that turn out to be wrong, and it's the clearest and the most proximate risks which tend to be missed. At the time, our big fears were whether growth in China would be sustained, whether the US current account was unsustainable, or whether the oil price would stay so high. The fact that investors, central banks and governments were worrying about those issues and adjusting their behaviour accordingly probably meant they were less likely to happen. The problem was they were not worrying about the US subprime housing market and the shadow banking system.

Because every major crisis in the last fifty years had been driven by inflation and inflationary pressures in the housing and labour markets, the fact that inflation was low and stable in Britain, and the labour and housing markets were operating relatively normally, gave us a confidence that we shouldn't have had. We weren't worried enough about whether banks on our high streets were sound and whether our financial system was stable. We weren't even asking those questions. We were scanning the horizon for global risks, rather than focusing on the risks at the end of our nose.

We have certainly now made huge strides in improving the strength of the global banking system. Reforms in the Federal Reserve, the Bank of England and the European Central Bank are ongoing, but they are definitely moving in the right direction. Yet there's always a danger that, just as we were focusing on inflation ten years ago, we are focusing on the wrong things now.

And if that's the case, we must be willing to make the mental leap to assume that the risks we are addressing now are not the ones which will cause the next major crisis. So yes, we worry about a collapse in confidence in the Chinese banking system, more volatility in oil prices, or a sharp drop in London house prices. But, equally, we must continue to play war games, to prepare for something totally unexpected: a major breakdown in the electricity power infrastructure, a new global virus, or a flood in London which overwhelms the Thames Barrier.

I said to a very knowledgeable banking friend recently: 'Does China worry you?' He said: 'China should worry everybody. But what keeps me awake at night is not their level of growth, but that China has had three of the four worst earthquakes in human history, and they're about due another one. Can they cope with that as well?'

I've certainly learned over the last few years that you must challenge your most strongly held assumptions every day, and keep scanning the horizon for global risks. But that doesn't give you an excuse to take your eye off the danger right in front of you.

22

Opposition

_____

*Governments get to make all the important decisions – so can it
really ever be good to be out of power?*

The only good thing about opposition, and I literally
mean the only good thing, is the moment you discover
something the government doesn't want you to know; the
hairs on the back of your neck stand up, and you think: 'I've
got them.'

During the first month of the coalition government in
2010, one fell into my lap.

With the general election lost and Michael Gove in his
early weeks as the new Secretary of State for Education, we
were causing an almighty row about his decision to cancel
the Building Schools for the Future programme (BSF),
effectively shutting down all the school improvements and

new school building plans that I had commissioned and budgeted for in government.

It was very unfair on schools who were already well down the line with their plans for expansion and development, and anticipating the extra investment in teaching that came with them. The cancellation symbolised the lunacy of the Tory approach to the economy: cutting back on the public sector projects that were helping to drive jobs and growth in the private sector.

Part of the Tory excuse was that I had authorised spending projects before they'd been approved by the Treasury. In other words, they had no legitimacy in Whitehall terms and so it was really my fault they were being cancelled. It was a complete lie, and one I had to expose. So I asked David Bell – the now renamed Education Department's Permanent Secretary – for permission to come and look through the file on how my decisions on BSF had been reached, so that I was at least able to defend my record with authority.

It's a very strange feeling returning to the department you used to work in. A bit like a divorced husband having a nose around at how his old house has changed when he drops by to take out the kids. Some of the old officials were happy to see me, some looked embarrassed or confused, and some just stared.

I went up in the lift, met the private secretary, and he left me in his office to read the old papers. They quickly confirmed, as I thought, that the Treasury had indeed approved the spending. I took notes to show that the Tory charges against my decision-making were nonsense, but as I came to the end

of the file, I realised I was reading a few pages of correspond-
ence that didn't seem to fit. Mystified, I read on, trying to
work out what they were, and realised I was reading emails
sent between Michael Gove and his advisers discussing the
risks that the decisions they were taking to reverse existing
BSF commitments could be overturned at judicial review by
the local authorities to whom they'd been made.

At the very least, this was proof that they knew they were in
trouble, and it could be the evidence we needed to force a
U-turn. My head was scrambling and I wasn't quite sure what
to do. There were, I thought, three possible reasons for the
papers being there. First, I was being tricked by the Tories into
making a fool of myself by exposing what was a deliberate
hoax. Second, someone had slipped those pages into the file.
Or third, and probably most likely, it was a cock-up: nobody
had thought to check what was in the back of the file.

My reaction was simply to write down in my notebook
every word of the emails, hope I didn't get caught doing so,
and decide what to do afterwards. It was potentially a vital
piece of information in the campaign to challenge the
cancellation of BSF, and not just for what I was doing in
Westminster, but for several large lawsuits that local councils were planning in the courts.

And the fact was we already had the Tories on the ropes on
this issue. We'd used every tool in the opposition box: points
of order and urgent questions in the House of Commons;
taking the TV cameras to stand outside decaying school
buildings with the leaders of local councils; and the mobil-
isation of students, parents and teachers all across the
country. Maybe this would be the tipping point.

So even though I was slightly wary, I thought I was justified to use what I'd learned, given how high the stakes were, adding to the pressure and clamour for a complete U-turn.

But it never came. Michael Gove was badly damaged, the campaign helped get my Labour leadership campaign up into second gear, and my fight on the issue won me the award for the *Spectator*'s Parliamentarian of the Year, presented to me by none other than David Cameron. But what did it ultimately achieve – all the speeches, and urgent questions, and petitions, and subterfuge?

Absolutely nothing is the truth. Michael Gove stayed on as Education Secretary, and pressed on with his cuts and his free schools programme. The government refused to change its mind. The judicial reviews came and went in the courts. The schools and children who would have benefited from the rebuilding programme remained disappointed.

It was a really important lesson for me about the futility of opposition: whatever the little victories you achieve in the media, the big battles are rarely won; and being known to be good at opposition is in the end not the kind of accolade to which any politician should aspire.

There are of course rare occasions when good opposition can make a difference. When I joined Labour in 1994, Gordon Brown and Harriet Harman were well into a brilliantly organised campaign to stop the Tories raising VAT on gas and electricity from 8 to 15 per cent.

In Gordon's memorable phrase, it would 'force pensioners

to choose between heating and eating', and the campaign achieved something unprecedented in modern politics – defeating the Budget in the House of Commons, and in the process forcing a total capitulation on that policy by the Chancellor who inherited it, Ken Clarke. We had a similar success eighteen years later as the collapse of George Osborne's Omnishambles Budget led, day by day, to U-turn after U-turn.

But when those occasions do occur they're usually reliant on a fair amount of support from the government benches, as we saw when Ed Miliband had a similar victory in the vote over taking military action against Syria in 2013. It was a decision which many Labour MPs were very equivocal about, but it was ultimately won because substantial numbers of Tory MPs voted with Labour.

It's also true that backbench campaigns can have equally big impacts on important but very specific issues, from Peter Mandelson arguing for the proper commemoration of the D-Day Jubilee in 1994 to Stella Creasy's very effective campaign against payday lending which forced the government to bring in tougher regulations.

And sometimes of course, even if they don't change policy, oppositions can define how the government is seen. Back at the beginning of his leadership, Tony Blair's emotional and highly effective response to the tragic murder of James Bulger succeeded in portraying John Major's government as out of touch with the public mood, a strategy which David Cameron repeatedly attempted to replicate, often in a rather unseemly rush, during his own period as opposition leader.

More successfully, in the run-up to the 2010 election,

George Osborne managed to lodge in the public's mind the false idea that the national deficit was caused not by the financial crisis but by Labour's excessive spending in the years that preceded it.

All of the above are examples of what can be called 'successful opposition'. But there is one fundamental truth: when you stand back and think about it, George Osborne alone didn't win the 2010 election, any more than it was Tony Blair or Gordon Brown who won it in 1997.

Oppositions don't win elections; governments lose them. Every opposition victory for the last fifty years has generally had to be preceded by the government losing either its economic or its political credibility, and sometimes both. The opposition simply needs to be in the right position to take advantage.

I've taken criticism for being too much of a doom-monger on the economy in the last Parliament, voicing fears about growth and unemployment, which turned out be pessimistic. I remain convinced that such an outcome was only avoided by maintaining loose monetary policy for far longer than was desirable, not just in Britain but around the world, whereas fiscal action to invest in infrastructure to boost growth and create jobs would have made for a more balanced response and even got the deficit down faster.

But aside from my economic analysis during those years, my political rationale was clear: we were only going to win the election convincingly if another economic crisis hit, and if it did, I wanted to be sure that Labour was on the right side of the debate, with our fingers firmly pointed at Cameron and Osborne on the other.

I didn't want to end in the same place that Labour found itself in following Britain's exit from the Exchange Rate Mechanism in 1992. As much as Gordon Brown railed against the Tories for mismanaging the situation, he could only get so much traction because Labour had – foolishly in my view, and I said so at the time – supported the Tory policy to join in the first place.

I'm not suggesting opposition parties should oppose the government position no matter what, but they do need to ask themselves constantly: what are we doing today that will help us get back into government? After all, it's not a debating society.

In government between 1997 and 2005, sitting on the other side of the fence, I can honestly say we didn't care about what the Tories were doing in those first two Parliaments, bar the temporary wobble over the fuel crisis in 2000. With Labour enjoying large majorities, and the Tories demoralised, divided and unfocused in their attacks, we could simply afford to ignore them. If they'd opposed us on Iraq, the 2005 election might have been a different story, but they didn't and it wasn't. Even after David Cameron's election as leader, he only gained serious traction after the 'election that never was' in 2007.

In other words, the Tory Party spent ten years in opposition – from 1997 to 2007 – as a total irrelevance. If that sounds familiar to Labour supporters, it is meant to. We were irrelevant for more than a decade after 1979, and we are well on our way to matching that record again.

My fear is that too many in the current Labour Party feel much more comfortable with the simplicity of opposition, the purity of protest, the black-and-white world view of the veteran outsider or the chanting student. Successful politics is about combining principles and values with the inevitable compromise and professional discipline needed to win. Refusing to listen to the electorate has never been a winning formula, any more than Jeremy Corbyn thinking the volume of the cheering from your core supporters is a reliable guide to wider public opinion.

Yes, it is absolutely true that the precondition of winning power – the incumbent government losing their economic or political credibility – has not yet happened, despite the referendum defeat, so the Labour Party would face an uphill battle if the election was imminent, whoever was in charge. However, there is a much graver danger afoot; the Labour Party cannot and must not start to regard itself as a party of opposition.

In politics, it is no good simply saying: 'Our job is to stand up for the underprivileged and dispossessed against the government'; the only way to stand up for the people you represent is to be the government. It is useless forcing occasional U-turns to stop bad things from happening. You need to be the one making good things happen.

Yes, being in opposition is hugely important from a constitutional point of view, but it is a futile, soul-destroying, utterly unproductive place to be. And a place no MP should ever want to stay for anything other than the shortest possible time.

Take an example: I'm sure Caroline Lucas has the best of motives serving as the only Green MP in the House of Commons; she has an important platform to make her arguments and represent the party's voters. But she has little chance of changing anything as a Green MP in the House of Commons. Huge pressure is put on the government to make the right choices on climate change, but it comes from the media, academia, civil society and the wider public, and usually to little avail. Caroline Lucas makes a contribution, but it's a small one, and can be easily ignored by the government.

Then take another example: the Liberal Democrats. For most of my adult life, they have been in a similar predicament to Caroline Lucas, a party of seemingly permanent opposition and irrelevance.

Which, of course, is why back in 2010 – the first time in forty years we had a hung Parliament – Nick Clegg saw his chance to turn the Liberal Democrats from a party of opposition into a potential party of government. The chance to make himself deputy prime minister, and take colleagues into the Cabinet and to the ministerial ranks. To try to pursue Liberal Democrat policies as part of a coalition with the Tories, and – as all politicians dream about – to make a difference.

Many of my Labour colleagues, not least Gordon, were angry with the Liberal Democrats for making that choice. 'How could a progressive, centre-left party prop up a Tory prime minister?' they asked. But the Liberal Democrats had a chance to be in government and they took it. And I think rightly so. So I fully respect Nick Clegg's decision back in May 2010. Nor do I have any problem that he shared power with the Conservatives. There was realistically no prospect of a workable Labour/Lib Dem majority, and it was clear from the very beginning of our coalition discussions with them that they had no intention of striking a deal with us. We were simply there so they could get a better bargain out of the Tories.

For that reason, I was hugely irritated, if not surprised, by the account given of those negotiations – presumably with Clegg's consent – by the former Lib Dem MP David Laws, who claimed that it was obstructive and rude behaviour by me and Ed Miliband which scuppered Labour's chances with the Lib Dems. In politics, everyone is used to people stretching the truth to fit their narrative, but Laws' accounts of those discussions were truly baffling to read for everyone who had been in the room.

But the wisdom of their decision to take power should not be confused with the wisdom of what they did with it.

My real frustration with the Lib Dems and Nick Clegg was the way their position shifted pre-election: from agreeing with Labour that the Tory plans for deep and rapid spending cuts would be premature and counterproductive, to signing up full throttle to George Osborne's plans. Promises which couldn't be delivered, weren't delivered, and did huge damage to the economy in the process. Nick Clegg's decision to ignore Vince Cable's warnings about George Osborne's fiscal plans and instead sign up to them lock, stock and barrel is a classic example of bad economics proving to be bad politics, and the Liberal Democrats certainly paid the price.

In our coalition discussions, Clegg was clear that his most important aims were to deliver proportional representation and to cement Britain as an effective member of the European Union. His referendum on voting reform was a catastrophe, and, following the equally catastrophic vote on the EU, how can he claim that his participation in government was a force for good on the European issue?

And, of course, along the way, he ended up breaking promises on tuition fees, and cuts to tax credits and housing benefit. He doubtless persuaded himself that these compromises were required to keep the coalition together, and perhaps that they were necessary to fund what became his obsession with the Lib Dem 'achievements' of free school meals for infants and a higher income-tax personal allowance.

But by signing up to the Tory rhetoric that the coalition was fixing the mess left by Labour and that an immediate lurch into austerity was in the national interest, he didn't just damage Labour, he boxed himself in, and gave up the ability to act as the counterweight to Tory plans on which all successful coalitions rely. In other words, Clegg fell into Osborne's trap, forcing his party to go along with decisions which undermined the social justice of our country, and as a result totally alienated the Lib Dem support base, leading to their crushing defeats at the 2015 election.

So while I have no doubt that Nick Clegg and the Liberal Democrats made the right decision in 2010 to choose government rather than opposition, I think that the way they went about it, the extent to which they aligned themselves with the Tories, the promises they broke and the decisions they signed up to, all amounted to an act of political suicide.

And looking back on the five years they spent in government, it's not really clear what their big, historic and uniquely Lib Dem achievements actually were, what they can point to and say: 'Well, it was worth it all for that.'

The reality of British politics is that while opposition is futile and frustrating, so is governing for government's sake, putting in place reforms which don't last beyond the Parliament in which they are enacted, or not putting in place reforms at all.

That was true for the Lib Dems, but you could also look at the first year of the new Tory government after 2015, and ask, given that it proved to be their last in power, what actually do David Cameron and George Osborne have to show for it? The expansion of nuclear energy, stalled. Forced academisation of schools, ditched. Budget welfare reforms, unravelled. And on Europe, a divisive and disastrous referendum defeat.

But perhaps there is one thing. In September 2015, on the Sunday of the Tory Party conference, I received an email from a Labour colleague in Parliament highlighting an announcement which had just been briefed to the newspapers, the day before George Osborne's conference speech. He had asked Lord Andrew Adonis, the Labour peer, to chair a commission to help set long-term priorities for infrastructure, an idea that I had first put forward in opposition three years before, having developed it with Lord Adonis himself and Sir John Armitt, the man who delivered the Olympic Games as chair of the delivery authority.

Our vision was to take long-term infrastructure decisions outside the political debate, and make it harder for successive governments either to take the short-term route of cutting capital spending, or to ignore the major long-term infrastructure decisions which were vital for the country but would yield no short-term electoral benefit, prime examples being the rebuilding of the Thames Barrier or the modernisation of the National Grid.

We wanted to break the logjam caused when essential infrastructure decisions were delayed for purely political reasons, as successive governments have done over the building of extra airport capacity in the south-east. Far better to have public proposals from an independent commission, reporting to Parliament but outside the political process, which can then hold the government's feet to the fire to deliver them.

It was one of the few Labour policy proposals in the last Parliament which turned out to be extremely successful with business. The CBI, the Institute of Directors and the British Chambers of Commerce all praised it, and just a few months before the 2015 general election we held a very successful conference in Westminster to discuss the idea. We published the draft legislation, we set out the priorities for the Infrastructure Commission's work, and appointed Sir John to chair it. The only barrier to it being enacted was, of course, if Labour didn't win the general election. When we didn't, I thought that was the end of it – another grand case study in the futility of opposition.

But then George Osborne decided to pinch the idea, appoint its co-creator Lord Adonis as the head of the commission, and make it the centrepiece of his party conference speech. I didn't know whether to feel gratified or annoyed, but I was certainly pretty frustrated. A few months later, after a trip to Iceland with the International Monetary Fund, I sat on the plane returning home reading their latest report on the UK economy. There was a paragraph in which the IMF commended Osborne's 'foresight' in coming up with the proposal for the Infrastructure Commission. I smiled wryly, and thought: 'That's the trouble with opposition.'

In the end it is only government which can enact change, and has the opportunity to build the public and political consensus which ensures that change will last. In those instances, oppositions can lend support, and even ideas, but that is about it. The only purpose of opposition is to propose an alternative, win the public's trust and get in to power. The rest is just the noise of protest, opposition for opposition's sake, and almost always worth nothing at all.

Whether the Lord Adonis commission can become one of those lasting, fundamental reforms that change our country remains to be seen; and given the impact of Brexit on investment intentions in the UK, he has a mountain to climb. But I wish him the best of luck.

23

Mistakes

We all get things wrong – but which are the errors you should be able to avoid?

As someone who's had plenty of experience of both, I've found that the mistakes you make in politics are a little like those you make in cars.

There are careless lapses of concentration, like tweeting your own name when meaning to search for it, or forgetting the surname of a businessman you've just had dinner with under the pressure of a live TV interview, two of my more notorious gaffes. They're the equivalent of lazily joining the motorway from a familiar slip road, and not thinking to check whether the usual speed limit is in force, or answering a phone call from the Prime Minister when stuck in traffic – driving offences which cost me a few points on my licence as well as a few predictable headlines.

Then there are mistakes you don't know you're making at the time, and only become aware of after the fact, like the time I bumped a parked car when reversing, and drove away. Or in political terms, the 75p pension increase, or the decision to sell a portion of the UK's gold reserves just before the world gold price jumped. It's easy to blame the politicians responsible in both cases, but there was no malice or even carelessness in our intentions or those of the civil servants who advised us, more an inability on any of our parts to see the mistakes we were making.

But then there are other mistakes. The political equivalent of getting behind the wheel after one too many drinks or speeding because you're late for a meeting. The kind of mistakes which cost lives – and elections.

In 2014, I was witness to one such catastrophic mistake – a mistake which reinforced the relentless Tory campaign that Ed Miliband and I were in denial about the deficit, and couldn't be trusted to take over the economy. It happened in Manchester at what we knew was the last Labour conference before the election. We were just ahead in the opinion polls, but our private polling told us that we still faced big challenges on the economy, public spending, immigration and leadership.

In the weeks before the annual conference, I'd hardly seen Ed, as he'd been so consumed with the referendum on Scottish independence – and we'd barely discussed his leader's speech at all. But unlike Gordon and Tony, we always swapped our speech drafts well in advance, which usually prevented any problems and misunderstandings.

I say usually, because even that didn't always work. At the

2013 conference, when I issued a tough warning that Labour would only support the High Speed 2 rail line if the costs came down and the value-for-money case was proved, some of Ed's advisers briefed after the speech that the leader didn't support what I'd said, despite Ed and I discussing the precise words at length the previous day.

When I read Ed's vital 2014 draft, I was concerned that it wasn't doing enough to tackle our weaknesses and suggested that it needed a lot more on fiscal discipline and the deficit to echo the tough speech that I would be making the day before. I felt he was doing too little to show we understood the concerns the public had about us. His office agreed, and sent a new draft through shortly afterwards. The new passages were much better.

I always enjoyed doing my annual conference speech – the packed hall, the media interest, the platform to make an argument – and I would like to think I got much better at it as the years went by. And my speech on that Monday went as well as a Shadow Chancellor's speech can go the year before an election. I spent the day before ringing my Shadow Cabinet colleagues to tell them that we were going to extend the 1 per cent cap on child benefit increases for a further year and that we would be freezing ministerial pay if we won the election. No one raised a word about the former. But I was surprised that more than one colleague got very agitated about the latter. In the hall there were the usual grumblings when I said that we would be making no promises to increase spending, but even the Unite general secretary, Len McCluskey, was forced to laugh at my jokes about George Osborne and Michael Gove.

The evening news bulletins went pretty well, with the tough message prominent. And the next day it was Ed's turn. During every leader's speech, I was always so absorbed in what I would be asked in interviews following it, and in trying to look attentive and happy in case the cameras cut to me, that I didn't often focus on what was being said, especially if I'd read the speech several times in advance.

It was the same with Gordon's Budget speeches. I'd spend the hour he was on his feet looking at the reactions of the MPs and the hacks, and thinking about the press briefing I'd do immediately afterwards. Gordon could have been reading out the shipping forecast and I wouldn't have noticed.

So when Ed Miliband delivered his speech at that 2014 pre-election conference, I'd like to say I listened in horror when he failed to deliver certain key passages, but the honest truth is that I'd completely zoned out. At the end, I rose to my feet to applaud along with the rest of the conference hall and was immediately grabbed by John Pienaar for an interview with Radio 5 Live. I found myself congratulating Ed for setting out his plans for a fairer, stronger economy, built on a platform of tough fiscal discipline.

When I finished, Alex, my media adviser, took me to one side, summoned up all his professionalism, and told me calmly that Ed had in fact missed out the entire section on the deficit, and – to add salt to the wounds – forgotten to mention immigration. It's strange how your emotions lurch around in situations like that: disbelief, astonishment, fury, and sympathy, imagining how angry Ed would be at himself.

Sometimes in politics you know instantly that one picture or one story will cement a perception in the public mind which no amount of other pictures or stories can unpick. This was one of those times.

At the end of the conference, Yvette and I followed our usual ritual, jumping straight in the car, getting onto the motorway, and listening to music until we could find a service station with a McDonald's. After a week of eating posh dinners with journalists, that's all you crave. There were some Labour students in the same service station so we had our final selfies of the conference season with them, then sat in the car, eating our burgers, listening to Nick Robinson on the PM programme giving his verdict on the conference, our last before the election.

And surprise, surprise – the only thing Nick wanted to talk about was the fact that Ed Miliband had forgotten to mention either immigration or the deficit, the biggest issues Yvette and I had on our respective plates; and how this just confirmed everything the electorate thought about Ed. We looked at each other, and I said: 'I'm afraid he's absolutely right.'

Most supposedly big moments in politics, however fevered the Westminster reaction, take place in a bubble, with only other MPs, journalists and people interested in politics listening. But you know there are certain events in politics that cut right through. One had come straight after the 2010 election when the outgoing Chief Secretary, Liam Byrne, had left a note for his successor wishing him luck and saying 'I'm afraid there is no money.'

It was intended as a joke – there is a long tradition dating back to the 1960s of outgoing Chief Secretaries leaving comical handover notes – and Liam thought he was leaving it for his pre-election Shadow, Philip Hammond, who by then he knew well. But when the coalition government was formed, that job went instead to the Lib Dem David Laws who promptly gave it to his new boss George Osborne to be gleefully announced at a press conference.

Leaking that note – and pretending it was in any way serious – was a pretty shabby thing for Laws to do, but it certainly worked politically. And just like that note, the fact that the Labour leader hadn't mentioned the deficit or immigration once in his most important speech before the election was undoubtedly going to be a very big issue for people up and down the country.

Nick Robinson's point was unambiguous: the omissions were a symbol of Labour not being willing to face up to the problems the country was worried about, and proof that we were trying to brush difficult issues under the carpet. We weren't ready – and didn't deserve – to return to government. It was incredibly frustrating.

As always with these kinds of mistakes, it wasn't just a momentary lapse, but a product of a whole parliament. We had collectively failed to agree and broadcast a settled position on the deficit or immigration, and to deal head-on with our perceived vulnerability on managing those two pivotal issues.

I had already come face-to-face with the divisive impact of the immigration debate. Back in April 2010, on the day the whole Cabinet launched an election poster manifesto – immortalised when a car ominously crashed on a roundabout just a few yards from our photo call – I'd had to dash up to

Morley to do a lunchtime hustings. It took place in the town square in front of a baying mob, with the BNP candidate whipping them up from the platform and the Tory responding by talking about migrants 'swamping' the area.

Since then I had held close to twenty public meetings in my constituency and it was clear to me it wasn't a case of people wanting to shut the borders, it was just that they feared that immigration was not being properly managed. In the weeks and months before the European elections in 2014, I consistently said to Ed that, based on what I was seeing and hearing going round the country, we had to address the issue of immigration. I said: you've got to talk about it, show that you understand and that you're willing to talk about tougher controls.

But while compared to previous Labour leaders Ed Miliband did talk regularly about immigration 'reform' and tackling exploitation, he didn't want to mention the word 'control'. As far as he was concerned, anything that suggested we might be questioning the principle of free movement would cause us big problems with our European partners, and could cost us the votes of ex-Lib Dems.

The only political positive about the immigration debate was that the Tories were seen as equally hopeless at dealing with the problem, with David Cameron's foolish 2010 pledge to reduce net migration to the tens of thousands openly ridiculed in my public meetings. So I didn't believe that issue alone would cost us the election.

The economy, however, was something different. From when we lost in 2010 onwards, Labour struggled to arrive at a unified approach on the deficit and the economy. Should we accept the Tories' deficit plans and spending limits and then try and talk about something else? Should we apologise for spending too much in the past and say we had learned and changed? Or should we go on the offensive, rebut the Tory attacks, defend Labour's economic record in government and set out a detailed alternative?

I was urged to follow all three strategies by Shadow colleagues. A couple of them, at different times, advised me to follow all three. But I came to believe all three options were wrong, and indeed, it was our collective obsession with which one of these flawed analyses was correct that proved to be the real problem. It is a lesson politics needs to learn from science: if you are constantly testing the wrong hypotheses, you'll never learn the truth.

Option one was to conclude that, in the end, winning the debate on the economy was an impossible task for Labour, because the financial crisis was such a fundamental knock to Labour's economic credibility that it was simply too big to overcome in a mere five years, just as John Major's government never recovered from the ignominy of sterling's exit from the ERM on Black Wednesday in September 1992. It's certainly true that I regularly had to explain to my parliamentary Labour Party colleagues and the Shadow Cabinet that for us to get anywhere near parity with the Tories on the issue would be a huge achievement, and I had to remind them that right until the 1997 election, and even after the ERM disaster, Gordon Brown had trailed Ken Clarke on public trust on the economy.

The trouble is that advocates of this argument concluded that we should either treat the 2015 election as a lost cause, or – as they phrased it – try and neutralise the issue by accepting all the Tories' tax and deficit plans, and attempt to shift the election debate instead to competing visions for the NHS or education.

To my mind, neither giving up on the election nor giving in on the economy was acceptable. The NHS was definitely a potent campaigning opportunity for Labour. But every election in modern British history has ultimately been decided on the economy, tax and public spending. If Labour was going to accept that the Tories had the right approach on all those issues, surely the electorate would follow suit.

I was certainly in no mood to sign up to George Osborne's rapid and, in my view, wrong-headed deficit reduction plan and his goal to eliminate the deficit by 2015. I thought it was completely undeliverable – as I had set out back in 2010 in my Bloomberg speech – and would hamper the recovery. And, for all his tough rhetoric and punishing spending cuts, that's how things turned out.

The second option argued that the only way for Labour to deal with the issue was to admit that we had made mistakes during our time in office, that we'd borrowed and spent too much and that excessive spending was to blame for the financial crisis. Essentially, advocates of this plan wanted us to say that Liam Byrne's note was telling the truth, not making a joke, that our spending had contributed to the financial crisis, that we accepted full responsibility for that and were willing to apologise to the British public.

That was a popular theme of some of the old Blairites after 2010, but I have to say I was never clear how much they thought it was a strategy for Labour to win the next general election, or just to pin the blame on Gordon and Gordon alone for why we'd lost the last one. From my perspective, this argument was both completely inaccurate and politically suicidal.

Factually, as I got very tired of saying over the years, while, of course, we made lots of individual mistakes on spending during our time in office – remember the Dome? – the overall level of public expenditure was never excessively high and the national debt had fallen, and it was only as a result of the financial crisis that our borrowing and our debt levels ballooned. That would have happened regardless of whether we'd been running a small surplus or a small deficit in 2008.

Many people, friends and colleagues included, would get frustrated by my stubbornness on this issue, and thought I would have had an easier ride from the media if I'd just conceded the point and tried to move on. But the journalist and the economist in me simply wouldn't allow me to 'admit' something that I didn't and still don't believe to be true. In addition to which, the politician in me thought it would again hand the Tories the election on a plate. They made enough hay with the Liam Byrne note without us formally conceding they were right.

Of course, to my mind, these two options shared a common problem – they were both economically flawed. Neither matching George Osborne's economically reckless austerity plan nor pretending that Labour's spending record had caused the global financial crisis made any economic sense. And on the basis that bad economics ends up being bad politics, as I have always believed, they were easy to reject.

But the third option – defending Labour's record and setting out a detailed alternative on the deficit – was hugely problematic. I knew it was the right thing to do economically, but I wasn't convinced that I could make it work politically.

The difficult issue was not how much time to spend defending Labour's record – Ed Miliband and I both agreed that if we turned the election into a debate about what had happened in the past, we'd be sunk, no matter how robustly we fought our corner. Our goal was to focus on what the economy, society, living standards and public services were going to look like in the years up to 2020, and which party people wanted making the decisions to realise those goals, not to have a constant discussion about who was to blame for what happened between 1997 and 2010.

It was frustrating in the run up to the general election to have some of the same colleagues who had urged me to apologise for Labour's record back in 2011 now urging me to do much more to defend it and talk up the role we had played steering the world through the financial crisis. I had people criticising me in 2015 for not saying often enough a phrase that they'd criticised me for using in my 2011 conference speech: 'It wasn't too many police officers or nurses or teachers here in Britain that bankrupted Lehman Brothers in New York.' I just took that on the chin.

But while my economic instinct was to set out a clear alternative to George Osborne – a slower pace of deficit reduction, a public investment programme to rebalance the economy, taking advantage of very low long-term interest rates, opposing his increasingly desperate and irresponsible efforts to fuel a new consumer and housing boom through government mortgage subsidies – my political antennae said this was an argument that just could not be won.

I knew in my heart it was economically right, but unlike the euro – where public opinion and the right-wing media were instinctively with us – my head told me it would be impossible to win this argument and that, bizarrely, it would further damage our 'economic credibility' with the voters and the media if we tried. All our polling showed us that extra help for first-time buyers was very popular. And while the voters were worried about George Osborne's strategy and wanted a more 'balanced plan', whenever Labour talked about more public investment and slower deficit reduction, the public just heard more borrowing, more risk and higher taxes.

So I took a slower, more defensive approach, convincing myself that if we could get into government, we could start turning the argument around from within.

I had learned over the past three decades that the government and the opposition play by different rules on the economy. We had shown after 1997 that a Chancellor can set out a sensible and economically sound strategy of balancing the current budget – matching day to day spending to tax revenues – while borrowing to invest to help grow the economy. But the media and the voters expect the opposition to show in an election campaign that – like an ordinary household managing its monthly spending – its tax and spending plans match up. Having been involved in three winning election campaigns, I knew the economic credibility argument ultimately relied on the ability to prove that the opposition's sums did not add up, and to expose what their plans would translate to in potential tax rises and spending cuts.

I vividly remembered Michael Portillo and Oliver Letwin walking into that trap before the 2001 and 2005 elections, to such an extent that we couldn't believe our luck. We were able to cost their planned spending cuts in exactly the same way as the 1992 Shadow Budget allowed the Conservatives to win that election by scaring the public about Labour's tax rise bombshell.

So my determination was never to give George Osborne a single opening in terms of unfunded promises or overambitious forecasts, and instead to try and turn the tables and expose his own weakness on those fronts. Everything I did – from imposing rigid discipline on my colleagues' spending commitments, and supporting the continuation of the 1 per cent cap on public sector pay settlements back in 2012, to asking the Office for Budget Responsibility to audit our manifesto, and promising to get the current Budget back into surplus and the national debt falling again in the next Parliament – was done with that in mind.

I concluded, following my announcement on the public sector pay cap, that the decision of my trade union, Unite, who had supported me in my constituency at the 2010 election, not to give me a penny of support for 2015 was just evidence that I was getting my message over, at whatever personal cost to my chances of staying an MP.

Being Shadow Chancellor is a pretty thankless task, with lots of saying no and enforcing message discipline. But I was lucky to have talented and media-savvy Shadow Chief Secretaries in Angela Eagle, Rachel Reeves and Chris Leslie. And I was hugely helped by having a brilliant team with old stalwarts like Alex, Balshen and Julie joined by new recruits. I brought in Gary Follis, a Labour veteran of the Whips' Office, to be my Chief of Staff. Jon Newton made sure all the trains ran on time. And Karim Palant checked every Labour speech and press release to root out any spending commitments, a job Yvette had pioneered working for John Smith back in 1991.

So we were resolute in our own discipline on public spending. But I was equally clear that signing up to George Osborne's impossibly austere deficit reduction plans would be disastrous – both for our chances of winning the election, and for what the hell we'd do if we managed to win. While the Labour left later tried to claim that I signed up to Osborne's austerity, I was clear that his plans were undeliverable, a fact that he himself belatedly recognised when he scaled them back in his first Budget after the election and then saw them jettisoned entirely under Theresa May.

For me the important thing was to make sure we were not boxed in and had the flexibility to pursue the right economic strategy in government. I would never have contemplated signing up to George Osborne's deficit plans as Shadow Chancellor John McDonnell advocated in the autumn of 2015. Instead, a year before the election, I set out fiscal rules which committed us to balance the current budget, excluding investment, by the end of the decade. They would allow us to take longer than George Osborne proposed in order to keep supporting public services and to continue to borrow to invest. But while I was preserving our room for manoeuvre, I resisted signing up to a full-throated pre-election call for more spending paid for by borrowing – an argument I knew at the time we could not win politically, whatever the economic logic.

Instead, we set out to argue that Osborne's failure to secure a stronger recovery and rising living standards was the reason he was failing to meet his own deficit reduction targets. Our aim was to contrast our plan for growth with his risky and unfair spending cuts and contend that the only way ultimately to get rid of the deficit was to get rid of the Tories.

But Ed Miliband was still torn: between his pollsters and advisers telling him we needed to deal decisively with the deficit issue by matching the Tory plans, his own personal instincts to make the case for 'borrowing to invest', and me in the middle desperately trying not to hand the Tories an advantage, either by signing up to their plans or opening up a damaging 'extra spending paid for by more borrowing or tax rises' flank.

And that is the truth behind his conference slip-up. At a time when Ed was still struggling to decide what to say, it's perhaps understandable that – in the ultimate Freudian slip – he ended up saying nothing at all. Whereas for my strategy to work we needed Labour's commitment to fiscal discipline to be a core part of his narrative, running through his speech like words through a stick of rock – not simply a couple of paragraphs which could so easily be forgotten.

As for me, I have never been afraid to push the boat out and go against the consensus when necessary: opposing joining the euro, pushing tax rises for the NHS or challenging Osborne's fiscal strategy in my Bloomberg speech. But I don't like getting either the politics or the economics wrong. And this time, with political and economic logic pulling in opposing directions, I decided that if we were to have a chance of winning the election, I had to put the politics first.

Was that a mistake? My answer is still no. Arguing for a detailed jobs plan paid for by more public borrowing just wouldn't have worked. For Labour in 2015, still dealing with the aftermath of the global financial crisis which happened on our watch, it was an argument we just couldn't win.

The irony is that in the first few months of 2015, and the first few weeks of the election campaign, my strategy appeared to be working. The line we'd established on our approach to the deficit and public spending was holding, viewed as 'tough' but not the same as the Tories, so we weren't under any great pressure. George Osborne's January attempt to expose Labour's spending 'bombshell' had imploded as we had successfully shown his claims were totally invented. In the election campaign proper, he was never able to land a single blow on us about the unaffordability of our Budget plans.

But if David Cameron wanted to 'prove' we had no economic credibility, he didn't need data, he could simply point to Liam Byrne's note or – even worse – Ed Miliband's conference speech.

And this perception that Ed did not care about fiscal discipline left us vulnerable to the inevitable Tory attack that the SNP would be deciding our first Budget if we ended up with a hung Parliament. Once the Tories put our weakness on economic credibility together with the fear that the SNP would be calling the shots, we were sunk. We became the risky choice. I believe millions of English voters – most crucially ex-Lib Dems – genuinely felt that their taxes were going to be hiked at the whim of Alex Salmond and Nicola Sturgeon, and the only way to stop that happening was by voting Tory.

Of course, some people will argue that the real underlying problem we failed to deal with was the idea that people just couldn't see Ed Miliband as a potential prime minister, or me as a potential Chancellor, and that our record in the Treasury before the financial crisis was playing a role in that.

For my part, I was sufficiently worried that I constantly asked Labour's pollsters to test the extent to which I personally was to blame for the slump in the party's economic ratings, and I attended focus groups to watch behind the glass and hear the views from potential voters first-hand. I used to say to Yvette that I would stand aside in a heartbeat if I thought I personally was going to cost the party the election.

But the answers I heard were that, while there was no doubting the negative opinions of Labour on the economy, it dated back at least ten years, and wasn't personal to me or Ed Miliband. If anything, when people were asked what they knew about me and my past in politics, the association was with my time as Children's Secretary, and in particular the Baby P case, not anything to do with the Treasury.

It may be why the Tories gave up portraying Ed and me as

puppets of Gordon Brown, or the men who 'crashed the car' during the election campaign – we knew those adverts just left many voters a bit baffled. But when they struck on the idea of billboard ads portraying Ed Miliband as a puppet of Alex Salmond, that really did hit home, because it combined the persistent worries about Labour's economic management with the new fear that Ed wouldn't have the strength as a leader to stand up to the SNP on tax and spending in a hung Parliament.

Every politician has problems they brush under the carpet, hoping either that they'll go away or that solutions will eventually present themselves. But, just like ignoring the alcohol limit or going too fast, it's an unforgivable mistake. Whatever problems the current Labour opposition are debating, they have to confront them head-on, not wait and pay the price at the next election.

24

Civility

————————

Politics today is too aggressive and divisive – who's to blame and can it be fixed?

I never usually questioned the purpose of a life in politics. Except for occasional Wednesdays at 12.35 p.m. from 2010 onwards, when I'd sit alone in my Commons office thinking: 'Why am I doing this? Is this really a productive way to spend my life?'

I would have just emerged from Prime Minister's Questions and, invariably, an angry clash with David Cameron. I'd taunt him, he'd hit back at me – and our respective sides would cheer or heckle as if we were pantomime dames.

For all his early talk of 'ending Punch and Judy politics', Cameron was more partisan – and evasive – at the dispatch box than any prime minister I'd ever seen. And while the statesmanlike thing for the opposition to do may have been just to sit there smiling quietly as his tirades and insults flew across, there was a real danger of ending up looking weak and irrelevant.

I was torn. I knew every time I got under David Cameron's skin and he lashed out angrily at me, it was a small victory for our side. I didn't think we could let him get away with his partisan bluster. But I would sit there afterwards with my head in my hands, asking myself: 'Is this why you came into politics?' And when I felt a strange sense of relief at losing my own seat in 2015, it was avoiding a return to all that rubbish that I had most in mind.

I grew up round kitchen tables alive with debate about politics, football, the state of the world, anything really. It was always a good way to forensically test the weaknesses in my arguments. At Oxford and Harvard, whether in the lecture halls or the political societies, I loved that intellectual cut and thrust; the desire to posit theories and challenge them. I joined the Oxford Conservative Club and the Liberal Club as well as the Labour Club, not because I had any sympathy with their politics, but because they gave more opportunities to hear outside speakers and engage in debate.

Labour colleagues used to ask me why I attended the annual meetings of the Bilderberg Group, alongside the likes of Kenneth Clarke, George Osborne and senior US Republicans, horrified that I was taking part in what they saw as some shadow Parliament of the plutocracy. I would explain that it was practically the only environment I knew in world politics where people with opposing opinions and theories could debate them in a calm and reasoned atmosphere, and learn and develop their thinking accordingly.

Prime Minister's Questions is the exact opposite. I'm sure every PM feels the same way. They hate it because they have to spend so many hours and days preparing, and still go in not knowing how or when they're going to be caught off guard, and – in David Cameron's case – not knowing at what precise point he'd say something bad-tempered or rash that would become the story.

I think Ed Miliband was always a bit unsure whether he liked me sitting next to him, or regarded it as a distraction. Every now and then a message would come through just before PMQs to say he was doing questions on some specific topic, and would like the responsible Shadow minister next to him instead. But the economy and austerity were invariably such hot issues in those early years of opposition that his line of questioning couldn't diverge much, plus later on – when stories started to appear saying that he was considering sacking me – it would have become a problem if I wasn't sitting next to him. And he would usually dig me in the ribs and urge me to wind Cameron up to get our side going.

On television, you never get a sense of how small the House of Commons actually is, how close the opposing benches are to each other, and what a cauldron of noise is created. The microphones pick up only a fraction of what is going on, as do the journalists up in the press gallery. It was perfectly possible, and common, for George Osborne and me to have a whispered chat throughout the PMQs exchanges.

I'd observe how little David Cameron understood the issues; George would ask in response why then were we unable to lay a glove on him?

Of course, Cameron could also hear what I was saying, and would become gradually more and more irate, especially when I had the temerity to address him directly, and ask repeatedly – in the manner of a disappointed schoolmaster – why he didn't just work harder at his job. Nothing annoyed him more than the simple phrases: 'You're supposed to be the Prime Minister. You're supposed to know these things. Why can't you answer the question? Why are you floundering around? Are you sure you're up to this?'

Naturally, a small part of me wished I could be in Ed's shoes, and pose the questions myself. And a big part of me just wished that we were tougher and more aggressive when attacking the government's record on cuts, the deficit and economic growth, especially in those first three years in opposition when we could have won that argument.

But while I couldn't ask Cameron questions, I could certainly use my low-level heckling and visible body language at PMQs to put him under pressure: using my outstretched hand to signal that the economy was flatlining, for example – a gesture akin to the smoothing of a bedsheet.

If you believe you're born to be prime minister you probably don't think that anyone else has a right to question the way you do the job, let alone treat you with disrespect, or – when it comes to your own civil servants – question the wisdom, practicality or legality of your plans. Among the media, his own ministers and MPs, and behind the closed doors of Downing Street, Cameron's temper was even more notorious than Gordon Brown's. But that was a side of his character that the public rarely got to see, and PMQs became one of the only occasions we could expose it.

I'm absolutely certain he never came into a session on Wednesday intending to say something nasty or patronising – you'd sometimes see him visibly trying to calm down and control himself – but eventually his inner Flashman would win out. In the Commons, I always knew I'd got him when one of his own backbenchers was asking some patsy question he didn't even have to listen to, and he'd instead glance over at me and hiss: 'Why don't you just shut up?' or 'Stop waving your stupid hand.'

It wouldn't be long after that before he'd allow that rising anger to boil over, going red in the face, snarling personal abuse at Ed Miliband or Dennis Skinner, telling Angela Eagle to 'Calm down, dear,' or announcing that I was a 'muttering idiot' or 'the most annoying man in politics'. Down the front bench, Sadiq Khan would look at his watch and say 'Well, it took him twenty-two minutes today' or 'Seven minutes! That's a new record!' So when Cameron finally lost it, it's true that it always gave me some temporary satisfaction. But without fail, I'd always go back to my Commons office afterwards and have those solitary moments of despair.

On the days when Ed scored a good hit, I was quieter, but on the days when he didn't, I'd try harder to catch Cameron out. If there's a comparison with close fielders sledging in cricket, it's that you don't bother when your spinner is turning them sideways, but you have to try everything when it's 200–0 on a flat pitch.

★

From my side, outside the Chamber, there was no personal animus between me and David Cameron. But in the ten years we shared the same corridors in Parliament, he never said a word or even gave a nod when we passed – he'd just stare ahead, or look at his papers or his phone. I can't think of a single other Tory MP who did the same, even the ones who were equally hostile in Commons debates. Even post-election, that attitude continued. The first time afterwards that our paths crossed directly, I could see he was a little puzzled at my presence. As he walked towards me, I gave him a nod and a smile. He ignored me and looked away.

In stark contrast, George Osborne was always friendly and civil. We had some very heated and bruising exchanges in Parliament and in the interview studios over the years, but immediately afterwards we'd be able to have a little chat about our kids, or about staff moves at the Treasury, almost a bit of a ritual to show there were no hard feelings.

I certainly wouldn't go so far as to call him a friend, but there was definitely a mutual respect and enjoyment of the political tussle, the same way you shake hands and go for a pint with your opponent even after a bad-tempered football match.

And yet there were times when things did become raw and difficult, behind closed doors as well as in the Commons Chamber, including when George made factually untrue allegations about my supposed role in the Libor scandal in a *Spectator* interview and then refused to withdraw them. Eventually, a few days later, he let it be known through his aides that he accepted he was wrong; but he didn't say so publicly, which prompted Tory MP Andrea Leadsom to call on him to apologise in an interview.

I profoundly disagreed with Michael Gove on education policy when we were up against each other, but I found him equally civil; we had tough exchanges but, again, there was mutual respect, and it was no surprise, but much appreciated nonetheless, that both Michael and George sent me very personal and thoughtful messages after I lost my seat in 2015.

Theresa May, on the other hand, was much harder to deal with. I expected her to call to congratulate me when I was appointed shadow home secretary, which is the usual form, but after a few days wait I gave up and called her instead. I wanted to reassure her that I would work with her closely on national security and counter terrorism. I had been involved with many highly sensitive issues at the Treasury and DCSF and knew how important it was to work closely with the opposition. But back then at least that was not her way. She kept me at arm's length, and the one time she rang me to give me a supposedly confidential briefing, it turned out she had already briefed the press. We had a civil relationship, but it was as distant as any working relationship I have had in politics.

George Osborne and Michael Gove weren't the only Conservatives I had good relationships with. More Tory MPs than Labour sponsored me to run the London Marathon, and – given that I was the Father Christmas for ten consecutive years at the annual Commons Christmas party – I'd guess that more children of Conservative MPs have sat on my knee than on any other politician's in Britain. Many Tory MPs who attended Treasury debates in the House of Commons also used to enjoy the very civilised and often quite humorous exchanges we'd have when I was taking their interventions during my speech, and some would seek me out afterwards to tell me so.

In some ways, it's a shame that – obsessives who follow Parliament TV aside – this is a side of politics that the public never see. All they know is George Osborne and me snapping at each other on the *Marr* programme. They wouldn't know our respective kids would be hanging out backstage, and that we'd all go for breakfast afterwards.

It's a shame and also a problem – because when all the public see is the uncivilised side of politics, they've got no reason to be civil to you themselves, especially when they disagree with your politics.

In previous generations, the political world was more remote. Politicians were people whose pictures you saw in the newspaper, and who very occasionally you saw in the flesh, making a speech to a large audience, or doing an election walkabout. But these days, first of all, people can see what you get up to in the House of Commons. Second, they see you appear – or discussed – on television much more often, not only on the news but on a whole range of interview and entertainment shows. And third, because of Twitter and social media, they have that sense of being able to engage with you and react to you whenever and however they want.

That all creates a sense of familiarity for them which is obviously very one-sided. So when you're going about your ordinary life – walking to a football match, sitting on a train going to visit your parents, or waiting at the airport to go on holiday – people you've never met can come up to you and talk in a very direct, very personal, and sometimes very abusive way. They're just continuing a conversation they've already been having with you on and off in their own head, sometimes for years.

The reality of being a well-known politician is that people come up to you all the time, but you never know until they open their mouths whether it is going to be a friendly greeting and a request for a selfie, or a tirade of abuse. The week after losing my seat in 2015, I went to the Norwich v Ipswich play-off match at Carrow Road, and walked to the ground with my young son. As usual, lots of people smiled or said hello or just stared as I walked past. But one man spotted me, marched up, put his face very close to mine, and spat: 'You're unemployed – ahhh!' and walked off.

That kind of personal abuse was particularly bad in 2009, when Labour was dealing with both the financial crisis and the fallout from the expenses scandal. I remember a very respectable-looking older man in a tweed suit and waistcoat having an ordinary conversation with his wife on a train before getting up for the toilet and realising I was in the next row of seats. He immediately turned very aggressive and abusive, telling me I was a disgrace and a shit, in a way that I think even shocked his own wife.

As well as a Goldilocks skin – not too thick, not too thin – you also need a Worzel Gummidge head as a politician, as I used to tell my fellow door-to-door canvassers in my old constituency. In the 1980s TV series, Worzel used to have different heads he'd put on depending on his mood: happy, sad, funny.

Whenever I was about to embark on that rather strange process of knocking on the doors of strangers, something that makes even the most experienced campaigners a bit awkward and nervous, I'd always tell new members joining the team that they needed to swap their normal head for their campaigning head, and be ready to go to each door with equal enthusiasm, no matter how many were slammed in their faces.

The trouble is, if you don't have a campaigning head, you can't survive in politics, but if you never take it off, you stop being a real person. The only alternative is just to shut yourself away. There were some MPs who did exactly that during the expenses scandal, in part because they so hated the painful reality of their spouses, children and friends having to see them take abuse in public.

The other thing every politician has to learn is to confront and challenge your preconceptions and see everyone as the individuals they are. Whether it's a bunch of teenagers on a street corner or an audience of people about to hear you make a speech, you can't project your worst fears onto them. If you stand up in front of a thousand people at a conference, and assume they all hate you and want you to fail, you inevitably will.

Every time I spoke at a teachers' conference, I would always ask the organisers to get together a group of twenty teachers in advance and we'd have a chat for half an hour, or I'd consciously go into the tea break where all the delegates were gathered before my speech and have a chat with some people at random.

What that would tell me was that even if some people wanted to grill you or were a bit sceptical, they were still decent, friendly, welcoming people who just wanted to talk, be listened to, and hear what you had to say. And once you know that, it's a much easier environment to approach. As I got more used to being on Twitter, I adopted the same mode of thinking. I'd sometimes look at my timeline, and I'd see twenty or thirty comments which were hideously offensive or abusive, and it's easy to make the mistake of feeling: 'Well, that's what everybody thinks.'

But if you put them all together, they would only fill the upstairs room of one pub, and then I'd ask myself: am I really going to forget all the hundreds of decent, reasonable people I encounter every day – including on Twitter – and worry instead about a couple of dozen very angry people in the upstairs room of a pub?

That day outside Carrow Road, when I met the 'You're unemployed!' man and instinctively thought to myself: 'Is it going to be like this all day?', I knew the answer was 'No', because, in the end, that was one person in a crowd of 25,000, and even if many more of them felt as happy about my political demise as that guy, they would probably be too decent to say so to my face, or in front of my son, especially when we were both there to support Norwich against our most bitter rivals.

In an ideal world, no one would behave like that, but that's a bit too much to wish for. However, the one thing politicians can control is how they themselves behave, and the manner in which they conduct their debates.

Yes, people enjoy the cut and thrust of politics, they want a decent argument, they sometimes want opposition MPs to show the government how angry people are about some of their decisions; but ultimately they want good outcomes for themselves, their families and their communities, and those are rarely delivered when Westminster is just an exercise in mutual name-calling and acrimony.

I know, speaking to people, that David Cameron is great company with his close friends and devoted to his family. But when it comes to politics, he saw it as a tribal, gladiatorial, contact sport. I fear he most definitely brought out that side of me too. But I always enjoyed the Commons exchanges more when they were founded on humour and intellect rather than aggression.

But it's not good enough for Cameron, me or those who will now come after us to complain that it's impossible for us to change the culture of politics. After all, we see a far different House of Commons often enough when it comes together to mourn the loss of a well-loved figure or some fresh terrorist outrage. I'd see it as well in the good-natured debates I'd have with Tory backbenchers on the economy.

I was definitely partly to blame with my sledging of Cameron at PMQs, playing up to the Tory caricature of me, rather than trying to challenge it. But responsibility starts at the top. If Theresa May wants the atmosphere at PMQs to be more statesmanlike, less partisan and less aggressive, it's up to her to set that tone – and stick to it.

PART FOUR

Learning To Move On

All careers in politics end in failure, but there is more to life. It's important to stay human and balanced and remember why you do it, so you can move on when the time comes, and do your best to help the next generation step up.

25

Hinterland

―――――――――

Most of us have a midlife crisis — so how do you turn the crisis into an opportunity?

'The bigger your empire grows, the more you have to look after your hinterland.' That was one of the best pieces of advice I ever received, and it came from a politician in a position to know – the late, great Denis Healey, Labour stalwart, former Chancellor and an MP for more than forty years.

It was one of the highlights of my trip to Denis' house by the Sussex coast with Bill Keegan, and he expanded on his point: 'You play the piano, you're running marathons, that's great. My hinterland was so important to me, it sustained me throughout my political career.'

Denis Healey was the Chancellor of the Exchequer who played the piano on television, live on *The Mike Yarwood Show*. His wonderful biography, *The Time of My Life*, describes his deep love and appreciation of poetry, music and theatre. At times of great stress, he wrote, he would wander over to the National Gallery to look at some paintings.

I'm afraid that, while I certainly came to be known as a politician with many outside interests by the end of my time in Parliament, I didn't do anywhere near as well as Denis Healey in managing and enjoying my hinterland during my time in government. And I've come to see in recent years what a mistake that was.

Too many politicians fear that admitting to any hinterland beyond family and children might suggest they're not fully committed to the job. But so many times over the past few years, when I've talked publicly about playing the piano, running marathons or my stammer, I've had people say: 'We knew you were a politician, but it's so good to know that you're a human being too.' And when they go on to say: 'You're so very different from what I expected,' you realise quite what a mountain politicians have to climb to be seen as real people and not just caricatures.

I was always a bit of an all-rounder when growing up – good at many things, not the best at anything. At school I played the violin to Grade 7, I was in the orchestra and choir, and played rugby, football and cricket. Aged fourteen, I even pole-vaulted for Nottinghamshire in a county match, not because I was particularly good at pole-vaulting but because only three of us turned up to the county trials. I quickly discovered how limited my pole-vaulting skills were when I was told that a number of sixth-form high-jump competitors were getting over higher heights with their Fosbury flops than I was with a pole.

At university I played football, rugby, cricket and darts for my college – I even competed in the inter-college ballroom-dancing competition – and also played in the Oxford Classical Orchestra. In my early twenties at the *Financial Times* and then as a young opposition adviser, I played football during the week for the FT team and at weekends for a brilliant team called the Hampstead Heathens, in the Southern Olympian League. But starting a family and moving into government in 1997 killed all that off.

Travelling backwards and forwards between Yorkshire and London every week made playing regular football impossible. Every now and then I got out my old violin, but even those odd occasions soon stopped. The long hours in the Treasury with Budgets, Autumn Statements and Spending Reviews meant there was little time for anything else. The birth of our first child in 1999 made that doubly so, with two more to follow over the next few years. Yvette and I were just about OK managing our jobs in government and looking after the children, but that was all we had time for. Family, friends and outside interests were all inevitably sacrificed. And that only got worse after we became Cabinet ministers in 2007.

I found it frustrating, but Yvette just said it was inevitable. She thinks it is just very hard for anyone in politics to maintain a hinterland given these twin pressures and obligations of work and family. She also maintains that trying to do so is easier for a man than a woman in politics, but probably in any profession. And she's right – especially when, given the 'everyday sexism' in our society, it was seen as noteworthy and unusual when I confessed a passion for baking cakes or cooking, whereas if Yvette had said the same, it wouldn't have got a mention.

Juggling family and work was often hard enough. In my time as a Treasury adviser, during which all our children were born, we all carried pagers, meaning that we were never really out of contact. The boundary between work and home became increasingly blurred, especially for me, working for Gordon, and often acting as the interlocutor between him and Number Ten.

One Saturday morning I took our two children to the giant Castleford soft-play centre – a children's paradise of climbing frames, ball ponds, slides and giant coloured blocks. Unfortunately our son managed to get himself stranded in one of the climbing frame tunnels. And then I received a call from Jeremy Heywood through the Downing Street switchboard. Despite the odd squeaking, I don't think Jeremy suspected that I was crawling through a plastic tunnel to rescue a toddler while trying to negotiate the Home Office budget for the next three years, but that's how my life was at the time.

The only exceptions we made were summer holidays, bank holiday weekends and New Year, when we spent time with our families and close friends and I could indulge my passion for cooking and birthday cakes. And I occasionally managed to get to see Norwich City. Being able to go to the football, stand in the away end, have a pint before and go as mad as anyone when we scored helped to get me through the stress and pressure.

When I was a Cabinet minister I did try to keep up my interest in music as well, usually just by having choral music playing quietly out of my computer in the department, often to the confusion of visiting civil servants who thought it was drifting over the road from Westminster Abbey. But that was about it. There was little time for anything other than work, what with early-morning starts, late finishes at the Commons, a few hours of paperwork from my red box at night and the whole family doing a 400-mile round trip on the train each and every week. To my shame, I would frequently go four or five days without seeing our children even though we were living in the same house, let alone make space for anything else. It's why our train journeys and weekends were so valuable.

But that all changed when we lost the general election in 2010. Despite the result not being a huge surprise, Labour's defeat, and the challenge of returning to opposition in my early forties, for the first time since my late twenties, hit me hard.

Over that summer I had the distraction of the Labour leadership election. I found the early weeks very tough as I established my pitch, assembled a team and dealt with question after question about my relationship with Gordon Brown. But my campaign launch, organised by Vernon Coaker at a packed community centre in his Gedling constituency, was brilliant.

Alex stayed with me as my campaign media chief, but what meant even more was Balshen Izzet leaving her safe and well-paid Civil Service role at the Department for Education to come and support me on the campaign trail. And I really enjoyed spending the summer touring round the UK going to hustings after hustings, meeting after meeting, fuelled by service-station toasted sandwiches, never knowing whether we were going to have an audience of twenty or three hundred when we arrived.

I was sponsored by the CWU who provided us with a people carrier covered in my campaign branding. The only trouble was that it had no fourth gear and I and my road team – Balshen, Ellie Gellard and often Jo Coles too – travelled thousands of miles just above seventy with the engine screaming at us. But what I remember most is the passion and interest and commitment of the audiences, young and old, and their determination that Labour would win again. It was liberating and uplifting.

I may have lost to Ed Miliband, but we did have the best end-of-campaign party the night the result was announced in Manchester, with karaoke in a local hotel in which the highlight was a pair of 'Endless Love' duets – I sang Diana Ross to CWU general secretary Billy Hayes' Lionel Richie, and vice versa. We were finally closed down at 3 a.m., supposedly after several complaints from an unsuspecting Polly Toynbee trying to get to sleep upstairs, yet by 10 a.m. I was on the football pitch for the annual MPs' football match, a little hungover but upbeat.

Afterwards, though, for the first few weeks and months following Ed Miliband's election, I was exhausted. I was appointed Shadow Home Secretary, and tried to throw myself into my new job to the best of my abilities. But it was a struggle, I was worn out and, after thirteen years of government, being in opposition felt frustrating and purposeless.

Eventually, I think I realised I was probably staring a midlife crisis in the face, and I made a conscious decision that – if that was going to happen – I needed to try and do something constructive with it.

That autumn I was invited by the disabled children's charity Whizz-Kidz to speak at a fundraising dinner with a group of donors in the City. And at the end of the evening, after I'd said my few words, their inspirational chief executive Ruth Owen announced that, once again, Whizz-Kidz would be sponsoring a team of runners for the 2011 London Marathon and that she was very pleased to announce that I would be one of them.

She even pulled out a Whizz-Kidz running vest with my name on it. Everyone clapped and started pledging money in support of my run. As much as I admired Ruth's chutzpah, it was news to me as well as to the rest of the room. And having done no proper sport other than one annual football match for the last decade, I was in no position – or shape – to agree.

Yvette helpfully confirmed that view when I got home, telling me I would likely collapse well before the finish. So I asked my office to politely decline the invitation; but as the weeks and months passed, and my midlife crisis continued, I began to think that running the marathon might not be such a bad idea, especially if I could do it for both Whizz-Kidz and another charity I supported, Action for Stammering Children. So I contacted Ruth and accepted her offer – begging for another year to get myself prepared.

I thought I should start running immediately, but was told

by a marathon training expert, Nick Berners-Price, that it would be unwise until I was halfway fit. So the whole of that summer I spent every other day jumping up and down on a step, wriggling a long flexible bar to 'strengthen my core', and doing sit-ups, press-ups and star jumps to try and get my body working again. I slowly started running in October, and by January I was up to doing ten-mile circuits.

Despite making steady progress I could never envisage running twenty-six miles, and really wondered if I'd be able to get all the way round. Which is fine if you're a fun runner giving it your best shot. But if you're the Shadow Chancellor, it's rather more high-risk. 'It's a marathon, not a sprint' is not a bad description of opposition life. However, to start the real marathon and fail to finish would have been a PR disaster.

Just two weeks before my first marathon I did my final long-distance run – twenty miles round Pontefract racetrack on a clear but windy Saturday morning. I arrived at 8 a.m. and started my slow plodding run. After half an hour, a van arrived, and the driver began to mark out a two-kilometre circuit along the track.

Not long afterwards runners began to gather for the local parkrun, dressed in vests and track shoes. A starting gun fired and about sixty runners were racing towards me, zipping along and giving me quizzical looks as they passed by. The last runners had completed the race in a little over an hour. They took photographs, had a small barbecue and drinks, held a prize-giving ceremony, cleared up the cones, and drove away at around the time I hit mile 16. It was honestly one of the loneliest, most hopeless experiences of my life. I spent four hours looking at my watch working out how far I had gone and how far I still had to go. Once I'd got through it, though, I felt more confident I would be able to get to twenty-six miles on the day.

People say the first time you run the marathon is one of the most exciting days of your life. It's completely true. The tension in the hours before the start was enormous. By that time, I'd managed to raise a good amount for the two charities, so I knew that as long as I was able to get round I had already succeeded.

And when the gun fired, I set off with my running partner, Bev, allocated to me by the marathon organisers to make sure I got round OK, and I was just carried along by the enormous crowds lining both sides of the route. Feeling sufficiently comfortable at mile 8, I was able to do a live interview on LBC with Iain Dale while still running. But by the time we got to mile 13, things were getting tougher. An old ankle injury began to flare up and to compensate I was putting too much pressure on my other knee, which then started to get incredibly painful.

I knew that Yvette and the children were standing at mile 14 to wave me through, but I was in so much pain I could hardly acknowledge them as I ran past. I also thought that if I stopped, I might not be able to start again. Bev said: 'You need some painkillers or you're not going to finish.' I was cursing myself for not listening to the advice of fellow runners who'd told me exactly that. But Bev started yelling to our fellow runners and the spectators on the pavement: 'Drugs, drugs, has anybody got any drugs!?' It was not an appeal I'd ever expected to be made on my behalf. Luckily a runner near us generously supplied some ibuprofen, and it worked. The pain eased, and while I failed to meet my five-hour target, getting round in five hours thirty minutes, I did finish, the charities had their money, and the potential PR disaster was averted.

It was exhilarating, exhausting, draining and, given that I was officially slower than a four-legged camel running for WaterAid and a woman who did the hula hoop the whole twenty-six miles, rather chastening. But I'd caught the bug, literally. I ran the marathon in 2013, having nearly pulled out the day before because of a lingering flu virus, and then in 2014 as well, finally breaking the five-hour barrier by three minutes and getting my total raised for Whizz-Kidz and Action for Stammering Children up to £160,000. I was the slowest marathon runner in Parliament, but the best fund-raiser. And I was in sufficiently good shape that each time I finished I was able to go live onto Sky News within ten minutes, unlike 'the whippet' Jim Murphy who I am reliably told was unable to speak for over half an hour.

Sadly in 2015, my office was clear that trying to do a marathon in the middle of the election campaign wasn't going to work. Which was a shame, because I found running those marathons immensely therapeutic. I got fitter and healthier, and I found the hours of training beneficial mentally, giving me time to reflect, think and plan.

Running became part of my new life in opposition. And so did the piano. In early 2012 I gave an interview to Patrick Wintour of the *Guardian*. As I talked to him beforehand, I mentioned that my children had recently taken up the keyboard, and how jealous I was. I'd always wanted to play the piano when I was younger but I'd never lived in a house with one to practise on and so took up the violin instead. Patrick's face lit up, and he said he'd just begun. He encouraged me to rent a proper piano and learn. We spent so long talking about it, we were halfway through our allotted time without the interview even starting, the kind of thing that always made my staff roll their eyes.

But to my surprise, after Patrick's interview was published – mentioning my interest in taking up the piano, but my fear of learning a new skill in my forties – I found it resonated with many other people who had either tried or thought about trying to do the same thing.

I spoke to Lola Perrin, my children's teacher, and she agreed to give me some lessons too. While she was clear that I simply had to enjoy my playing if I was to make progress, I knew that I would only really practise and commit if I had a challenge – so I decided I would do the official music board exams. Soon enough, I was ready for the Grade 1 test. Lola asked me whether I'd be happy sitting it with a group of her other pupils, which of course I was, although it gave me a bit of pause when she said the others were all under ten years of age.

Unfortunately, just a week before the exam, we were told by Ed Miliband's office that his long-awaited speech on banking reform was scheduled for the same morning. I protested and said to my office that my exam had to come first. Alex, patient as always, gently explained that was definitely not a good enough reason to miss Ed's speech.

Luckily Lola rode to the rescue, and managed to get me another slot three days later. I sat in on the speech and passed my Grade 1, and went on to pass Grades 2, 3 and 4 while I was Shadow Chancellor.

Of course, as more of the media found out about my new hobby, I was in prime territory to be ambushed by interviewers with a request to play live on air. I gave a less than impressive performance on Iain Dale's show, a slightly better one on Jeremy Vine's, then – most nerve-racking of all – came an invitation to play in a concert at Kings Place with a mix of professional pianists and amateurs like myself.

I had three months to prepare, but that just gave me more time to get stressed. Worse, George Osborne made his Autumn Statement shortly before, and my stammer-affected 'shouty' response was widely lambasted by the media, the Tories and even some of my Labour colleagues.

We decided I needed to do a Sunday TV programme to get back on the front foot, so I agreed to appear on Dermot Murnaghan's Sky show at 10 a.m., an hour before the Kings Place concert at 11. It was probably the easiest interview I've ever done, and I was famously combative, saying I didn't 'give a toss' about the criticism of my Commons performance. Which was true: I was so overcome with nerves about the concert in an hour's time that the interview was the least of my concerns.

The performance itself however was probably the most frightening thing I have ever done. The piece I had agreed to play from Schumann's *Kinderszenen* came at the end of the programme and my hands shook from the first note to the last. I remember vividly the aching silence of the packed audience before I played a note, and the huge relief when they finally applauded at the end.

Then a strange thing started to happen. I found my House of Commons postbag filling with very personal letters from people in their forties, fifties and sixties either encouraging me to keep going at the piano, telling me how they'd only taken it up late on, or – even more hearteningly – telling me that hearing me play on the radio or talk about it in the papers had inspired them to have a go at it themselves.

In the weeks and months that followed, often when I got into a black cab or was sitting on a train, the cab driver or train guard would say, just casually: 'By the way, I really enjoyed listening to you playing the piano on *Jeremy Vine*.' It was striking the interest it inspired, and the same was true of my marathon running and my baking, once the cakes I made for my children's birthdays became a bit of a hit on Twitter.

What I learned was not only that these new hinterland activities were helping me to manage my midlife crisis and give me new, different things to do, but people were interested in hearing about them, or at least about a politician talking about something other than politics. It reached the bizarre stage where even a throwaway remark I made about an episode of the *Antiques Roadshow* being the last thing to make me cry found its way onto the front page of the *Daily Telegraph* and became the subject of numerous radio phone-ins across the country.

It was a time when politics was becoming ever more

unpopular, Labour politicians were the most hated of the lot, and I was a particular bête noire for many people, but my new passions added an extra dimension to my communication with the public, and, from what they said to me in response, changed a few minds. And interestingly, I'd been able to do it without taking the default option for many politicians and talking about my family and children instead.

It did make me wonder whether Gordon Brown had missed a trick in his own public communications. I think the general view of him was that he was obsessed with politics and power, and it made for some very ungenerous revelling in his discomfort whenever he was under pressure as Chancellor and even more as Prime Minister.

The truth is he had an incredibly well-developed hinterland, but not one that he allowed anyone to see. The fact that he kept his family entirely private was understandable, but there were sides of him – his enthusiasm for poetry and classical music for example – that he never spoke about publicly. And even though he was known to be an avid fan of football, rugby and other sports, he was never quite able to show the public just how much of a passion they were, especially for someone so workaholic in every other aspect of his life.

For Gordon, that self-restraint flowed from an almost regal sense of duty. On a long flight to Bangkok in 1997, his new principal private secretary announced that he had booked a first-class seat so he could sit alongside Gordon, explaining that 'the Chancellor should not fly unaccompanied, in case he needs to work during the flight'.

I rolled my eyes, knowing what was coming. We were barely a half-hour in, I was choosing my in-flight movie and meal, when the PPS came down and said to me: 'Gordon wants us to swap seats, he wants to discuss his speech with you.' I sighed, gave him a long look, and then walked up to first class. Cue eight hours of discussion with Gordon about the global financial system.

Now Gordon could have chosen to have a brief chat about his speech, then we could have talked about football, music, family, or any of our other shared passions. We could have just had a drink. But he had a reflex in him that – even in that relatively private situation, with flight attendants approaching and other passengers looking over – he had to be seen to be working at all times. He would only ever sleep on flights if he was genuinely overcome by exhaustion.

And that sense of being constantly on duty used to affect his ability to show other sides of his personality. He believed the Chancellor – and anyone contending for the position – had to convince the public he was up to the job. So even when he spoke about football in interviews, he'd focus on its importance for British exports, not Wayne Rooney's best position.

When he was off-duty it was a different story. Arriving in Johannesburg back in 1997 we left the airport and took a taxi to the hotel. All Gordon could talk about was whether he'd be able to watch Newcastle United play Partizan Belgrade in the Cup Winners' Cup. Unfortunately, the hotel didn't have the appropriate subscription, and explained there was nothing they could do.

That would have stopped most people. But not Gordon. We ended up with one of the hotel staff up on the roof speaking to the TV company and retuning the satellite dish, just so Gordon could catch the game. It was obsessive all right, but it also spoke volumes about how Gordon was much more than a simple career politician.

We regularly saw this side of him in private, but the only time you saw him show it in public was on his trips to Washington or New York, especially the ones we'd try and arrange – despite the freezing temperatures – in the run-up to Christmas. He loved the freedom to stroll around second-hand bookshops in Georgetown, or to wander into a random bar to watch football or have a proper drink. In his mind, he was anonymous over there, he was most definitely 'off duty', and for that reason he always resisted staying at the British Embassy on our trips, much to the consternation and disappointment of successive ambassadors.

But here was the contrast between Gordon's hinterland and mine. I found liberation in being able to show the public a side of myself at odds with the stereotype. Gordon found liberation in being able to enjoy that side of his life without anyone knowing about it. Who was right, it's difficult to say.

At a time when politics is seen as so one-dimensional, for me being able to publicly enjoy my hinterland was a way of confronting that, and it became humanising as well as liberating. But the fact that I obviously had a life outside of politics, and hadn't let politics consume my life in opposition as I had in government, undoubtedly helped people see my future differently after the election defeat in 2015.

It meant that I could become chairman of Norwich City

Football Club, pour my heart into Sport Relief's *Bake Off* and present an award at the BBC Music Awards, without anyone thinking those kinds of activities were rather odd things to be doing. It also means when I tell people my life almost certainly lies beyond politics now, they don't take it with a pinch of salt.

Most importantly, I've been able to have the midlife crisis many of us go through, even losing my job in the process, without letting it overtake me, and even enjoying it (mile 14 of the marathon aside). I like to think that Denis Healey would be proud.

26

Purpose

_____

Being an MP is a stressful and unpopular job – why would anyone ever want to do it?

'Do you think we can do anything about this one?' my constituency office manager asked. 'It's so unfair. I think we've got to intervene.'

Walking into my constituency office – first in Normanton, and then in Morley – I never knew what to expect: what letters would be waiting; what case meetings would be organised for that afternoon.

That summer day in 2013, Jo Coles passed me a letter from two foster-parents in my constituency, clearly desperate with worry and frustration. They had been fostering two young children who, for complex reasons, had been moved by their sponsoring local authority many miles from their original

home, and the courts had decided they were to be permanently adopted.

The foster-parents had decided they wanted to adopt the
children themselves but, even though they were happy in
their new home and school, the sponsoring local authority
wanted the children to return to their own area for adoption.
The foster-parents had argued the case, but there had been a
procedural problem and they had now been given a date
when the children were to be taken away.

Once I looked into the case, I agreed it made no sense: it
was just the wheels of bureaucracy turning without anyone
thinking through the human impact on the children and on
the foster-parents too.

It was so upsetting all round, and given I knew from the
inside how the system worked, my office intervened with our
local Director of Children's Services and his counterpart in
the sponsoring local authority. We explained the situation,
and a hold was put on the move until the decision could be
looked at again. I wasn't hopeful we could keep this new
family together, but we were going to have a damn good try
and, as it turned out, a successful one.

A few weeks later, I received another letter – this time not
from the foster-parents but from the two children. It just
said: 'Thank you for keeping our family together.' The right
outcome had been reached: the family had stayed whole, and
I like to think those two children are growing up now as
happy as they sounded in their letter to me. It was a classic
situation where – without the intervention of the local MP –
things can just get stuck in the system, and will never work

out without a great deal of pain, upset and difficulty on all sides.

The fact is that the worst thing you can ever say to a politician is: 'You're all the same, nothing any of you do makes any difference to me and my life' – worse even than someone telling you they hate you, or they're glad you're out of a job. At that point, all the sacrifices you make as an MP – the exhausting hours, the media intrusion, and everything else – suddenly seem like some self-inflicted madness.

Why the hell do we do it? Why would anyone want to go into politics? Why would you put up with all the abuse?

But then there are times when you remember why.

I still remember the surge of pride I felt standing next to the returning officer at my count in Wakefield as she announced that I had won the ballot, and that I would be the next Member of Parliament for Normanton. Watching Yvette be the local MP for the previous eight years, from the start I had been quietly angling to take over from her next-door neighbour, Bill O'Brien. Indeed, I'd had to intervene to make sure he didn't stand down prematurely in 2001, as I still had the euro assessment to oversee.

For me, at that time, becoming an MP was simply a means to an end. Obviously I wanted to do good things in that position, but my starting motivation was about the big changes I could effect for millions of people, not the difference I could make to a few of my constituents. For other MPs, it's a platform to campaign on issues that they care passionately about, even though they might be pretty low on the radar of their own constituents, and for a few it's just the kudos of becoming an MP that attracts them, and the status it gives them.

But over time, I'm sure all our motivations change, and during the ten years when I was an MP, they certainly did. So when I now look back on my time, it's not just the big things I was involved in which give me satisfaction. The aspect of the job I came to enjoy the most, and find most rewarding, were the individual cases where I could make a personal difference to my constituents' lives. And the times I felt acutely painful were when I had a letter, an email, or someone sitting in front of me in my surgery, and I had that sinking feeling of knowing I could do absolutely nothing for them.

I have to keep reminding myself of the latter feelings because it's easy to wear rose-tinted spectacles when you look back. Most of the time doing constituency casework was just grindingly tough: routine issues about planning applications or parking tickets, where my job was simply to tell my constituent what the proper procedure was; and the occasional person who was persistently aggrieved at the world, and just wanted someone to listen to them.

That listening task was not only, or even mainly, performed by me. Jo Coles, her predecessor Carol Moran and my case-workers Julie Ward, Jolene Hodgson and Rory Bickerton worked tirelessly, day after day, solving problems, writing letters or just listening. But for all those routine cases, there were the 10 per cent where I knew my intervention was not only justified but could be influential: a letter to the chief executive of Abbey National pointing out that a constituent had been unfairly treated by the bank, short-circuiting all of the bureaucracy that would be caused on both sides by referring the matter to the Financial Ombudsman; an email to social services about a disabled constituent who needed a ramp installed to enable them to get down their front doorstep.

You do enough of those things, and it changes your perspective of what politics is about. Throughout my ten years as an MP, when I was walking round the streets, I continually had people coming up and saying: 'Thanks so much for sorting out my mum's wall,' or 'Cheers, Ed, I got my money back from that holiday,' and I'd nod and say it was a great pleasure, often having no idea which particular case they were talking about.

By contrast, sometimes cases are intractable and impossible to solve. I'd spend hours sitting with women who were owed child support by a partner who'd gone missing, or a mum angry that her child had been expelled from school, and – as much as I could see their anguish – I had to explain that there was nothing I personally could do, except tell the Child Support Agency or the school what I'd been told, and keep pushing if I didn't think their answers were acceptable. Seeing the disappointment on the face of a mother walking away from those meetings was incredibly hard to take.

And then there were the very upsetting and painful cases: a brother who died in custody after what appeared to be terrible mistakes by the local police; a child who died as a result of a virus misdiagnosed, with treatment delayed because of an apparent dispute between two parts of a local hospital.

In those kind of cases, I'd have to start by explaining – even to very distressed people – that I couldn't take sides, and I wasn't a lawyer, but the one thing I could do was ask all the questions of authority that they were struggling to get answers to, and make sure that – if any failures were proved – the system was held to account and lessons were learned.

And again, that's where you see your clout as an MP: when your letter to the Secretary of State gets answers that a family's questions to the local constabulary or hospital never could. I look back on those cases, while often painful and long and protracted and where there was never going to be a good solution, as some of the most important things I ever did.

But of course they never made me happy. It would be bizarre if they had. The cases that made me happy were ones where you could make things better. There was the son of a local constituent, a huge achiever in school, just offered a place at Cambridge University, but because the father was three-quarters of the way through the immigration process and hadn't yet received his 'right to remain', they were told the student would have to pay international tuition fees, and pay them up front.

His choice was to give up his place and try again in a year once his dad's immigration status was finally confirmed, or go to another university where he could afford the fees. Instead, a letter from me to the warden of the college, setting out the case, offering to talk it through, and asking for some flexibility, was enough to secure his place. I've been receiving updates on his progress ever since.

Even better than those individual successes was when you could do something for the whole town. One year I was alarmed to discover our local mobile breast-screening clinic was set to disappear because the leisure centre car park it sat in was being rebuilt. The local health service concluded that – for efficiency reasons and because no public sector land was available – the clinic would be moved to a different town, a twenty-minute drive or two buses away. It totally undermined the purpose of having the screening clinic in a place where local Morley women could have easy access. It could well have cost lives.

Jo and I looked for all kinds of solutions, and we hit on the idea that the local Asda car park might have the room to host the clinic, and when we spoke to their brilliant community champion, and the store manager, they couldn't have been more eager. Three months later, the breast clinic was re-located to the Asda car park, even closer to the centre of town than it had been before, and as a permanent site, with all the accompanying utilities provided by Asda. I can't tell you how good that felt, and how good it still feels today.

And while every MP is different, there's nothing unusual about my story. Every MP I know personally tells exactly the same kinds of stories, has the same kinds of case meetings, and, for most of them, comes to the same conclusion about why they do the job.

That's why it hit us all so hard when the expenses scandal emerged on the front of the *Daily Telegraph* back in 2009. We were already dealing with the impact of the financial crisis and the anger everyone felt with those in charge. We were already dealing with the corrosion in trust that had come from the popularisation of the concept of spin, and the no-toriety of everyone who practised it.

But when the scandal hit with the leak to the *Telegraph* of every expense claim by every MP over the previous few years, we had to deal with the fact that every one of us, even the cleanest, even the best-liked by their constituents, was instantly seen as a crook. And not just any crook – someone robbing from them, the taxpayers.

The attitude towards all of us went from sceptical to hostile then furious overnight, and while that was entirely justified in the round, it didn't prepare me for someone screaming in my face: 'You lot, and your fucking duck houses and your fucking five-star hotels – I'm fucking paying for that.'

In that context, I couldn't explain it wasn't my duck house or hotel, because it didn't matter, it was about me being part of 'you lot'. It was a mood that didn't distinguish between what party you were in, what you personally had done, and certainly not any of the good things you might have done in the job.

And I did have my own personal 'scandal' to deal with over the report that I'd claimed the costs of a Remembrance Day wreath on expenses. Every single year I was an MP, I'd paid – as you'd expect – for the wreaths to be laid at memorial services in Normanton, Altofts and Morley. But one year in the middle of the Parliament, my office manager put that particular receipt into the wrong pile. It went into a claim that I signed, but which was then queried by the Fees Office; we realised our mistake, and I immediately paid back the money. But that was enough to create the story, the indelible impression, that I was the kind of MP who would claim a memorial wreath on expenses. It made me 'one of them'.

★

The fact is the old expenses system was difficult to manage and navigate. It was wide open to abuse for those who wanted to do so, and for the vast majority of MPs who didn't, it still required constant vigilance to pass the 'Daily Mail front-page test'. By that I mean, you could be doing something perfectly permissible within the rules, approved by the authorities, but that was not enough: you had to ask yourself: 'How will this look on the front page of the Mail?'

Yvette and I received a warning of how easy it would be to fall foul of that test when I became an MP in 2005. Together, we went to see the Fees Office to ask how we should manage our expenses as a couple in Parliament. They pointed out to us that there were a number of other couples where one claimed their London house as their main home and their constituency house as their second, and their spouse did the opposite, thus enabling them both to claim their full allowance. Bizarre as it seems, they almost seemed to be expecting us to pull that trick because otherwise we'd miss out on claiming our full allowances just because we were part of a couple.

Yvette and I said no, we would both designate our constituency home as our main home – that's where our children were born, that's where we spent most nights over the course of a year – we'd both designate London as our second home, and we'd split our expense claim for London 50/50. That was the right thing to do, but it came at a price, and I don't mean 'missing out' on the second allowance.

Two years later we moved house in London from Vauxhall back to Hackney. A couple of months after the move, I had a call from our accountant, the late and great Jeffrey Lent. He said: 'Ed, I've been thinking about your house move and I need to give you some advice.' He came down to my office and said: 'Look, you treat London as your second home for House of Commons expenses, but if you do the same for tax purposes, then in theory you'll have to pay capital gains tax on the move you've just made. It's not necessary and most people wouldn't, but I think you should.'

'How much will we have to pay?' I asked. He looked at his notebook: '£86,000.' We decided we had no choice but to pay it, even if we had to borrow from our families to get the money together. It was a salutary lesson in how easy it could be to get things wrong over expenses, and also – frankly – of the temptations that were inherent in the system to skew your declarations to suit your finances. That was what did for so many MPs when the scandal broke into the open a year later.

And when it did break and Yvette and I were accused of 'flipping our home three times', we told the *Telegraph* they were wrong: Yvette had changed her designated main home from our London to our Yorkshire home just once before I was elected, when the rules about how ministers had to claim were changed, me not at all. And we had moved house within London, which far from benefiting us had cost us an awful lot of money because of the capital gains tax bill.

The expenses scandal severely damaged the standing of MPs in our country. It contributed to a view that we were just out for ourselves, money-grubbing, only interested in what we could get out of the system. And in the aftermath of the financial crisis and perhaps the phone-hacking scandal, it reinforced a sense that there was a powerful elite – all cosied up together, able to operate under different rules to everyone else.

Worst of all, it offered up the most terrible answer in the minds of the public to that question: 'Why would anyone want to become an MP?' The new answer: 'So they can line their own pockets at our expense.'

It's a desperate shame, because politics is still a noble cause; it's still a fantastic feeling of pride being elected to serve your constituents, and the vast majority of MPs on all sides of the House work damn hard to do exactly that. And even if it often goes entirely unseen by most members of the public, MPs do make a difference.

In the final few months of my time as an MP, I received another letter from a local mum. She had lost her young daughter after a struggle with a terrible illness, and she wanted to buy a bench to put in the local park so she could sit there and think about her daughter; but, as sometimes happens, the bureaucracy of the local authority was getting in the way of her simple wish.

When I read the letter, I felt very moved and phoned her home. I spoke to her husband, who told me how frustrating it was, and how upsetting his wife was finding it. I immediately rang the chief executive of the council, the excellent Joanne Roney. I explained the situation and asked her to look into it.

She came back a few days later to say the delay had been totally ridiculous, and it would all be sorted out. I rang the mum, said how sorry I was about her daughter, and about all the upset she'd had to go through, but it was all going to be OK, she could have her bench put in the park whenever and wherever she wanted. And at that, this young mum broke down with emotion, and I sat at my desk with tears flooding down my face as well.

It's a tough job, politics. The standing of MPs is not high and may never be again, but for all the mistakes we make, it remains a noble calling. I don't really miss Westminster, I don't miss the House of Commons, I certainly don't miss Prime Minister's Questions, but I do miss making a difference to the people in my constituency. I miss that very much.

Postscript

I signed off my final edit of this chapter on 15 June 2016. The very next day, Jo Cox was shot and killed while doing her job as an MP, arriving at a constituency surgery in her Yorkshire seat. She was my next-door neighbour when campaigning in 2015; she was my colleague and my friend.

She devoted her all too short life to saving or changing the lives of others, and while she could have had any position she wanted in the charity world, on far better pay than an MP's, she chose to go into politics because she knew that is where you get more of a chance to try and save or change the lives of millions of people.

But the day Jo died, she was doing what matters most to any of us: coming to help the constituents lining up to see her in a library in Birstall; trying to make things happen for people who can't do it on their own. This chapter is dedicated to her.

27

Future

Politics is in crisis in Britain and across the developed world —
has anyone got a plan to turn things round?

In the summer of 2010, I left our family camper-van holiday early and flew back to a Labour leadership election that I knew I was losing. Five years later it was Yvette's turn.

As the dust settled on our 2015 election defeat, I knew there would be one candidate to succeed Ed Miliband from the centre-right of the party and another hoovering up the union votes by representing the centre-left. And I could have guessed that Liz Kendall and Andy Burnham would fulfil those respective roles. In that climate, I believed Yvette could win the contest by running down the middle, and offering the kind of strong, confident, unifying leadership that people felt was lacking with Ed Miliband — a potential outcome that left me and the children feeling both excited and worried about what it would mean for our lives.

What I never anticipated was a far-left insurgency, and by the time Yvette and the others realised 'Corbynmania' was taking over, it was too late: he had the momentum, the new £3 members and the unions; and under Ed Miliband's new electoral system and with a good ground and social media campaign, that guaranteed a massive victory.

A few weeks later, with the votes cast and Corbyn installed as leader, I landed again in the US to start my fellowship at the Harvard Kennedy School. The talk was of Hillary Clinton's troubles with emails and the surprise rise of celebrity billionaire Donald Trump, then topping the polls to be the Republican presidential nominee.

My Harvard friends were quick to dismiss Trump, a maverick with far-right views on immigration, taxes and foreign policy. They would invariably opine: 'He'll have gone by October − these outsiders always do.' I would reply: 'Everyone said the same about Jeremy Corbyn when he first entered the Labour race. And now he's taken over the party.'

If anyone had told me on the day I lost my seat that Jeremy Corbyn would be the next leader of the Labour Party, I would have laughed out loud and bet thousands of pounds against someone from the hard left, who had opposed almost everything the Labour government achieved, winning the leadership election. Then again, if you'd told me back in 2010 that the UK would almost break apart in the Scottish referendum, that the SNP would win fifty seats in Westminster, that the British population would vote to leave the European Union and that Donald Trump would win the race to become the Republican nominee for president, I wouldn't have believed any of that either.

What times we live in. Trust in politics has slumped. And outsiders have been building support and winning elections, not just in the UK and US but across Europe. France, Austria, Denmark, Sweden, Italy and Germany have all seen the rise of new populist parties, left and right, threatening to over-throw the established order.

So how has it come to this? Who's to blame, and what can mainstream politics do to turn this around and rebuild trust?

I grew up in a household that was shaped by memories of John F. Kennedy and Martin Luther King, and the models of inspirational leadership they gave to America in the 1960s. For good or bad, Ronald Reagan and Margaret Thatcher dominated politics on either side of the Atlantic in the 1980s and certainly reflected the aspirations of many people and their desire for change.

And in the 1990s, Bill Clinton and Tony Blair showed how governing from the centre and bringing divided coun-tries together could provide equally compelling leadership. Those were all times when, with mainstream politics working, the leaders of the major parties always sought to embody the hopes of people for the future, and convince the public that they themselves were the agents of change who could help realise those hopes.

In many ways, Barack Obama has been the child of all

those political giants: as inspiring as JFK and Martin Luther King; as strong a communicator as Reagan and Thatcher; and as pragmatic about how to deliver change and win elections as Clinton and Blair. And like all of them, also empowered with a real sense of principle and vision, and an innate ability to put himself alongside the hopes and dreams of ordinary people. The irony is that – instead of sparking a generation of imitators – he may be the last of that kind.

Because when trust slumps, when people in vast numbers believe their country is going in the wrong direction, when people say that politicians are just out for themselves and not on the side of the people, then mainstream political leaders lose that ability to represent the aspirations of large sections of the population, and instead outsiders, mavericks and extremists take the stage.

What is really striking over the last few years is how, for all the very different national contexts and past political histories, the language of these outsiders is very similar. From Donald Trump in America, through Nigel Farage and Jeremy Corbyn in Britain, to Marine Le Pen in France, there is a common narrative: a corrupt elite, a rotten establishment has run the economy for their own ends, while ordinary people, playing by the rules, have suffered. Now it's time for change.

The bugbears differ across the political spectrum, the right blaming welfare scroungers and immigrants for holding ordinary people back, the left blaming capitalist bosses and multinational companies. But there are some common targets which transcend the political divide, and, of course, at the bullseye are governments and bureaucrats.

The populist backlash has one thing right: the elites, be they prime ministers, senior politicians or business leaders, have certainly failed. They failed to prevent a financial crisis; and they failed to maintain public trust in their ability to provide answers for the future. And in a country where, for the first time certainly in my lifetime, the older generations believe that the younger generations will be worse off than they were, not better, something has clearly gone wrong.

But while conspiracy theories have been a part of our politics in every generation for centuries, it is not a mode of thinking I am inclined to follow. Yes, politics has failed, but I don't have time for the idea that Donald Trump or Nigel Farage are really exposing a rotten, corrupt elite of which they are not a part, and that the only people who can overthrow it, on behalf of the people, are a celebrity billionaire or a former stockbroker.

Nor do I believe this is simply the product of 'mediocre growth and mediocre political leaders', as one senior European policymaker put it to me recently. Deep and jarring though the global financial crisis was, and slow as the recovery has been, these angry and populist forces and pressures were in evidence beforehand – the rise of the BNP and UKIP in Britain, the National Front in France, and the Tea Party movement in America all pre-date the financial crash. This is a crisis which is several decades in the making, not a post-crisis phenomenon.

The other common explanation is that social media and the Internet have changed politics and given the outsiders a platform to reach the public that they never had working through the mainstream media before. Email lists are easier to compile, campaigns are easier to organise, and the public will readily give those campaigns a momentum of their own. A well-organised social media 'surge' can recruit new members and generate excitement much faster than was ever possible before, as Jeremy Corbyn showed in the summer of 2015. And then, with just a click, you can sign a petition or even vote in a leadership contest.

But social media cannot begin to explain, at root, why politics today is in such turmoil. It is a magnifier of events but it doesn't change the fundamentals. It can't explain why we lost the EU referendum or why every mainstream Labour or Republican candidate fell by the wayside in the face of the Corbyn and Trump campaigns, and why Hillary Clinton had to fight so long and hard to defeat Bernie Sanders.

Nor can we simply blame Tony Blair, Gordon Brown and Ed Miliband, as the left in Britain are inclined to do. Of course, that generation of Labour leaders made some mistakes. Every generation does. Public anger about Iraq, the financial crisis and the expenses scandal is real and lasting. But none of that explains the rise of Donald Trump or the rise of far-left and far-right movements across continental Europe. Deeper things are going on.

Returning to the Kennedy School after twenty-seven years away, I was struck by how often I heard academics and economists lamenting the fact that 'politicians' are failing America. They talked as if it was now their job to find ways around elected politics and Congress to mitigate the damage.

Their scepticism about politics and politicians was more profound than I remembered and surprising in an institution named after one of the most inspirational political leaders in US history.

That attitude is an affront to the democratic process. But I also take it with a big pinch of salt. It suggests to me a striking lack of introspection and self-awareness.

Yes, politics has failed to adapt to new trends and pressures. But so has the world of economics and policy analysis. It's not enough just to lament a dearth of political leadership or to believe that better communication can save the day; that a new generation can easily fix the failings of the past one; and that with a few tweaks, 'business as usual' can get things back on track. Economists and policymakers have failed as well as the politicians, and we need to understand why so we can work out what to do.

And that starts with going back to the most basic rule in the book: take care of the economics and the politics will follow; get the economics wrong, and the politics will go out of control. That's exactly what's happened over the past three decades.

We didn't see that technological change and the digital economy would hurt the middle classes as much as unskilled workers, and lead to the stagnation of wages. We didn't see that globalisation would lead to a massive movement of people as well as capital and trade, and turn immigration into such a heated political issue. And we didn't see the financial crisis coming, ensure a fair recovery for the majority, or take all the steps required to reform our banking system.

So what do we do now?

Certainly not bury our heads in the sand and assume that things will return to normal. That approach is highly dangerous. These challenges are not going to go away. If we do not take the right steps now, the damage will become irreversible, whether it's Britain leaving the EU single market, or the resulting threat that the UK itself will fall apart.

Telling people that life is good, the status quo is working and their concerns about living standards or migration are unfounded hasn't been working, and it won't start to do so now. It's insulting and foolish when economists or politicians tell the public: you need to understand that migration is good for our economy, because we all benefit; or that technological change is good for our economy, because we all benefit. When people don't see how they are benefiting and are fearful about the future, patronising lectures are not the answer.

But nor does it work to feed and pander to the forces of nationalism and isolationism which are stirred up at these times. Not only does that lead to nasty, divisive and destructive politics, it is also plain incompetent, because no country – certainly not Britain – can solve its problems of growth and wages, let alone climate change and security, by trying to cut itself off from the international community when cooperation between countries is more important than ever before.

So, post-referendum, we are going to need a new approach. One that starts with the people – their concerns, their worries and their fears. An approach that shows people that politics can get a grip and can provide answers but that does not cut us off from the modern, changing world. A strategy that seeks to unite the country and not divide it. A plan that instils confidence that we can have growth and fairness and tackle inequality, that we can rebuild the social contract between people and government.

It means we have to show how technological change can deliver more good jobs, encourage entrepreneurs with great ideas, give people the skills they need to compete in the digital world, and also increase the value we place on the kind of skills and contributions that machines can't deliver and only humans can.

It means rewriting the rules around corporation tax, international taxation and executive pay, and rebuilding trust that not only does everyone play by the same rules but that people face the same penalties when those rules are broken.

It means rethinking the function of economic policy and independent central banking in a world where financial risks are as important as inflation risks, and where the financial health of large companies and private institutions and the risks they pose for the stability of our world needs to be monitored, challenged and regulated just as intensively as governments are themselves.

And it means accepting that the free movement of people across national borders is unsustainable; and showing instead that governments together can manage borders, set tough and fair rules for our respective welfare systems, and retain the benefits of managed migration without the instability and imbalances caused by unrestrained population movements.

These are all big challenges, but they are all essential. Throughout my life, I have seen that political speeches are never, ever powerful enough to overcome economic realities. It was economic logic that prevailed when we decided not to join the euro; it is economic logic, even more than history, tradition and identity, that dictates why it is right to hold the UK together as a union. And it is sadly economic logic that was ignored when Britain decided to leave the European Union in June 2016.

But economics only works when it leaps from the text-book, engages with the world in all its complexities, and accepts that behaviours and outcomes are also profoundly shaped by people's own experiences and their sense of iden-tity. Our task is to understand the powerful economic forces at work, shape them, and manage their political conse-quences so that we can rebuild public trust in our ability to deliver rising prosperity for all.

It's a big challenge for politics too. We can't leave vision and leadership to outsiders, to those who diagnose problems but can't propose solutions for fear of fracturing the fragile coalitions upon which their simplistic appeal is based. Populism can only ever propose fantasy solutions or no solu-tions at all, and my experience is that the public are deeply sceptical about any fantasies they are peddled. Which is why political leadership means being honest about the challenge, open about the difficulties and building a consensus, step by step from the inside, as to how problems can be solved, aspir-ations met and trust rebuilt.

This challenge is especially difficult for Labour. The EU referendum has exposed big divides in world views within the two main parties. Both have a challenge to unite again. But for a party which wants to occupy everything from the centre to the left of politics, it is a harder challenge to offer a vision of the future around which all sides can coalesce: because to succeed, progressive politics has to be about hope and optimism as well as harsh realities. In a time without hope, a right-of-centre party can still flourish by exploiting fear; a progressive party cannot.

So Labour will only now succeed if it can show it has solutions on wages, jobs, growth and globalisation which appeal to affluent city-dwellers and also deliver real substantial change for hard-pressed families in communities up and down the country. And I never believed that the 'them-and-us' class-conflict politics of Ed Miliband in 2014 or Jeremy Corbyn in 2015 could do that job.

Labour has to become a uniting party of the centre ground again, comfortable dealing with markets, business and the global economy, but determined to tackle inequality and make the market economy work for the long-term, in a way that is fair to all and not just a few.

It must always offer radical answers to the challenges we face; but in tough times, it cannot itself be a source of risk and uncertainty. Credible and Radical was the policy platform that secured election for Labour in 1997; and while the policy solutions are different now, the message contained in that slogan is as relevant today as it was twenty years ago.

Caution will not win the day; but nor will a hard left utopian fantasy, devoid of connection to the reality of people's lives and the need to make tough decisions on tax, budgets, immigration and welfare. Labour has to show that you can be principled and true to your values, but also competent, politically savvy and in touch with mainstream public opinion.

That, too, is why I never believed Bernie Sanders was the right person to take on Donald Trump and why I believe Hillary Clinton is – although to succeed Hillary will need all the policy cunning, strength and determination I sensed when I first met her at a 'third way' summit hosted by Tony Blair at Chequers back in 1998.

It's going to take a tremendous effort to turn this around, and all at a time when being a politician is harder than it's ever been. We have to start by exposing the anti-politicians for what they are: quick with the stump speech attacking the so-called corrupt governing elite, but unable to engage with the complexities of policy, its trade-offs and tough choices, lest their followers think they may be joining the elite they so despise.

It's tempting to think we need superhuman political leaders. But as I hope I have demonstrated, they just don't exist. And trying to be a superhuman politician can be counterproductive.

Being part of the 'not the usual politician' brigade, with a great back story and an easy style on a stage or in a studio, can work for a while, but only if you also have answers, substance, policy and something to say. And while it's good to be highly professional and media-trained, don't be so cautious about making mistakes or revealing any hinterland that you don't make an impact.

So my advice to the next generation of politicians and leaders is accept your flaws, look after your family, cherish your friends, learn from the past, don't duck the hard choices and never try to be anyone but yourself.

And remember, the economics always comes first.

As for me, I will continue to try and make my contribution to debating and solving these big policy issues, I'll continue watching Norwich City as chair of the board, I'll enjoy exploring and expanding my hinterland, and I'll enjoy being challenged by all the young students at Harvard and King's College London wrestling with their own views and futures.

I've had my chance in politics and – while you should never say never – I don't expect that chance to come again. That doesn't mean I don't miss it, but it's the turn of others now. Though I hope that the next generation, especially the Labour one, can learn from the experiences, lessons and insights I've tried to set out in this book. I'm deeply loyal to their cause, their task is hugely important, and I'll always contribute in any way I can.

Just a few months after the 2015 election, as I sat on a British Airways plane, flying off to start my new fellowship at Harvard, I sipped on a gin and tonic and thought back to the flight I took there in 1988. A 21-year-old, sitting on a plane for the very first time, also drinking a gin and tonic, full of excitement, ambition and hope.

What a journey it's been since then. I'm definitely older, I'm definitely wiser, and I'm definitely more worried about the future than I was back then. But I'm no less optimistic about everything we can achieve as a country, and what a difference a good politician – with sound economics – can make to people's lives.

My goodness, how I've learned – both from all the successful things I've done and from all the mistakes I've made. And what a lot of flowers I've smelled along the way.

ACKNOWLEDGEMENTS

I thought writing a book for the first time would be the hard bit, but thanking all the people who have helped make this book happen, or supported me over the last two decades and more in Westminster and before, is much more daunting.

First things first – this book couldn't have happened without all the team at Penguin Random House, most importantly my editor, Tom Avery, who has been patient and brilliant in equal measure, and my wise agent, Jonny Geller. Thanks to Catherine, Emma, Patrick and Balshen for keeping us on track, and Hugh Tomlinson for valuable counsel.

I was also hugely grateful for the early advice and encouragement of those with a bit more experience in this game, including the wonderfully supportive Ken and Barbara Follett, Jonathan Freedland, Damian McBride, Nick Robinson, Ed Victor and Phil Webster.

Now it gets really tough. And unlike the book, I am going to have to go in chronological order.

At Nottingham High School, the late Peter Baker encouraged and inspired me to study economics; at Oxford, Tim Besley and Tim Jenkinson taught me what economics really was; Jim Griffin encouraged me to follow his example and secure a Kennedy scholarship; at Harvard, Larry Summers, Larry Katz and Martin Feldstein showed me a wider world; and at the *Financial Times*, I will always be grateful to Geoff Owen, Richard Lambert and especially Martin Wolf for giving me my start.

It was hard to leave my colleagues at the FT, but I made friends for life in Gordon Brown's 1994 team, especially Sue Nye, Charlie Whelan, Ed Miliband, my two office mates, Dan Leader and – yes – Peter Mandelson, and of course Gordon and Sarah. What a team we made.

At the Treasury, there are too many people to mention but I must pick out and thank the outstanding Permanent Secretaries I worked with: Terry Burns, Andrew Turnbull, Gus O'Donnell and Nick MacPherson. In my own private office, heartfelt thanks to Julie McCandless, Ben Kelmanson, Julie Fry, James Bowler, Richard Hughes, Hermione Gough and all my private office team. I helped recruit three superb Heads of Communication and good friends in John Kingman, Michael Ellam and Damian McBride, and on the political side, I learned a huge amount from all the ministers I worked with and from Chris Wales, Shriti Vadera and Paul Gregg; and I was always grateful for the advice and companionship of Ian Austin, Bob Shrum and Spencer Livermore.

At the DCSF, my permanent secretary David Bell, was a vital support. Mela Watts, Sinead O'Sullivan and all my private office team were brilliant. I was lucky to have a superb team of ministers to work with, and a succession of excellent PPSs to support me in Parliament. My political team – Alex Belardinelli, Francine Bates, Caroline Abrahams, Richard Brooks and Jo-Anne Daniels, all went way beyond the call of duty. And what a difference Jan Logan made.

While I can't name all the backers and staff involved in my 2010 leadership campaign, thanks to you all and especially to my good friends Vernon Coaker, Jim Knight, Sarah McCarthy-Fry, Anne Snelgrove – and also Simon Burgess and Ellie Gellard – for keeping the whole charabanc on the road.

And then, through five years' hard slog as Shadow Home

Secretary and Shadow Chancellor, huge thanks to Alex Belardinelli, Balshen Izzet, Gary Follis, Karim Palant, Julie McCandless, Barbara Keeley, Richard Hincks, Charlotte Dunn, Jon Newton, Leo Haigh, Patrick Dougherty, Bex Bailey, Steph Driver and everyone who worked in my shadow ministerial team. Big thanks to Deborah Mattinson, Peter Hunt, Jon Mendelsohn and the Shadow Chancellor Advisory Group; thanks to Will Straw, the team at the Center for American Progress and all the members of the Inclusive Prosperity Commission; and also to all the Labour party staff at HQ and round the country.

Plus a heartfelt thank you to the Speaker, John Bercow, for his generosity, to Jo Hunter, Ruth Owen and everyone at Action for Stammering Children and Whizz-Kidz, and to all the hundreds of staff and parliamentarians, from all sides of the house, who laughed at my jokes, tolerated my Father Christmas routine, and sponsored me to run marathons.

No MP can function without a strong constituency base. My agents Gwen Page and Neil Dawson and my constituency office managers, Carol Moran and Jo Coles, held it all together alongside Nicola Leslie, Victoria Silver, Kate Williams and Anna Wright in Westminster. Judith Cummins, Fiona Gordon, Leonie Mathers, Keir Cozens, Rory Bickerton and Jayne Hill worked tirelessly on the campaigns, while Julie Ward, Jolene Hodgson, Heather Adams and Jess Riley worked harder – and chopped more onions and garlic – than was fair and reasonable. Huge thanks to all the interns, councillors, volunteers and friends who were always there for me.

I received very many letters, texts and emails when I left Parliament, from fellow MPs, media contacts, former colleagues and old friends. I hope I replied to them all. And many people have given generous advice and support over the last eighteen months, particularly Nick Butler, Howard Davies, Mohamed El-Erian, Peter Mandelson, Manny Roman, Paul Tucker and especially Larry Summers and Chris Keates.

At Harvard, Anna Stansbury and James Howat have been excellent collaborators and Scott Leland and Michael Walton and Isabel Guerrero have all been fabulously generous. At King's, Eleanor Hallam and Jon Davis and his team have been superb, and the Harry Walker team excellent. At Norwich City, Delia and Michael and all my fellow directors and colleagues have become good friends, with Rachel Barnett always going the extra mile to fix things. And big thanks to Jon Newton for staying on with me after the election until his elevation to the Bank of England beckoned.

It's the nature of politics that your friends outside of it often have to put up with a lot. So to Tom and Brigit, Murray, Bill and Nick, Steve and Elin, Michael Holman, the New Year Group and the Millbank Wives – thank you and apologies for so often being late and all the missed dinners and birthdays.

The same is true of our families. Both mine and Yvette's parents have been there for us time and time again. And in Joanna and David, Bill and Erica, Nicky and Andreas and Dave and Alex, we have a great team of brothers and sisters.

As for our kids – what with all the nonsense and disruption and travelling they have put up with, I am immensely proud of them. They are who they are, they're defining their own paths and doing so with a talent and enthusiasm which constantly overwhelms me.

Above all, none of this would have happened without Yvette. From meeting for the first time in a London park, sharing an office together and then our Disneyland honeymoon, it has been quite a journey. Our political lives have been just like those Disney rollercoasters, but I'm so lucky I've been sat next to Yvette through all the highs and lows, holding on tight and laughing all the way.

PICTURE ACKNOWLEDGEMENTS

Morley Labour rooms (courtesy of Jo Coles)
2015 General Election count (© REUTERS/Craig Bough)
Empty sherry glasses (courtesy of Jayne Dawson)
EB aged 6 in Norwich City kit (author's own)
First official school picture (author's own)
With younger brother Andrew and sister Joanna (author's own)
Wedding Day, 10 January 1998 (© Ashley Ashwood, courtesy of
    Joanna Pinder)
Action for Stammering Children (author's own)
EB and Gordon Brown in Blackpool (author's own)
Peter Mandelson in full flow (© Peter Marlow/Magnum Photos)
Steve Bell Treasury cartoon (© Steve Bell)
With the Queen of Nashville, Dolly Parton (courtesy of Dolly
    Parton)
Third Way Summit, Chequers, 1998 (author's own)
EB and Ed Miliband, 1997 (© Martin Argles, *Guardian*)
EB, Gordon Brown and John Maynard Keynes cartoon (© David
    Simonds, The *Economist* Newspaper)
'Balls to the Euro' (© *Sun*)
EB, Vince Cable and George Osborne (© Stefan Rousseau/Press
    Association Images)
EB with ministerial team at DCSF (author's own)
EB with End Child Poverty Coalition (author's own)
Eyeing up the Budget box (© Getty Images)
Helsinki Ecofin Summit, 2006 (author's own)
EB and Ed Miliband cartoon (© *The Times*/News Syndication)
Quizzing Michael Gove (© Parliamentary Recording Unit)
'Goosed!' (© Andrew Milligan/Press Association Images)

EB with fellow candidates in 2010 Labour leadership election (© Mirrorpix)

MPs vs Press at the 2014 Labour conference (© Mirrorpix)

Backstage at the 2000 Labour conference (author's own)

EB and Yvette Cooper walking to Cabinet meeting (© Getty Images)

'Scanning the Horizon' FT cartoon (The *Financial Times* Limited August 2015)

Campaigning against abolition of BSF (author's own)

Working for Gordon Brown in opposition (author's own)

2010 *Spectator* Parliamentarian of the Year prize-giving (© News Pictures/Rex/Shutterstock)

Key members of my team on the set of *Coronation Street* (author's own)

Private Eye 'Balls Up' cover (© *Private Eye*)

G2 cover (© *Guardian*)

Labour conference speech (author's own)

EB in front of Labour campaign poster (© News Pictures/Rex/Shutterstock)

'Flat-lining' at PMQs (© Parliamentary Recording Unit)

EB as Santa Claus (author's own)

Completing the 2012 London Marathon (© Anthony Devlin/Press Association Images)

EB playing Schumann at Kings Place (© Getty Images)

EB delivering Maiden Speech, 2005 (© Parliamentary Recording Unit)

Celebrating bringing breast-screening unit back to Morley (courtesy of Jo Coles)

EB and Delia Smith celebrate a goal (© Joe Toth/BPI)

INDEX